THE

WHOLE STAGGERING MYSTERY

A Story of Fathers

Lost and Found

✦

SYLVIA BROWNRIGG

COUNTERPOINT

CALIFORNIA

THE WHOLE STAGGERING MYSTERY

First Counterpoint edition: 2024

Library of Congress Cataloging-in-Publication Data
Names: Brownrigg, Sylvia, author.
Title: The whole staggering mystery : a story of fathers lost and found / Sylvia Brownrigg.
Description: First Counterpoint edition. | San Francisco : Counterpoint, 2024. | Includes bibliographical references.
Identifiers: LCCN 2023052621 | ISBN 9781640096561 (hardcover) | ISBN 9781640096578 (ebook)
Subjects: LCSH: Brownrigg, Sylvia, 1964- | Brownrigg, Sylvia, 1964-—Family. | Women authors, American—21st century—Biography. | Authors, American—21st century—Biography.
Classification: LCC PS3552.R7867 Z46 2024 | DDC 813/.54 [B]—dc23/eng/20231109
LC record available at https://lccn.loc.gov/2023052621

Jacket design and illustration by Farjana Yasmin
Book design by Laura Berry

Counterpoint
Los Angeles and San Francisco, CA
www.counterpointpress.com

Printed in the United States of America

1 3 5 7 9 10 8 6 4 2

In loving memory of
Nick Brownrigg
(1932–2018)

Failing to fetch me at first keep encouraged,
Missing me one place search another,
I stop some where waiting for you.

—WALT WHITMAN, "Song of Myself"

CONTENTS

✦

PART ONE: A TALE OF TWO FATHERS

PART TWO: A DEATH IN NAIROBI

THE
WHOLE
STAGGERING
MYSTERY

FAMILY SECRETS AREN'T WHAT THEY USED TO BE. IN THE traceable age, second families are harder to hide, double lives easily made visible. Personal geographies can be tracked by a simple app on your phone, and disappearing takes a lot more work. If ghosts are in the machine, so is their data.

How many plot twists in novels or soap operas turn on revelations of paternity? "It is a wise child that knows his own father," goes the saying, but father-knowledge doesn't require you to be wise anymore. You can just spit into a tube and send your sample off to faceless people in a far-off lab, who will come back to you with discoveries about your father, or other ancestors. All over the place, hidden relatives keep popping up on screens.

There is something the science doesn't get at, though. Genetic tests can't tell you how it *felt*. Stories are still irreducible; the bots haven't caught up with us on those. If your parents won't tell you what happened to them when they were young, then their childhood is fenced off from you, no matter where you spit.

In 2012, at the Berkeley house where I lived, a place cluttered with books and shoes and backpacks and dog toys, a box arrived that contained PRINTED MATTER. Inside was a jumble of items: wrapped volumes, sepia portraits, papers within papers. Musty, brown, unpromising, the items had languished in a Los Angeles basement for over fifty years, a production from a time when print did still matter and seemed important to save. If your children were born in a different century than you, as mine were, the gap between your upbringings is deep in a particular way. It's hard for twenty-first-century people to make out the shape of lives that started before the Internet. My friends and I could ask our parents what it was like during the war; now we try to tell our children what it was like when you couldn't sit at the kitchen table and google the war.

The bulkiest item in that cluttered box was a parcel wrapped in thick old ash-gray paper, with a hand-inked label that read *Sir Nicholas G Brownrigg, Baronet.*

That was my dad. The man who fathered me, not the one who raised me.

Long story.

You would be surprised that label could be meant for Nick Brownrigg, though, if you ran into him while he was packing groceries into his Subaru in the parking lot at the Safeway in Fort Bragg, in Northern California, or checking out of an oncologist's office in the logging town of Ukiah. Nick was a burly, jovial, blue-jeaned American with a large head, blue-green eyes under a jungled tangle of brows, and thick white hair and beard that made him Hemingway or Santa Claus, depending on the day and his mood. He spoke like a would-be Beat writer who once got drunk with Kerouac and Cassady, or a sixties holdover who used *man* and *cool* as conversational punctuation; like a Stanford grad who once read French poetry but had become more of a Tom Robbins, Colleen McCullough guy over the years; and, with a robust actor's voice, like someone who performed in community theater. Nick was all of those. He was also, though hardly anyone knew it, listed in the red British volumes of *Debrett's Peerage.*

On a film set a while ago, I learned that the art department often has to find or create a "hero prop," that special, perhaps magical, object key to the movie's narrative. Rose's necklace from *Titanic*, Bilbo's ring in *The Hobbit*, *Citizen Kane*'s Rosebud sled. In what passes for real life, that dusty package is the hero prop of this family story. Two men at the heart of the tale, Gawen Brownrigg and his son, Nicholas, turned away from each other: one wrongly thought that he would live long enough to turn back, and the other that it was safer to stay turned away. But not knowing your son, or your father, is a yawning emptiness in a life. No amount of lab work or internet research can fill it.

One of the two men did have the chance, though, to bridge that gap. The package that arrived at our Berkeley house included a wrapped scrapbook created by Beatrice Brownrigg, my dad's grandmother, with letters and photographs and accounts that mattered—to Nick. If he would look at them, that is.

Otherwise, it would be left to me to turn it all into stories.

PART ONE

✦

A Tale of
Two Fathers

Mike probably sent you that video . . . pretty good, huh? Young Nicholas evoked a tear, must say, must be getting dotty, but the little fellow is quite fetching and will never lack for parental love, kinda strange watching this baby human being, not even able to walk or talk and think of all his life unfolding ahead of him, all the steps on the way, the laughter, the tears, the . . . the whole staggering mystery of being alive for a nanosecond on this earth. Bonne chance, mon vieux, bonne chance.

—NICK BROWNRIGG TO SYLVIA,
JANUARY 23, 1994 (ABOUT NICK'S
FIRST GRANDSON, MIKE'S SON,
NAMED FOR HIM)

1.

THE INTREPID
BROWNRIGG PARTY

✦

"AS THE SUN SINKS SLOWLY IN THE WEST . . ."

The large bearded man would intone these words from the driver's seat of his Toyota truck as my brother and I settled into the hard-benched back. Tow-headed Mike in a plaid flannel shirt and jeans, me younger and scraggle-haired, likely in a tie-dyed tee under my jacket.

". . . the intrepid Brownrigg party finally makes its departure, heading out into the great unknown."

It might be a dark predawn, and we were heading off on a fishing jaunt over on the coast. Or we had had breakfast, cereal with blackberries we had picked from overgrown bushes out by the woodpile, and were now readying for an excursion into town to get more milk, meat, cigarettes. The point was, we were not leaving as early as our dad had hoped. Getting kids on board, something he wasn't practiced at, took time.

It wasn't real, though. He was speaking a kind of fiction. At nine years old, I didn't know what *intrepid* meant, but you could tell from his heavy, dramatic voice that he was making us part of a story, a joke-story about who we might have been. *The Brownrigg party.*

It was the only thing he ever said to my brother and me about the Brownriggs, at all.

I used to imagine Nick's voice, and that line, before some great embarkation of my own, especially one in a car, involving kids. As a parent packing up two little ones for a road trip, three if my stepson was joining us, rustling together snacks and gear and entertainment and car seats, I had the exasperated feeling that Scott or Shackleton could not have had to master this level of detail. That was when I heard my dad's dry irony in my mind; sometimes I even breathed it aloud, mostly to myself.

"As the sun sinks slowly in the west . . ."

The phrase came to me as I drove to meet my brother one morning in that year, 2012. Our dad had invited us to lunch, just us two, which was rare, possibly a first. And Mike and I had this package to deliver to Nick, about fifty years late, though that wasn't the reason our dad had asked us to join him. Death was the reason. Not imminent, but implied: he wanted to talk to us about his will. This was also unusual, discussing finances or the future with our dad in a way that suggested we were family.

Nick was not the man my brother and I had grown up with. He moved out when I was born. Our household had been a compact unit in the early years: my mother, my brother, and me, as well as a plump, unhappy dachshund who had learned how to nose open the refrigerator, so someone always had to bungie-cord it shut when we left the house. In addition to all the good things, ice cream cones or Los Angeles cousins or trips to the beach, I was aware in my small years of a hovering, anxious atmosphere at home, the air that comes from someone having been left. From someone having left.

Our dad lived an hour away from us in San Francisco, and we saw him intermittently. He did not have a regular job and was said to be working on a book. He had long brown hair and a droopy mustache, smoked, swore a lot. He was foreign to me, and I had a quiet, unspecified fear of him, an animal instinct like the sense for earthquakes. The uneasiness was mutual. To him, I was a soft-spoken mystery; to me, he was loud and alarming, though if I ever earned his approval—for instance, by catching one of his passes during a game of three-person football—I glowed. Sometimes he took my brother and me to a bowling alley, or to Candlestick Park, where we sat chilled in those sharp winds off the bay, eating hot dogs and cheering on the Giants, especially Willie Mays when he came up to the plate. Mike spent more time with our dad than I did and was allowed to stay overnight. My visits were limited to the daytime. There was no explanation for the difference;

it may have had to do with the convention then that "boys need their father," as if girls do not. Or, in leaving when and how he did, Nick may have been judged by a tribunal of one to have forfeited his rights with me. Whatever the reason, the policy changed once my stepmother came on the scene.

In 1971, Nick met Valerie Arden, a gifted pianist from Michigan who worked in San Francisco in the pre–computer industry. They got married in a barefoot ceremony on Mount Tamalpais in Marin. My brother and I weren't invited to the wedding, but we saw the pictures. Soon afterward, Nick and Valerie left city life and moved up to the Circle C Ranch, eighty forested acres reached after an hourlong dirt-road drive from the logging town of Ukiah. (HOME OF MASONITE read the proud sign as you came into the main streets.) The place was remote, beautiful, rugged: there was no electricity or telephone, hot water depended on keeping a fire burning in the kitchen stove, and the nearest neighbors were a few miles away. Our dad and his wife were close, in their fused solitudes, sharing the toughness and hard work needed to render their outpost life viable, making friends over the years with people "in town" and others who were carving out rebellious lives in the woods. They somehow got Valerie's upright piano out there, so on a good afternoon we could surreptitiously listen to her practicing Chopin's waltzes or Bach's Italian Concerto.

The ranch, with its risks and its freedoms, became above all the thing my brother and I shared with our dad. Gradually, the long-haired hippie who had planned to write a great novel about his urban, alcohol-fueled adventures became a rancher guy who hunted and cut down trees and made wine from grapes he had planted. But really no word or category quite matched Nick. He was someone who did what he wanted. In the early 1970s, he and his wife wanted to make their home off the grid in an elemental wilderness, and so that's what they did. They were intrepid.

2.

WINE O'CLOCK
SOMEWHERE

+

MIKE AND I MET IN A PARKING LOT OFF THE FREEWAY, after crossing our respective bridges, so we could drive the last hour of Highway 101 together. My brother, who still had his light blond hair, only slightly receding, wore glasses and the light business clothes of the Californian-in-finance he had become. As for me, well, somewhere along the way I had finally learned to brush my hair, so I no longer resembled the unkempt kid I had been, squirrel-cheeked like my dad and buck-toothed, mats at the back of my head that required periodic hours-long disentangling, or in the worst case, removal by scissors. (At a summer camp I once went to where everyone won a trophy, mine had been the "Can I borrow your hairbrush?" award.) As a girl, I never felt pretty and no one said I was; but eventually, after the interventions of orthodontistry and romance—being told you are beautiful transforms you—I grew into my appearance. Now, on a good day, I could achieve a kind of elegance and smile as the groomed blond mom I had become. People might assume things about me based on how I looked (my conventionality, my "normalcy"), but then that happens to anyone.

I had the package with me. Mike and I talked and joked about the laborious journey it had taken from my aunt in Los Angeles to our mother, and from our mother to me. Convoluted arrangements of this kind—handoffs of parcels, transfers in BART stations, keys hidden in tire wells to enable someone else to drive the car—are a hallmark of our non-Brownrigg family, the people we think of as family, on our mother's side. Any one of us has enough canniness and knack for logistical complexity to be a spy, or an operative. It is somewhere between a honed skill and a bad habit.

Nick had booked a table for us at a lively place in Healdsburg, a once-agricultural town in Sonoma County that now had wine as its lifeblood and was shaping up as a competitor to Napa. Limos glided darkly along the modest streets, carting tourists from new boutique hotels to surrounding vineyards, and restaurants and tasting rooms jostled round the central plaza by gift shops selling tea towels and aprons printed with jaunty sayings like *It's wine o'clock somewhere* or *You had me at Merlot.*

"Something to drink?" the waiter suggested.

"You guys should—they have a great list."

In host mode our dad was generous and gregarious. Formerly he'd have had a glass or three of wine at lunch himself, taking pleasure in his knowledgeable selection, not showing off but sharing his enthusiasm. That was one of his great gifts: rounded bloodshot eyes widened, shaggy eyebrows raised, he would exclaim about something—a dish, a drink, a jazz riff—*Man, that's good!* He had an experienced palate, though he never made great claims for the wine he had made at the Circle C ("It's not Premier cru, but it's not plonk, either"). He and Valerie had entered wine-tasting competitions for a while, and had a couple of victory certificates taped up on the weathered yellow walls of their dusty homestead kitchen.

"Days of gracious," my dad called them, the good decades before they had to leave the ranch, and before he fell ill with liver cancer. It is a very Dad phrase. Eventually, when he reached his sixties, they both had worn-out joints that made looking after so much land too hard, having to chop wood for the fire, maintain the dirt road, clamber up hills and deep into the woods to check the water lines. The couple had lived and worked at the Circle C mostly without help, except for the great late-summer cider parties they threw, when people came from all around to pick and press apples from their orchards, or on special projects, like the time they installed a windmill at the top of the hill above the house. One day in the late 1990s, Valerie "fell and did a number on her knee," Dad said, and a helicopter had to lift her out, since an ambulance could not make it over the curving journey of Low Gap Road. Miraculously, it was the only time a rescue was required in the over twenty-five years they lived there. Nick and Valerie sold up and bought a house on the north coast, moving back to civilization. That's where they were when he received his diagnosis.

Since the liver surgery he had stopped drinking, so while Mike and I enjoyed wine with our bistro sandwiches and beer-battered green beans, Nick got through without. The estate discussion was brief and somewhat awkward, mostly because this territory was so unfamiliar to us. Our dad covered provisions he had made for our stepmother, some new information about his younger half brothers, and the financial affairs of his late mother, Lucia. He probably made a dark joke about Lucia; there had always been plenty of those. Nick used to refer to his four-times-married mother as Jocasta, without elaborating. (Jocasta is Oedipus's mom, if you need a refresher.) His father, Gawen (pronounced GOW-in, first syllable rhymes with *now*), had been the first of Lucia's four husbands, right at the start of the series. Nick never spoke of him.

Someone watching our lunch together that day would have observed our easy joking manner with one another, seen the physical similarities. As adults, we had plenty to connect us. We all watched sports, had dogs, enjoyed the natural world, hated hypocrites. I have my dad's eyebrows, his sarcasm; Mike his height, his love of fishing. You would imagine Nick to be a regular old guy out with his kids, sorting through some business. My brother and I in our different ways willed that appearance, even if we did not feel it. It was another kind of fiction. We each knew what was missing; neither of us had ever counted on Nick, and we weren't about to start.

We did have our own revelation to offer, though, or we thought we did. Mike and I had agreed not to say anything ahead of time; it seemed better to explain in person the wrapped object waiting now under the table by our feet, in the place where a dog might lie half asleep or hoping for scraps.

After coffee and a couple of desserts—Nick, though diabetic, freely indulged his sweet tooth—my brother and I came to our unrehearsed announcement.

We made apologetic guesses of why this wrapped package had been lost or hidden until now. No one knew anymore how it had ended up on a remote shelf in the cavernous Los Angeles basement of our mother's family, Nick's long-ago in-laws. These people he had not been related to for decades had kept it alongside the several volumes published by various further-back Brownriggs. It seemed clear the mistake came not from malice but from carelessness, and certainly when my aunt found them during a late-in-life cleanup, she was embarrassed they had not reached Nick sooner.

Our dad showed no anger or surprise about this, but neither did he show any interest in what was inside. I don't know what went through his mind when he saw his formal name written in the hand of his English grandmother, a woman whom, I'd later learn, he had known and loved as a small child, who had cared for him when his own parents wouldn't.

To Sir Nicholas G Brownrigg, Baronet.

He made an unreadable face—pursed lips, brow raised in irony, his ever-ready mask over any deep emotion—and put the parcel back in the canvas tote bag we had carried it in. My brother and I could tell there was no point in pushing him, however eager we were to see the contents. Did it contain stories about his English relatives? Specifically, information about his father, Gawen Brownrigg, a writer who had died by suicide in Kenya when Nick was just a boy? We assumed he would take the package home and find out, open it with his wife, rather than under the curious eyes of son and daughter. We would hear about it later, probably from Valerie.

Our dad's greetings and goodbyes were always back-thumping and affectionate. "Hey, Syl, great to see you." *Thump.* He turned to my brother. "Muckle—carry on, old man. Carry on."

And taking the tote bag and its contents, he drove off north again, leaving Mike and me to head back to the Bay Area, deflated by the anti-climax. When I returned to Berkeley, and my own busy household of dog and kids, books and papers, it frustrated my husband that I had no dramatic tale to tell. He had floated the idea of our opening the package ourselves, to see what was in it before I took it up there.

I did not think we should have opened it, but I shared his frustration. What if somewhere inside that thick envelope was a crucial element that might explain the mysterious arc of my dad's life, how it came to bend toward Ukiah, unfathomable miles away from the English people he had left behind?

The sun sank slowly in the west; but the Brownrigg party remained none the wiser.

3.

LOS MUERTOS

✦

THE DEAD DON'T COME BACK, BUT THEY ARE NOT AS FAR away as you think.

I had to start losing people before I understood this. Older, wiser cultures than the one that formed me teach children about their ancestors: people sit around the fire telling tales of the figures who came before, make ritual cemetery visits to pay their respects, construct shrines for Día de los Muertos. My own kids, at their school in Oakland, learned about the Day of the Dead and were tasked with creating craft objects celebrating loved ones who had died.

But the Californians I sprang from looked forward, not back. You made yourself up from scratch. There was no talk of "ancestors," and ditto *los muertos*. My high school town, Palo Alto, later became near synonymous with start-ups, which is how we thought of ourselves. The angels mentioned in the Bay Area are usually investors; I didn't hear much about any other kind.

You miss a lot that way. You step across people's graves without even knowing you're doing it. It's a kind of cultural amnesia—related to pretending not to know who lived there before European explorers did. *Pioneer* is such a different word from *colonizer*. Wagons seemed fun and adventurous to a white California girl who liked imagining horses and cowboys and open spaces. Colorful histories of land being claimed by scrappy settlers did not then consider the people who were already living there and had been for years: this was true in both the American West and, half a world away, British East Africa.

Besides, divorce gives you an extra reason not to want to think about the past. Mike was three when Nick left our Los Altos house, begged him not to go. I was always glad I did not have any memory like that in my emptied mind. To the question people used to ask me—"How old were you when your parents divorced?"—I got some satisfaction from answering, "Zero." It was such a clean number. "And Zero at the Bone," Emily Dickinson wrote, though she was describing the chill brought on by meeting a snake, not the feeling brought on by the word *divorce*.

If we ever heard the word *family*, it often had the word *broken* in front of it. When you are told as a kid that you come from a *broken family*, it bugs you after a while. What's the alternative? Whole, pristine families, sitting like china teapots on some shelf? Who wants to come from one of those?

You don't want the pity, and you don't want to think of it as a big deal. The word *broken* has the sound of something violent and unfixable. For us it was more a question of a group portrait that you could not fully make out—an image half painted over, so some faces were blurred or unreadable. Over years, my brother and I made up for the absence in the ways we could. I wrote stories; he coached teams. There was not a field or diamond my brother's many athletic children played on that Mike did not stand on the sidelines of, cheering. As for stories: well, where my dad had tried writing books and then stopped, I tried and kept going.

Yet I guess it is not an accident that I am often drawn, in love and friendship, to people who are missing someone. They were adopted; or they lost a father young, to illness or suicide; or their parents rejected them for being gay; or they rejected their parents for being intolerant. Or simply, their fathers or their mothers drank, living behind that particular fortress, sober mostly in the early mornings, like my dad, or only out in their work lives but rarely when they were at home.

It was more years before Mike and I learned anything about what we had handed over to our dad that day in Healdsburg. Our own work and family lives, spouses and kids, tasks and deadlines, produced challenges and distractions. From time to time, my brother would ask Valerie if Nick had gotten around to opening the package, and she would tell Mike that it was driving her crazy, but she could not make him do it. Our father's health started to deteriorate and require more attention, and he suffered from memory issues, which maddened them both.

Chatting with them out on their deck by the dunes in Fort Bragg one day, I threw the ball for their busy, noisy border collie, who focused her fierce intelligence on the fate of that rubber ball, retrieving it from deep in the sandy brush alongside their winding, eucalyptus-shaded driveway. I listened to my dad trying to explain what was happening to him.

"I'm losing . . . I'm losing . . . ," he said, a man who had always been so inventive with words trying to find the right one.

"Well, you're losing your marbles, Nick," Valerie said.

He laughed a little, agreeing with her. They had always been pretty direct with each other.

"Maybe you can get marble replacement therapy, Dad," I suggested.

He laughed at that, too.

I did not ask about the package on that visit; I left those questions to my brother. It was up to our dad to decide when he would feel ready to open it. It had always been his decision. It should have been his story.

There was a problem, though. He was in his eighties, and he was running out of time.

4.

THE WELSH WORD FOR "LITTLE BIRD"

✦

THE EARTH WAS HARD AND DRY. NOT MUCH GREW ON THE small hill above our house in Los Altos but scratchy, dehydrated grass. I was seven, using a trowel and not making much headway as I knelt in my blue jeans, trying to chip away enough dirt to make a difference. But bit by bit, I dug a shoebox-sized hole. I was preparing to bury Sab.

Sab was my favorite chicken, a cute bantam hen with soft white feathers and an inscrutable blue-black face under a comical fluffy topknot. She was half Japanese silkie. My best friends, the Yu sisters, had shown me how, if you held a chicken in your arms and stroked it gently, the soothed bird would close its eyes and take a nap. This was something we did sometimes for fun, when we weren't playing imaginary games in the abandoned apricot orchards or dried creek beds nearby. It was how we became friends in the first place: I brought my pet chicken in to my first-grade class for show-and-tell, and afterward, when the teacher asked for a student volunteer to help me carry the cage back to the parking area where my mom waited, Jennifer Yu raised her hand.

We had gotten the chickens on a whim of my mom's, after she saw a listing in our local paper, *Los Altos Town Crier* (the *Crier*'s logo a smiley Pilgrim ringing a bell). Linda, our mom, asked the teenage son of a friend to come over and build us a basic structure and erect a wire fence around a scrabbly dirt area for the chickens to wander in. We lived in a cramped, irregular-angled, redwood-walled bungalow—its inventive but impractical architect was a fan of Frank Lloyd Wright—with little light and no neighbors, except for a doctor we never saw who kept giant poodles in her backyard. The coop was about ten yards from our house, past the clothesline, partly sheltered by a cottonwood tree and perched on top of another mild slope that led down to an unfriendly jungle of poison oak. The joke was that the chickens had the best view of anyone, looking out as they did to a slice of the bay. My first weighty responsibility in life was to lock up the coop every night after they had gone in to roost. After dark, predators came out.

I say "my favorite," and Sab was, of our first clutch of birds, but there was a child's narcissism in this, as I had named her with my initials. SAB had not seemed like much, before that. Mike had cool initials—MGB, like the sports car, perfect for a boy. Not only that, but his middle name was Gawen, giving him something extra in common with our dad, who was Nicholas Gawen Brownrigg. I knew Gawen was a "family name," whatever that meant, and that my middle name, Alderyn, was not. Mine had been found in a book, and my mother told me it meant "little bird" in Welsh. This pleased me, as I loved birds. I found out she was wrong only many years later when, applying for a reader's card at Oxford's Bodleian Library—as my mother once had—I was required to swear an oath that I would not harm the books. On hearing my full name the friendly librarian commented, "Ah, if only it were 'Aderyn,' your name would be the Welsh word for bird, wouldn't it?" My first research act in that hallowed, light-filled reading room was to find a Welsh-English dictionary. The librarian was right, of course. *Aderyn* meant "bird"; *Alderyn* meant nothing.

Still ignorant of this mistake, I called our new pet Sab, which did give me a personal connection with that hen and made me fonder of her than of the others.

The idyll ended in a bloodbath. I was spared seeing the worst of it; my mom warned me before school not to go out and look, and I took her advice. A raccoon had gotten into the coop. I must not have closed it up right. The raccoon tried to bite the chickens' heads off, but it did not succeed in killing all of them, and at least one lived on, blind in one eye. (It was the hen we called Fuzzy.) "They don't even do it for the food," my mother told me, disgusted. "They just drink the blood." I am not sure where this wildlife fact came from, but the vampiric nature of it stayed with me. Don't tell me raccoons are cute. They're monsters.

The shoebox for Sab's stiffening feathered body was to prevent any other creatures from smelling it underground and trying to dig up a free dinner. The hills around where we lived, now famous for housing tech billionaires in mansions that look more like movie sets or county museums, were then scrappy and unfenced, dotted with nondescript ranch houses and populated by deer, snakes, and coyotes. People who chose to live up there, some distance from town or city, might be doctors, like the Yu girls' father, or engineers. Our situation, a single mother working on getting her PhD in English, was unusual.

The Yu family, in part inspired by us, took the chicken idea and ran with it, gradually building an empire of coops and cages and a small pond, populating their land with ducks and chickens, peacocks, and even a glamorous pair of golden pheasants. They eventually brought a few of their bantams to the Santa Clara County Fair. I spent a lot of time at the Yus' house, often slept over, went with them to drive-in screenings of Bruce Lee movies, and learned to eat salty dried plums for a snack. A warm and lively family of five, they generously made room for a kid at loose ends after a divorce. Connie Young Yu, a lifelong activist who worked to expand awareness of Chinese American history, volunteered in those days at the Peace Center. She would take her daughters and me with her in the family's spacious station wagon, then let us go get comic books and beef jerky while she did her shift. It was a time when Palo Alto had such a thing—a Peace Center.

What is it they say about that trio of the most stressful things to go through—divorce, death, moving? We had a sampling. Some time after the chicken massacre, my brother and I were given some unexpected news: we were relocating to England, where we would live and go to school.

5.

ALL SOULS

✦

ONE REASON GIVEN WAS THAT OUR MOTHER NEEDED TO do more research for the PhD she was working toward at Stanford. Linda was a medievalist and had to go to British libraries that held the various Anglo-Saxon manuscripts she was studying. Long before I used the word *manuscript* for my own hopeful stack of xeroxed pages sent round to agents, I associated the word with centuries-old pieces of vellum covered with beautiful, obscure calligraphy and colorful outsized initials, and harbored in different faraway European cities. They had led us to England the summer before, 1971, when we stayed for a while in a damp basement flat in London, from where you could watch suited legs walking by behind black metal railings, giving you the feeling that you were in an underground jail. Posted signs on the fenced, well-tended greens of city squares read TRESPASSERS WILL BE PROSECUTED, which alarmed me since I thought *prosecuted* meant *executed*. It was a barbaric country, where you heard stories about people's heads getting chopped off—maybe not recently, but it made sense to be careful. I kept off the grass. There were chilly rules and stern accents, which people used to tell you things like "It's disrespectful to step on someone's grave" when you were caught playing tag in a small cemetery outside an Oxford church. A few streets away from that particular church was a darkened, spire-shaped monument called the Martyrs' Memorial, built to honor three religious Englishmen who had been burned at the stake there. The monument was put up by other Englishmen who came along later, who decided that burning the men had been an error. Like I said, it was a barbaric country.

The other reason, which maybe emerged as the real reason, that we were moving to England, and specifically to Oxford, was because of my mother's new "friend." On our summer trip, she had met a gentle legal academic named Philip, and over the winter break he had come out to visit us in California. (She was so excited to pick Philip up at the airport that she forgot she had left a pile of undergraduates' papers she was supposed to grade on top of the car; off they all flew, when she got on to the freeway, never to be retrieved.) Philip was a Fellow of All Souls College, a title that suited his companionable, inclusive nature, and he was Jewish, though the significance of that was obscure to me. Sharing a household with a new person and changing countries to do it was a dramatic shift, though the parental bribe was, comically, architectural: we would finally live in an ordinary house, the kind with an upstairs and normal, rectangular rooms. There were neighbors and parks nearby, and you could ride a bike without killing yourself on the steepness of the slope. It wasn't as if "No thank you" were an option—it never is when you are shuttled around as a kid—but right angles did sweeten the deal.

Oxford was our home for six years, in two stretches. I never got a sense that our dad complained about the geographical displacement of his two children. He and Valerie were busy settling the Circle C, buying trucks and gear and books about how to kill and cure game. Mike and I were living in the country Nick's father and the Brownriggs had come from, a fact that went unmentioned. By everyone.

So we did what you do: we got on with adjusting to the differences. Biking on the left-hand side of the road, Mike learning how to bowl overarm for cricket, and best of all discovering a *sweet shop*— translation: candy store!—on the walk to school, where you could buy a handful of morning sugar for a *ha'penny*, a small brown coin that looked like pretend money. We reorganized our slang: *you guys* had to go, kids laughed if you said you were *mad*, and *bloody* was a swear word that might get you into trouble. At our local elementary school, we sang Anglican hymns every morning at assembly, and learned the Lord's Prayer. They still slippered or hit children there who misbehaved. It happened to me once: the teacher called me up to the front of the class, then glared me into holding out my hand for the slap. On the playground everyone, girl or boy, had to have a football team to support, so I picked the Wolverhampton Wanderers, not because we lived anywhere near Wolverhampton but because their nickname was Wolves, and I liked animals. Also, I tended to wander.

In December we went home to California and visited our dad, spending a memorable holiday at the Circle C, on which we chopped down our own Christmas tree from the woods nearby and learned how to read by the light of kerosene lamps, amid storms and mud and a deep, old-fashioned cold at night fended off with a huge weight of blankets. The two places were old in different ways: one had Gothic churches that housed marbled nobles lying on stone tombs, their arms crossed; the other a weather-beaten schoolhouse that had stood since the turn of the century, a rusted-out truck down in the meadow, and pearl-bright abalone shells half buried around the perimeter by long-ago members of the Pomo tribe or else the Coast Yuki.

Our day-to-day life in Oxford's outskirts was fairly suburban; it was only in the center, where the colleges are scattered, that the city's antique grandeur made itself felt. If our mother took us in to go shopping, we'd walk along narrow alleys and around golden-stoned buildings to enter the covered market, where they hung big slabs of dead animals at the butcher's and for some reason had a stuffed fox, wearing glasses, in one display window. A neighbor, whose daughter roller-skated with me along our road's bumpy sidewalk, ran the boathouse by Magdalen Bridge, where you could rent punts to take out on the River Cherwell. On one side of the bridge was the boys' school Mike went to when he turned eleven, where he had to wear a tie and attend class on Saturdays (more barbarity), and which taught us that *Magdalen* is pronounced "Maudlin." On the other side, Magdalen College's iconic tower marked the juncture where the Oxford of postcards and famous gargoyled buildings began.

I was a dreamy kid, often inhabiting an alternate world. In the town center it was easy to imagine ghosts along those ancient streets, shuffling along cobbled alleys, pacing the quiet cloisters, or haunting the riverbanks where weeping willows drew mournful leafy fingers through the water. In those parts of the city you could see why so many tourists came to soak up the history of the celebrated university and ogle the rounded glories of the Sheldonian Theatre or the Radcliffe Camera (confusingly, not a camera).

It is too bad I didn't possess the telepathic powers I wished for; if I had, I might have seen Gawen around there somewhere. My grandfather had himself gone to Magdalen College in 1929 (I believe the crash was one reason his family was strapped for cash). He is in the college's books for that year, and his second novel opens with a scene set at Oxford, a disaffected student assessing the damage in his rooms the morning after a raucous party.

If someone had told me then, I could at least have imagined Gawen. The knowledge would have changed the color and feel of those streets.

6.

DEEP THROAT

+

THEY STAYED "FRIENDS." THEY NEVER BECAME EXES OR enemies—my mother and Philip were together for forty-seven rich, loving, adventurous years—but neither did they become husband and wife.

To live with your mother and her "friend" gives your household an amiable feeling, rather than a familial one. Their partnership was warm, cooperative, largely egalitarian. I loved Philip; everyone did. He was a funny, generous, deeply considerate person, as well as a great listener. He was a payer of attention, and a master of tact. But it was Philip plus us. My mother, my brother, and I were the *us*.

You could not tell this from the outside; ostensibly, Philip and my mother were regular parents. Philip shopped and cooked, something you notice as a child because food governs so much of life. (You don't ask, after hearing of a girl in your school called Longrigg, *Why do I have such an English name?* You do ask, or at least wonder, *Do I really have to learn to like blancmange? And custard?*) Philip went to our matches, Mike playing rugby, me playing netball or tennis; he was interested in our homework and attended parent-teacher evenings. He took pride, and let us know it, when we did well. There were parental roles he deliberately avoided, such as any real disciplining, leaving that to our mother. And if anyone ever referred to him as my dad, I was quick to correct them, or he was. With us, too, he positioned himself as a friend.

Family shapes have always been elastic, and of course vary hugely culture to culture, but for people like me who grew up during the worries and threats of the Cold War, with a lingering memory of the Cuban Missile Crisis, it always seemed eerie that *nuclear* was the word assigned to an ideal, "normal" form of family. Especially if you did not come from one. When, thirty years on, my own kids had a unit in second grade devoted to "nontraditional families," they were made aware of nonnuclear options.

We did not call Philip our anything: there was no correct word. He was simply Philip. Eventually, when I was older and taking our collective reality into the wider world, I started using the word *stepfather* about him, since it described the role he played and since the fuller explanation was cumbersome. ("You see, they've never married . . .") But Philip, a stickler for accuracy and the truth, never referred to himself that way, over all those decades—not until the last six months or so of his life, when it became impossible for me to help with making doctors' appointments and getting medical information if I did not have some specified relation to him. I felt the irony: although my father's surgeon spoke to me, as Nick's daughter, without suspecting how tenuous my relationship with Nick had once been, there were greater obstacles with the man who raised me. When I found my way to a Santa Clara hospital to visit Philip, by then frail and ill, the internist at his bedside saw me in the doorway and asked warily, "Who are you?" Neither the patient nor I had a ready answer, though Philip finally said in a faint voice: "She's my partner's daughter."

In the 1970s, even previously conventional people were doing a lot of living together. It was not that big a deal, though at first our beloved older babysitter and some of Philip's relatives muttered with discomfort, and my father told me years later that he considered taking some stand against my mother living with her partner unmarried. The idea that our dad—hippie, drinker, iconoclast who never gave "a rat's ass what people thought" about one thing or another—could have had a moral qualm about my mother and Philip's arrangement seemed laughable to me. Though it now seems related to the origin story Valerie told me, a few years ago, of their own marital union. Nick and Valerie had been dating for a while when his mother, Lucia, in Albuquerque, had invited her son to join her on a trip to Morocco. He asked, "Can I bring my girlfriend?" to which she replied, "Not if you're not married, no." So Nick went back to Valerie with a double proposal. "Do you want to get married? And then go with my mother and me to Morocco?" She said yes to both.

One by one, the other cohabiting couples we knew got married, while my mother and Philip never did. When people asked me why, I had to shrug. Marriage seemed to be something that had damaged my mother so badly that she would never return to it, like a foreign country you once went to where you almost died from a terrorist attack or a parasite picked up at a restaurant. Getting married again was off the table for Linda. She preferred to shape a more free-spirited life with her friend.

This meant that on paper my mother appeared to be related to Nick, not Philip. Names often fracture after a divorce, but my mother has stayed Linda Brownrigg throughout her life, even though she was infuriated by the man whose name she carried and indifferent to the story of his English family. Lately, I have considered the strangeness of her keeping his surname after such a short marriage (it lasted five years) and such a bitter split. Then again, the name she had grown up with was not exactly available to reclaim. My mother was Linda Lovelace until she married. By the early 1970s, a different Linda Lovelace had become famous, you could say notorious, for her role in the porn flick *Deep Throat*, so for our mother there was no easy return to a name you could not really call "maiden." (My businessman uncle, Jon, occasionally asked if he was related to Linda Lovelace, took mischievous pleasure in saying that he was.) The times I have tentatively begun writing fiction about any of this, I have squandered hours looking for a suitable parallel name for a seventies porn star that might also sound elegant and southern. A name like Lovelace. It's not as easy as you might think.

7.

A PERSON IN A PHOTOGRAPH

✦

IN 1980, RONALD REAGAN WAS ELECTED, I TOOK MY O-level exams in Oxford, and a different three of us (my mother, Philip, and I) returned to California so that I could finish high school. My brother was away at college, and we reorganized an American life. Again my slang was off, my clothes were wrong, and the music I liked, English ska bands, seemed weird. I learned how to drive, on the right-hand side of the road, and adapted to a culture of fake IDs. In Oxford teens drank freely in pubs and elsewhere; even at my girls' school, the ordinarily prim headmistress, who might issue a reprimand if your navy-blue trousers were not of the proper polyester, jollily served beer and hard cider to us at a dance held one night in the assembly hall, where that morning we had prayed and sung hymns. My transition to being an American teen was awkward, underlining other adolescent awkwardness. I did not feel I belonged anywhere, though at least I could say "you guys" again without getting hassled.

One day, as my mother was clearing out cabinets, she came upon a box of photographs from her wedding in 1959. The nuptials took place in Los Angeles, with a reception afterward at her parents' spacious Spanish-style house, a place I knew from visits to our Lovelace grand-parents (I thought of myself as only having one set: my grandfather a man generally suited and remote, the founder of a successful investment firm). My mom brought the box into my narrow polygonal bedroom, herself amazed by the forgotten images. A trove of family memories, not unlike the one carefully produced and intended for Nicholas that my brother and I would be combing through one day in our late middle age. But a time capsule makes much more sense when interpreted by someone whose earlier self it contains.

I sat on the carpeted floor staring at pictures of an event I had never contemplated. The marriage question was so remote that I had not considered the fact that my mother must have once had a wedding. The idea of weddings had not crossed my mind. I wasn't a girl who dreamed of myself being a bride one day; it seemed as unlikely as my becoming an astronaut or a murderer or a princess. *Really?* was my skeptical thought as I browsed the photographs, the way some people must feel about the moonwalk images. *Yes, but those pictures might have been faked by NASA.* Certainly the round-faced, clean-shaven man in a tux bore some resemblance to the bearded mountain guy who lived at the Circle C, and the lovely, silk-gowned young woman was definitely Linda. (We have the same smile.) They were a handsome couple, though it made me shiver to think so, as if I were feeling a faint breeze from the multiverse. Corroborating the photographs' authenticity, I recognized older Lovelace cousins in cute roles as flower girl and ring bearer. What startled me most, though, was one particular stranger: a stout middle-aged woman with protruding eyes and a wolflike smile. She looked exactly like my dad. She was a female version of my dad.

I yelped.

"Is that—is she—"

Yes, it was. She was. My other grandmother, the mysterious one who lived in New Mexico. I had never met her. My mother told me her name, Lucia. Originally, Lucia von Borosini. Half-German, I was told, though her father was actually Austrian.

Lucia's picture provoked shock in me and a hint of distaste, as when your favorite novel is turned into a film and you can't stand the actor cast in a key role. She was stolid and matronly, not pretty, and if I still felt alarmed by my dad at times, I felt wary, too, of this hungry female impersonator who stood and smiled, blackly and whitely, in the Los Angeles house I knew. My mom's tone made it clear that she had never much liked her mother-in-law, and I was then still close to and aligned with my mom, so out of loyalty to her I developed no curiosity about Lucia.

I accepted passively that she would remain, for me, a person in a photograph. No one urged me to claim Lucia as a grandmother—my dad had been mute on the subject—so I might as well continue living in the counterfactual world created by my mother and father both. Accepting someone as a relative appeared to be optional, so I rejected Lucia.

8.

"I HAD A FARM IN AFRICA"

✦

AT SEVENTEEN, I WENT EAST FOR COLLEGE, WHERE I learned that in the Ivy League there are plenty of people with a powerful sense of the families they come from, whose names are like badges, or cudgels. That was not a culture familiar to me, and those were not the students who became my friends. Brownrigg was, for me, just an unspellable mouthful. I took women's studies classes and became a feminist, organizing protests, cooking lentil soup in a shared off-campus apartment, denouncing sexism, and fretting about my own racial privilege. I told my mother I had a girlfriend, which caused her great consternation and launched a years-long rhetorical battle to get me to change course. My hair was short, my clothes were thrift, my jackets were mannish. I got annoyed when my brother told me I could look pretty, if I would only try.

It had already been a bad period between my dad and me, and it got worse. In my late high school visits to the Circle C, when I had to go up without Mike, Nick and I got into arguments of a predictable kind. I played the adolescent part, trying out new righteous politics, like railing against the American obsession with guns and lack of gun control, and Nick got the redneck role of brushing off my spoiled suburbanite opinions, defending their need for firearms at the ranch. Probably somewhere in the script, in small print, was a note clarifying that I was partly representing *effete Europe*, and people in his family I had not yet heard about, though mostly the furnace blast of my dad's disgust seemed like it came from a hot, still-burning anger at my mother. "Los Altos Hills," the place he and Linda had once lived together with their young son, was a name uttered by my dad with tart contempt.

And of course we had already begun another classic dad-daughter argument that would run for several seasons and be repeated in the next generation: Did sexism still exist? Was it really a problem? I felt that Nick accidentally clinched this win for me when after too much wine he began complaining about women he had known who were "twats" or "prick-teases" ("Nicholas!" my stepmother interjected occasionally, though it did not stop him), the start of an adult habit he took up of telling me, in a murmur, which women he found attractive—gallery assistant, waitress, actress in a local production. When I read, recently, some letters he wrote to his mother over the years, I discovered Nick liked to make similar shock-worthy comments to her. It was something he spared my brother. Nick and Mike might have been in literal locker rooms together on the few occasions we went swimming in public pools, but our dad's locker-room talk was saved for his mother and daughter, from both of whom he was partially estranged.

Late in my freshman year at college, I was asked to co-edit the feminist student journal. Proud of the honor and of a piece I had written for its pages, I made the rookie mistake of sending my dad a copy. Did I really think that a goddess-named, smearily printed rag with sapphic poems and calls to action would win him over? It didn't. Rather, he duly mocked its contents in a long rant of a letter that mixed in casual anti-Semitism with the sarcastic rest. *Caustic* is the word that comes to mind about that letter, and like that sort of substance, it burned. At my brother's graduation dinner in 1983—a historic gathering, all four parental adults around the same table—Nick indulged in a boozy diatribe against a student who had spoken up for gay rights. It included a memorable, uniquely Nick-inflected riff: "If she really thinks George Washington is gonna applaud from his grave because some lesbian wants the right to go bed-hopping from one bed to the next . . ."

I kept quiet with him about having a girlfriend. It seemed like a good call. The announcement had been met with baffled distaste by my mother and brother, and for that matter Philip, so it seemed best to leave the news there for the moment.

In December 1985, I turned twenty-one, the age Nick was meant to be when he was to receive Beatrice's scrapbook about Gawen. Like all of my other college birthdays, the occasion was obscured by the stress of final exams, but after they were over I flew home to Los Altos. My dad offered to drive down and meet me nearby. He and I had some patching up to do. I think we shared an instinct that we had reached a juncture when our relation could get either better or terminally worse. Was it worth the effort to fix it? Our political differences and suspicions had corroded the bond between us; our affection was at its weakest point. The temptation to allow the gap to widen into a chasm, to simply let go of each other, flitted through our Brownrigg minds. There was precedent.

I had a farm in Africa.

We decided to go to a movie together, often the safest choice for a reunion when conversation is risky. I met my dad and stepmother at a large outdoor mall in Mountain View. Google was not yet a twinkle in the eye of Larry Page or Sergey Brin, and brightly colored work campuses with sushi bars and kombucha on tap were years away. Dad and Valerie drove down from the ranch, a chainsaw in the back of their Subaru in case they encountered downed trees blocking the road. The lights in the theater lowered, and Meryl Streep's seductive Danish voice drew us in as the camera panned over the lush, intoxicating landscape of Kenya's Rift Valley. It was a country that she (playing the writer Karen Blixen, who published as Isak Dinesen) would never forget. She would never forget her lover, Robert Redford, either. Who could? Redford played the charismatic English pilot Denys Finch Hatton, though the American actor did not attempt to sound English. Playing across from the empress of accents, he may have feared being shown up by her, or going the mockable route of Dick Van Dyke's cockney in *Mary Poppins*. In any case, Redford's suave, rugged American turned his and Streep's romance in *Out of Africa* into a European-American affair. I knew something about those, having grown up around one, that of my mother and Philip. I had not considered that my dad had been the product of one, too.

After the movie ended and the house lights came up, we sat in the dim theater and he spoke to me about it, while a teenager circulated, collecting candy wrappers and Coke cups.

"You know, Syl—my father, Gawen, who was English, died in Kenya. In Nairobi."

No, I had not known. Blixen's farm had been in Kenya, a country I could not have located on a map. All I knew of Kenya came from the film we had just watched.

"How?" I asked. "How did he die?"

"Drug overdose." My dad kept it simple. "It was suicide, they said." He raised his eyebrows, pursed his lips. His characteristic expression, which created a distance from any straight emotion. From grief, in particular.

The word *suicide* caught my attention. A close high school classmate of mine, who had attended freshman year at Harvard, had died that way. I was a reader of Sylvia Plath, of course. Any dark story of that kind plants itself in your imagination if the idea has ever occurred to you, as it had to me. Suddenly there was a solidity to it. My grandfather had *committed suicide*, as the phrase was then. Was that why I had not heard more about him? The shame of it? The pain of it?

"How old were you?"

"A young boy. I didn't know him. He and my mother had already divorced."

His mother: this was one of the first times I had heard my dad mention the scary woman in the wedding photograph, who lived in New Mexico. Before I could follow up that rare line about his childhood, Nick added another unexpected detail.

"Gawen wrote a novel that might interest you. It's called *Star Against Star*. I'll lend you my copy."

So Gawen Brownrigg was also a writer! Like my father had hoped to be. Like I hoped to be. I had known writing was what I wanted to do since elementary school. I had been warmly, unstintingly encouraged by my mother and Philip and kind teachers who read my stories, up to and including the novella I determinedly wrote at fourteen (a fable about the break in harmony between mankind and animals). But at Yale, a university crowded with confident young people aiming for, and achieving, early success in New York, I became almost furtive about my fiction writing; I wasn't yet ready for the competitive arena, certainly not for New York. I felt almost as far away from those students as from the scions of the Bush family, or the Hoovers.

This new fact, however, rearranged my thinking. There had already been a novelist Brownrigg. Gawen—not Nick.

That day in the movie theater my dad decided to draw a connection between these two shadowy relations: his long-dead father and his half-lost daughter. He might never have made that link. He could easily have allowed both of us to drop; it was doubtless his first instinct. In going the opposite way, Nick had no model. But it makes you like someone better when you choose to trust them with something important to you. It raised me in my dad's estimation—that I might receive this gift from him.

"That would be great," I said.

"I'll send it to you. But be careful with it."

"I will be. Thanks."

He was passing the baton to me. You could be grandiose and call it a scepter, if you wanted to go with Brownrigg-themed imagery for a minute, like the scepter Sir Robert Brownrigg brought back to Britain in the early 1800s from Kandy, as the island country later renamed Ceylon and, still later, Sri Lanka, was then known. (The scepter ended up at Windsor Castle, as such colonial objects I guess often did.) It was General Robert Brownrigg's actions for the Crown in "securing" Kandy for Britain—in a period when countries were thought of as wares available for imperial invaders—that earned the Englishman a baronetcy, a hereditary title. There was a Brownrigg coat of arms, a family motto. *Virescat vulnere virtus*, "Valor strengthens from a wound," a kind of Latin version of Nietzsche's "What does not kill me, makes me stronger." (The point is, pain is good for you.) In the peerage books that listed Nicholas, his first wife, Linda, gets a mention, and Michael and I do, too. Then Valerie. After Sir Nicholas died, Michael Gawen Brownrigg would become the sixth baronet, at which point Sylvia Alderyn Brownrigg, with her misspelled middle name, would fall out of the record.

I knew these basics, had seen our names in those red-bound books, and it had always seemed fictional to me, part of the same imaginary world as my dad's campy pronouncements about the "Brownrigg party." Nick did not tell me anything else, then or later, about Gawen or about Gawen's parents, his own English grandparents, though as a tiny boy he had lived with them in Maidenhead, near Reading, in the period when his young parents' marriage was already falling apart. I find it hard to believe Nick had no thoughts or memories of his grandmother Beatrice. But in that year, 1985, Beatrice's scrapbook was still lying unclaimed, wrapped up on a shelf in a Lovelace basement. We were thirty years away from seeing it.

My grandfather's novel, the physical book, was a family gift my dad was offering me—a first. Perhaps, even more than that, it was a writing gift. I don't know if it marked my dad's drawing a line under his own ambitions; certainly he was making a gentler offering than the sharp critique he had sent me some years earlier about my novella, a letter written with the brusque impatience of a literary agent returning an inadequate manuscript. (Something I now know Nick had himself received, which created a permanent discouragement and doubtless fed his unfettered mockery of his teenage daughter's effort.) I can't know, and of course I didn't ask him, but his sending me his father's book seems to me now a way of giving me his blessing.

One wintry January day, wearing jeans and a long navy peacoat, I collected a padded envelope from the student post office and found within it his copy of Star Against Star. I held the weight of the book in my hand, then took it to the library and started to read.

Within moments, I understood why my dad thought I might find my grandfather's work of interest. I had not told Nick anything about my romantic life, but he might have guessed or, more likely, heard the news from my brother.

My grandfather's novel told the story of two women in love.

9.

THE PROBLEMS OF ABNORMALITY

+

"RARE INDEED IS THE NOVELIST WHO CAN TURN HIS AT-tention to the problems of abnormality," notes the jacket copy of the 1935 edition, "without assuming the mantle of judge or censor. Gawen Brownrigg, however, in this his first novel dares to tell without partiality the story of a girl who, by virtue more of circumstance than of heredity, becomes, with full awareness of what is happening to her, a Lesbian."

Which would be worse, though—becoming a capital-L Lesbian by circumstance or by heredity? This was precisely a point that had haunted my mother since I told her about having girlfriend. Linda, distressed by my deviant path, fretted over what she could have done differently. What had gone wrong? Could she blame Nick?

> He traces the emotional development of Dorcas Castro from infancy to womanhood, showing the various influences actually moulding her destiny,—an oversexed mother, a significant incident during her childhood, a disastrous affair at school, her eventual meeting in Paris with Conseuelo Sinclair, a woman of morbid loveliness and a brilliant writer.
>
> In working up to the dramatic climax of his story—the tragic liaison between Dorcas and Consuelo—the author has steered an unsentimental course. His style is mature and understanding, unhysterical, free from cant and propaganda. He is

concerned only with his story. His book, refreshingly free from plea or condemnation, is a fearless examination of a life story of a young woman, all the more remarkable in that the author is a very young man. He wrote this book at the age of twenty one.

The book was published by Obelisk in Paris, a press run by an Englishman, Jack Kahane, who took advantage of French openness to bring out works that would have been caught up in British obscenity laws, or already had been. Kahane took on Radclyffe Hall's *The Well of Loneliness* after it had been banned in Britain, as well as other titles, including James Joyce's *Pomes Penyeach* and Henry Miller's *Tropic of Cancer.*

The copy notes that Gawen Brownrigg was twenty-one when he wrote it; I was twenty-one when I read it. I would like to say that my grandfather spoke to me through his fiction, but if so, it was something of a strangled warning—though whether about intrusive parents, the perils of Lesbianism, or just the risks of publishing your first novel too early, it would be hard to say.

If I hoped for an involving romance, I was disappointed. The preamble is lengthy and disturbing. Many pages are devoted to the main character Dorcas's troubled upbringing in the grand house of her poet father, a man with "the eyes of a visionary, deep, dreamy pools in which his brave, fantastic thoughts were reflected," and the aforementioned "oversexed" mother, who is "eager, insatiable, and very desirable, in her aloof, vicious way." Desirable to whom? The point of view is as unstable as some of the characters.

At sixteen Dorcas is sent off to a Swiss boarding school, where she falls under the influence of a willful American girl named Shirley. The two are discovered together—"*Eine Shrecklichkeit!*" the untranslated exclamation of the German teacher who spies on them. (The expression means "a terror," though Wikipedia helpfully mentions it being used not by Germans but rather by English-speaking people to describe Germany's ruthless policy toward civilians in World War I.) The girls are thereafter expelled for "immorality," though not before the defiant Shirley tells the Swiss headmistress, "Dorcas and I have loved each other, with passion and devotion, for many months. We offer no excuses, and why should we? We have found happiness in each other. What more need I say?"

In London, Dorcas is met off the train by her mother, who is not scandalized but rather empathizes with her daughter in her predicament by confiding, over dinner at the Savoy Grill, about her own many extramarital affairs: "Then came Juan Mascareñas, the painter. He was a satyr, insatiable, bestial, fascinating . . ."

The reading made me queasier and queasier.

By the time Dorcas finally meets Consuelo Sinclair, a brilliant, beautiful blonde with jade-green eyes, wearing black suede shoes "above which were ankles arched and small-boned, showing breeding," I was reading in an alienated state, keeping myself at arm's length from prose I judged overdone, and from a depiction of the pampered English upper classes that made me cringe. Any nascent excitement I had about my newfound relative and his sapphic fiction flickered out.

I majored in philosophy, not literature, at college, so I did not yet have Bloomsbury's literary and sexual innovations intellectually to hand. I lacked both the family history and the cultural awareness to understand how a young British aristocrat might have come to write such a novel, or the contours of the society in which it was published. So I responded in classic undergraduate fashion: I laughed at it. To be fair to my snarky younger self, the book had plenty of prompts, as at the women's first embrace: "There was fierceness in their kiss, the virility of possession, the sweet impuissance of surrender." I had inherited my dad's wry, high chuckle—it unnerved me when I first heard myself utter the sound, involuntarily—and soon I would get to know Lucia's sharp sarcasm, hearing in it something like a house style. I responded to Gawen's novel with that chuckle, and that sarcasm.

Showing off the book became a kind of party trick. Look! "An oversexed mother"—"A woman of morbid loveliness"—"A tragic liaison." Was there any other kind for two women in love? As I told friends who asked whether the book was any good: "Well, put it this way: the last line is 'She lay down on the bed and sobbed and sobbed and sobbed . . .' *Dot dot dot . . .*"

The raised eyebrow. The pursed lips.

Was I a callow youth, or a shallow one? Probably both. I was not able to appreciate what was good and fluid in Gawen's writing: the vivid social descriptions of parties or soirées; the playful dialogue; the author's genuine interest in and sympathy for his characters, who were, against the odds, nuanced women. Ironically, the novel's submerged theme had to do not with sexuality or "abnormality," but rather with whether devotion to writing and to love are compatible. It's a theme I would find surfacing in my own life, and eventually in my novels.

My long-dead English grandfather's lesbian fiction became a passing curiosity among friends who were busy making the argument, at campus protests and beyond, that homosexuality must stop being pathologized. The AIDS crisis blew up during the time I was an undergraduate, hardly known when I arrived, wreaking its tragic losses by the time I graduated, including among fellow students. The pink triangle, taken from the Nazis' designation for homosexuals, was reclaimed as a symbol of pride, and rage. Gay people *did* have rights, whatever George Washington might have said about it. I heard Larry Kramer speak about his time on our campus as a fearful, closeted student in the 1950s, and felt part of a collective celebration when his play *The Normal Heart* became a breakout hit in New York. The sensitive, astute writer David Leavitt, a few classes above me at Yale and a graduate of the same public high school, Gunn, in Palo Alto, had broken ground publishing stories in *The New Yorker*, among the magazine's first that dealt with gay life in white middle-class families.

At that politically and personally charged moment, I was not mature enough to accept *Star Against Star* as the hero prop of my twenties, or a necessary chapter in the bildungsroman of my own life. If anything, I considered my grandfather's overwritten novel more of a cosmic joke, as if I found myself, say, to have some relation to Oscar Wilde. (That would come much later, when I discovered that my grandmother Lucia had a brief affair in 1930s London with Wilde's son Vyvyan Holland—another long story.) It was as though Gawen's novel cleverly proved my mother's direst predictions about my choices, presenting an advertisement, in both form and content, against love between women. Such passion would not make you happy, and besides, the only way to write about it was badly.

If *Star Against Star* wasn't quite the melodrama of *The Well of*

Loneliness—which I had read, and found dismaying—the story did share territory with that novel, not least the posh London and Paris milieux of its lovers. Gawen certainly knew of Radclyffe Hall's work and the controversy it had stirred, and he knew that his publisher, Kahane, probably hoped *Star Against Star* might ride the coattails of that scandal. Further ironic links appeared later when Gawen engaged as his divorce lawyer a man named Lancelot Joynson-Hicks, son of the very home secretary who had declared that publication of *The Well of Loneliness* was "gravely detrimental to the public interest" and who forced the publisher, Jonathan Cape, to withdraw it. Gawen's protagonists were not as tortured as Hall's "invert" Stephen Gordon (whom we might now think of as a trans man), but I found no kindred spirit in *Star Against Star*'s troubled Dorcas or even in the ambitious Consuelo, who eventually throws over her young lover to salvage her literary career. It is Consuelo, unable to achieve a satisfactory work/life balance, as we would now call it, whose rejection causes Dorcas's tearful collapse at the novel's end. *Dot dot dot . . .*

I did wonder what might have led my grandfather to write such an unusual story, though. Had he been a closeted gay man himself?

The only way to find out would be to meet the one person still alive who had known Gawen Brownrigg—who had, in fact, been married to him. My grandmother Lucia von Borosini Batten, a woman who for a few short years in the 1930s had been an earlier Mrs. Brownrigg.

10.

THE OLD ADOBE

✦

RECENTLY, AMONG MY GRANDMOTHER'S PAPERS, I FOUND
a Polaroid of my brother. Lucia kept, over her ninety-three years, letters from husbands, lovers, sons, friends, wine merchants, and book
dealers—categories that certainly overlapped. She kept old passports;
boxes of diaries (her own and her mother's); photographs; and receipts,
ticket stubs, and invitations. Because we became close in her later years,
and because I'm the writer in the family, this daunting trove eventually
came to me. I could set up a whole library for Lucia, if I had time and
a fully employed staff, and no doubt unearth yet more juicy material,
like the flirtatious letters I found to her from Vyvyan Holland. The
latter I was able to marvel at one afternoon in London with Vyvyan's
son, Merlin—Oscar Wilde's grandson, who has written and spoken
extensively on Wilde. Such a person would not, for obvious reasons, be
shockable about people's love lives, but Merlin Holland and I both were
a bit wide-eyed with surprise over the liaison between his father and
my grandmother: the age difference, yes (Vyvyan was twenty-six years
Lucia's senior), but also that she was still married to Gawen at the time
Vyvyan was writing her playful, mildly salacious notes.

In the Polaroid photograph Lucia kept, Mike is a lanky young man
with Shaun Cassidy hair, grinning by his silver Fiat up at the Circle
C. On the back, in my grandmother's distinctive, looping hand: *Michael Brownrigg on Nick's ranch, '80.* She used my brother's first and last
names to identify a relative not then in her life. Mike would have been

nineteen. What passed through her mind, I wonder, when she considered her unmet Brownrigg grandchildren who lived a couple of states away? She might have thought about seeing us. She knew her two other grandchildren, the offspring of her middle son, Victor (by her third husband). And it was clear that Nick and Valerie visited Lucia sometimes. But to this former Mrs. Brownrigg, Nick's children remained a closed book. Was it because we were remnants of Gawen? Was her first marriage such a bad memory that she could not bear to summon it?

My mother's story about why there was no contact had to do with thank-you notes. When we were small, our grandmother did send us Christmas presents, until one year when our thank-you notes were not up to standard—late, or never sent—which ended all grandmother-grandchild communication. I can't say if this is true, but from what I knew later of Lucia, who knew her way around feuds and grudges, it's plausible. As with any family matter, my dad had no story about Lucia's absence from our lives. He had his own contentious relation with her; at times they joked and were friendly, though for other long stretches they did not speak. At different points, in different conversations, both my mother and Valerie told me that they felt Nick's mother had done terrible damage to him, and it was hard to forgive her for it.

My dad's sending Gawen's book to me may have begun to unlock this situation, or perhaps our having reached adulthood made it seem safer to allow the connection to form. (Certainly, my grandmother had little feeling for children, wondering aloud once when I was with her why people couldn't train them better, like dogs.) I learned that Mike was going to blaze the trail first when he was passing through New Mexico with some college buddies. He met Lucia, who preferred to be known as Mrs. Batten, after her long-dead fourth husband, at her home in Albuquerque. When Mike emerged unscathed I felt brave enough to meet her, too, on a cross-country trip I took with my girlfriend to celebrate my recent graduation from college, an occasion my dad did not attend, as he was performing in a play in Ukiah. We drove in my first car, a used Honda Civic. Before we set out, my girlfriend's mother cautioned me: "I did not give birth to my daughter for her to become a smear on the road." She didn't. We drove all the way across and back, a speeding ticket in Kansas the only blot on our record.

It was a great road trip. The term *red states* didn't yet exist, but we drove through a lot of them, getting a sideways look from a motel manager in Alabama and never correcting people who guessed we were sisters. Texas was endless; generations of bugs had perished on the windshield by the time we crossed into New Mexico. As we drew closer to Lucia, I began to feel nervous about meeting this unknown person, who did not yet seem real. I was unsure whether my girlfriend would be an asset or a liability. Nick had warned me that his mother had old-fashioned manners, which helped explain his occasional streak of the same. We stopped outside of town so that I could change into nicer clothes. Nick and his mother, whom he called Mama, had already discussed what I should call her; they had landed on *Grandmother*. Rehearsing "Hello, Grandmother!" in a gas station mirror while I donned a skirt underlined the theatrical aspect of this meeting, which acquired an additional safari element as we drove up the dusty concealed drive to her house and a party of peacocks scattered, some flying colorfully just above the car, issuing their loud, distinctive cries.

Lucia Batten had lived for decades in a historic Albuquerque adobe, the Juan Cristobal Armijo Homestead, built in 1875. Over its acres of brush and cottonwoods roamed—and flew—eighty to a hundred peacocks, whose calls lit up the blue New Mexico sky. The house itself was so cluttered with art and books and antiques and kitsch that, years later, I wrote a children's book about it, and her, called *Kepler's Dream*. The peacocks had a starring role in my story, as did my grandmother's library, a newer, separate building that housed thousands of books, many extremely valuable. From my children's story I left out non-child-friendly details, certainly of Lucia's louche biography but also some physical objects like the cabinet where she displayed hundreds of miniature bottles of every kind of alcohol, pocketed after countless flights she had taken around the world. When the book became a film, the art director did his best to invent an atmospheric clutter for the character, but Lucia was never bettered at that form of curation. Her environment was un-re-creatable.

A tall, silvered, azure-eyed lady in her seventies greeted us at the adobe's wooden doors, which were painted turquoise and flanked by pots of vivid red geraniums. We traded pleasantries about the birds, some of which perched on the lower cottonwood branches, glaring down at us like security guards. Grandmother wore jewels but little makeup, a nondescript floral dress. She was not a model of elegance or of beauty, but she had a confident air, like someone who by wealth and temperament was used to getting what she wanted. She was American, though her German-ness was not far beneath the surface, expressing itself in her upright posture and a readiness to correct. She was funny, sharp, patrician. There was some physical resemblance between us; I had somehow not expected this and found it unsettling. Her eyebrow was frequently raised, and her delivery deadpan. She had a small dog she spoiled terribly, and finches that chirped and skipped in a cage in the kitchen, but otherwise she lived alone, though a part-time caretaker rented a small house on the property. The cute dog gave us all a conversation topic, though the salient thing my grandmother and I had in common was Nick, and neither of us knew how to talk about him.

I needn't have worried about Lucia's reaction to my bringing a "friend." It was clear that she was shrewd enough to understand our relation but was unfazed and did not mention it. I was grateful for both her acceptance and her tact, which predisposed me to like her. My girlfriend and I slept in the same twin room my father and stepmother had shared: their signatures were on the wall, where Lucia encouraged visitors to sign a permanent record of their stay. Higher up the list, several times, in his tiny British script, was the name of Alec Waugh, Evelyn's older, less famous brother.

My grandmother was an adequate host, formal rather than warm, and better on bar snacks than real food. There was a tub of roasted cashews by the front door, and she had a ready hand pouring wine, bottles of which were stored in racks stashed around the adobe, including one in a room decorated by a genuine tiger rug. Lucia did not cook—I found a can of corned beef left half-open in the pantry—so for an actual meal we had to go out. If there were any bread crusts or greens left on our plates, my grandmother had the restaurant box them up so that she could take them home for the peacocks.

Almost all I went in knowing about Lucia was how many husbands she had had: four. She had outlived them all. Gawen was far in the past, the start of a long line. She mentioned, knowing it made for a good story, that her last husband, the Philadelphia advertising executive Harry Batten, had been too busy to go away after they got married, so Lucia took a honeymoon trip to Europe on her own. It was Lucia's third, Edmund Engel, Albuquerque's city planner, who brought her to the southwestern city in the 1940s with their two sons, Victor and Peter. At that point, though I don't recall Lucia mentioning it, Nick was sent away to school. My uncle Peter, a gentle, friendly man, had come out to stay at the Circle C a few times while Mike and I were there.

Everyone who knew Lucia agreed that she was acquisitive—to put it bluntly, greedy. She collected art, wine, men, jewels, trinkets, countries. (Years after she died, the Albuquerque nonprofit to which Lucia donated the bulk of her estate was still auctioning off her fine linens, china, furniture, and silver.) One room at "the Hacienda"—as my dad sardonically called the place, in the city he nicknamed "Albujerk"—had acid-yellow walls covered with Haitian folk paintings. Another smoke-stained surface, above the ever-burning fireplace near the kitchen, displayed numerous santos, though Lucia was not conventionally religious. A mantel in a back room displayed a battalion of German beer steins, below it a drawer with countless loose photographs, including one she was proud to show me of the day in 1933 when, thanks to her well-placed Brownrigg in-laws, she was presented at the court of George V. Fifty years on, it remained a high-water mark of social achievement for her.

The daughter of a German baron and a midwestern American, Lucia was educated erratically, at schools in Switzerland and elsewhere, followed by a year at Scripps College in Southern California before she and Gawen married. She was smart, widely read, a quick study. She read and spoke German fluently and had passable French and Italian. She was a fearless, adventurous traveler to all continents. She taught herself about the stock market, subscribed to *Barron's* and *The Wall Street Journal*, and parlayed a decent inheritance into a sizable fortune. She told funny stories about past pets, including a couple of monkeys who once lived in her courtyard, and de-glanded skunks she named after famous perfumes.

My grandmother was interested in people but did not tolerate fools. Her blend of irreverence and convention was one I recognized from my dad. She was adept at putting others in a bad light, impatient with pretenders but also with those she considered poorly mannered. This was a broad category, and lots of people fell into it. She rolled her eyes to me about the clothes my dad wore or the way he kept his shirts half-unbuttoned, "showing off his shrubbery," and said of another son's companion, "She doesn't have a lot upstairs—I mean there is not much furniture there *at all*."

Yet I liked her. We made each other laugh. I felt a kind of defiance in appreciating Lucia, even in admitting, to my own surprise, that there was something of her in me. If previously I had accepted without question my mother's distaste for Lucia, at this point Linda's disapproval of my romantic choices had brittled me to her judgments. I was ready to make up my own mind. Besides, I was following a narrative now: I wanted to find out who my novelist grandfather, Gawen Brownrigg, had been.

In her thousand-volumed two-story library, Lucia showed me editions of her first husband's books, shelved near affectionately inscribed copies of Alec Waugh's thirty novels. I was not brave enough to ask what Lucia thought of *Star Against Star*, but she had kept Gawen's handwritten manuscript of it, a notebook filled with beautiful, neatly inked writing, not so very different from the notebook I had filled at fourteen with my novella fable, though my grandfather's was tidier.

Lucia had little to say about Gawen himself, though. She could not bring his character to life, or locate pictures of him to show me. Now and then she saw reminders of him in their son—she had caught a surprising detail of resemblance when Nick unconsciously played with his long eyebrows in concentration, a gesture identical to that of his father, though he would never have seen Gawen do it. Wasn't that interesting?

She described the difficulty she had had as a young American newlywed running a London household, and Atlantic crossings they made together, including one to California on which Gawen teased her for a seasickness that turned out to be the start of her pregnancy with Nicholas. She was proud of having played tennis up to the week before she gave birth. But after fifty years, she had few memories of my grandfather to share. She seemed keenest to mention the unfortunate circumstance of Gawen's departure and his death. She gave the clear impression that their divorce had been Gawen's decision, that he had left his wife and child without a backward glance.

"When he left, Gawen said he did not want to see his son again until he had grown up," Lucia told me, shaking her head. She summoned an air of being shocked still, decades later. We were sitting on the adobe's cool patio, drinking iced tea. "And all he left for Nick was just one dollar. Wasn't that strange?"

What a monster! What a cad! No wonder my dad had such a hard time being any regular kind of father: he had been coldly abandoned by his own.

She went on to explain that Gawen died a few years later in Africa of a drug overdose. In her telling, it was unambiguously a suicide. Gawen had been living in Kenya, researching a new book about drugs, and had left all his money to a woman in Nairobi, leaving none of it to her or to their son. Lucia had had to contest the will. Wasn't that terrible?

The image I formed of Gawen's drug-related death came filtered through famous celebrity overdoses from the seventies, icons like Jimi Hendrix or Janis Joplin who had, the papers said, "choked on their own vomit," that gruesomely exact description. In high school we were shown warning films about people getting addicted to heroin and ending up dead in some dark alley. I formed a hazy picture of a debauched aristocrat, possibly shooting up, one of those men who lounged around forming casual liaisons, having forgotten his son. Not aware of how unlikely this would be for an Englishman of his background, I speculated that the undeserving beneficiary of Gawen's will had perhaps been a native Kenyan, which might have explained the appalled intervention of his relatives. When I later watched a 1980s film about white Europeans in East Africa, *White Mischief*, its glamourizing of the careless, entitled British hedonists who settled in Kenya's "Happy Valley" between the wars led me to wonder if that had been Gawen's world, and might explain his end. There seemed to be no way to find out.

Proud that I was forming my own independent opinion about Lucia, I never considered that I was swallowing whole Lucia's disapproving description of Gawen. I did not bother to read my grandfather's second novel, *Later Than You Think*, and felt a vague shame about him altogether, due to the drugs, the upper-class narrowness, the suicide. Lucia was the lone grandparent in front of me, the one I could talk to and gradually get to know (my Lovelace grandparents having both died), and I did not doubt her memories of her first husband. If history is written by the victors—a line attributed to various people, including Winston Churchill, himself a great imperialist rewriter—divorce is written by the survivors. If your ex-spouse is dead, he cannot challenge your version of events. Lucia had that advantage over all of her former husbands.

There was someone, however, who might have questioned Lucia's story about Gawen, a person with a close-enough read on Lucia's character to predict precisely how Gawen's former wife would come to slander and condemn him. She was not alive either, but her voice survived.

Beatrice Brownrigg, Gawen's mother, did everything in her power to create an accurate account of her late son's life and death, to tell a story true to the young man she knew. She hoped that one day, when her grandson grew up, a fair and loving portrait of Gawen would emerge that might help Nick and any other Brownriggs who followed know who her beloved son had been.

11.

WITH LUCK, YOU COME OUT THE OTHER SIDE . . . OR, YOU DON'T

✦

WE'RE COMING TO THE END OF THE TIME WHEN PEOPLE will look to writers' letters to better understand their work. No one has the time anymore, and besides there won't be any letters; I doubt scholars will be hacking into Gmail accounts trying to harvest old emails. Friends of mine who work as biographers or literary scholars still journey to libraries or archives or people's attics, where the correspondences of the famous are stored; reading through and making selections allows them to illuminate the voice, the thinking, of their subjects, which often emerges more purely in epistolary form than even in the poetry, the plays, the fiction.

There were always greater and lesser authors who diverted some of their focus to their letters. I think of my dad as one of those. He corresponded with friends and family throughout his life, devoting consistent hours to the typewriter, and those missives became the real vehicle for his literary energy and imagination, though whether this was a deliberate decision or just what happened, it's hard to know.

He also knew that you can build or sustain a relationship through writing letters. He spent his life doing it. Living telephone-free out at the ranch, Nick used letters to connect to the wider world. He wrote surprisingly revealing letters to his mother—with opinions and tart comments about girlfriends, accounts of sobriety, descriptions of art and meals and travels, requests for money. He wrote comic, swashbuckling, and intellectually engaged letters to a few of his close friends, including Stanford buddies like the writer and editor Gus Blaisdell, and heartfelt letters of advice to Peter, the younger of his two brothers: "But this whole process of finding yourself is a very private thing and, really, is sort of what life is all about—and, finally, it doesn't have anything to do with Beatniks or wearing a gray flannel suit and working for a bank, but only the tiny, private voice that says 'yes' or 'no' and when you hear this voice you've come home."

And he wrote to his two kids. It was how he became, belatedly, a father to me—through the letters he wrote me throughout my adult life. From my freshman year at college onward, I received letters from Nick, typed on his distinctive buttercup-yellow paper, a sunny trail he sent out over the decades until he could no longer type and switched to handwritten decorative cards that were still legible, affable, and ironic right up to the point his mind and language gave out, and his writing finally ended. His early absence left a constant hollowness in me, a low-level ache, in spite of my stepfather's gracious stepping in to provide reliable attention, love, and care. But in his countless letters my dad was, paradoxically, present. He was honest and he was generous—his honesty *was* his generosity—as he offered up his irreverent, expressive, uncensored self. That gift changed our relationship. Gradually, we moved from the awkwardness of my childhood years— where I'd mumble around him out of shyness, he'd scold me for mumbling, I'd hate him for the scolding, and then I'd wander off to make up stories about animals, while he started pouring wine—through our near estrangement during my late teens and early twenties. We landed, finally, on affection. On humor, and freedom from bullshit, and the pleasures of description, given and received. I learned to swear and to drink and to write. All three of those, I connect with Nick. (None were Philip.)

November 1, 1992
Ukiah

Dear Sylvia,

Hmm, muted (very!) kerosene in kitchen, wet 5 A.M. wood in living room stove, the adjectives pertain to a torch singer: sultry, sulky, smouldering, no heat... "I'll take a double and, Jim, I'll catch you after the set, dig." It's always the same, radio confirms a fine storm, it comes, accompanied by rosy reports of clearing skies, sunshine in the afternoon and, up here, after a tantalizing windy interlude with flashes of blue sky it abruptly grows grey and dark and dumps all over again. Question: will we make our scheduled dawn shot wood run? Thumpety-thumpety, we shall see. Minor paranoia is having left, last week, a half-cut tan oak at the head of our road on LP [Louisiana Pacific] land and I don't want those jolly lads to accuse us of poaching.

Not that it's any big deal but, actually, it is, we're kind of trustees of their land insofar as we traverse it. And traverse the Masonite road (which they own, having bought out Masonite, lo these many years) which we've been allowed to do for the last six months. Did you ever go on the Masonite road? The entrance, for us, is right in front of the Yellow House—gate/key—and then it's all paved right into town emerging by the (still owned by) Masonite mill. Heresy to say, I love it. You can mostly drive without concentrating on the road (as you must do on Low Gap) and occasionally reach speeds up to 45 m.p.h. and it is beautiful, totally different from Low Gap with its ruined bastard forests of tan oak and equally crowded, spindly fir, twisting and turning until you reach the Michelangelo madrone with the glorious vistas of the valleys below and the far hills, only then does it lose its oppressive nature. But Masonite makes you think you're in Oregon or even a little the Sierra foothills, it's open, ordered, still mostly empty being taken up by large landholdings. On the ridges you can see some new solar type homes but mostly the old ranch houses are tucked away up canyons. Bob Burns, that sweet old man with the boyish face, lives close to town, Bob who used to be a bailiff and I pass him, sometimes, he always waves, placing his pint of Apricot Brandy carefully on his seat. There're some black moos hither and thither, a ton of deer (Valerie got hit by one the other night, slammed right into the side of the [Subaru] Justy, leaving a few tell-tale hairs and an $800 bill) and I have seen bobcats and watched a flock of wild turkey grown from clustering chicks to full-grown gobblers.

Many of his more expansive and reflective letters came after he quit drinking. In middle age, with his second marriage hanging by a thread, as he admitted to me one sour, resigned afternoon in the old yellow kitchen at the Circle C, Nick's oldest friend from Pasadena days came out from the East Coast to persuade him into an Alcoholics Anonymous meeting. Only someone who had known my dad for years could have succeeded in that mission, but it worked, and for close to a decade, for the first time in his life, he had lived without alcohol. (When her personal bitterness had finally leached away from her, my mother told me how awash the last unhappy year of her and Nick's marriage had been in liquor. She slowed right down, after their divorce; he didn't.) This dry period in the 1980s and '90s allowed my dad to fix things: let go of grudges, repair relations with his mother, take time to visit his kids, me in London, my brother in DC. You end up having more energy for other things in your life when you're not devoting a substantial amount of it to drinking. I expect it led to Nick's encouraging us to meet Lucia. Also, he became less aggrieved, causing that mocking, argumentative meanness to fall away from him like a sloughed skin.

It was a point of pride that he could continue to make Circle C wine even after he stopped sampling it himself.

October 27–31, 1993

Dear Syl,

Ah-um, Valerie's typewriter . . . bear with me. I take pen to paper at quarter to five in the morning, knowing it will not be light enough to work outside until nearly 7:30.

. . .

Wind rattles the leaves outside—I step out into a dark, balmy morning, realize it's an east wind, all right, a definite east wind harbinger of weather but the barometer is unchanged and there is nothing on the radio news. I tuck that away, sizing up my last free day (all the things I want to do—wood, plant leeks, water, get gravel, pick the white grapes) yesterday I got in the Zin at 23½ sugar and, since it's Zin with all its raisin clusters, it'll go up another point at least. Not bad. Start fermentation today.

. . .

Valerie is off to Michigan today—house is very empty. (leading into a light exegesis on the transformation of love, etc.) Valerie is my framework—without her, all would be da-da, emptiness, chaos.

I was very happy to hear of your energy to get into a new novel. Yes! Waiting for the mail . . . how many years I did that, God, I used to pace back and forth waiting for the postman's step. For years. Love letters, literary letters, a touch from on high that I exist and am, at least nominally, loved. Move on, my sere advice! Energy clones itself. An odd Moebius Curve, only trick is getting in! So, stay in!

. . .

River Phoenix is gone: what was that movie, A different Kind of Idaho? He was great. Very good. Yeah, drugs leap to mind but what to say? You break the umbilical, search for meaning, grow greedy for experience and, with luck, come out the other side . . . or, you don't.

In that last dense paragraph, picturing addiction as childish hunger, Nick was probably thinking of Gawen, or of his own experiments with drugs in 1960s San Francisco, which might have ended differently. In his days on the fringes of the Beats, my dad smoked opium and at least once injected a speedball, but luckily the cocaine-heroin mixture did not take. He did come out the other side.

I can't recommend reading your father's thinly veiled autobiographical fiction recounting sexual exploits in the final miserable year of his marriage, during the time his wife became pregnant a second time— with yourself—but I did learn a few things from reading Nick's unpublished novel, Moebius Curve. In it, the brandy-downing main character dourly reflects on "old Daddy, the sleeping-pill dropper," his English father who died in Africa, then notes: "A tiny chill swept through him; between sleeping pills and brandy there existed rather a fine line." Even when he was drinking, he was not unaware of the damage his drinking did. His novel is soaked in alcoholic regret over it.

My dad wrote me hundreds of letters, cards, and postcards up until a year or two before he died. Some of his last cards dwell, with comedy but also old-guy bite, on his anger at his doctor for declaring he could no longer drive. I wrote him back from wherever I was, through moves from coast to coast, at graduate school and after, to London and back, as I replicated in my twenties the restless pattern of my upbringing. Writing to him was how I became a daughter, too. I tried out my own views on art and meals and travel (if not women). Belatedly, we got to know each other. We were freer and more relaxed with each other in print, and it made our relation in person easier when we met.

In spite of that early rant, he had become tolerant and open about my having a girlfriend, and generally was jovial to and about the people in my life whom he met. "She's a terrific gal, Syl." He greeted changes in my circumstances, or Mike's—moves, marriages, jobs, books— positively, but from a curious, observational distance. You could call it novelistic. He loved us, but also we were characters to him, like anyone else. When Mike was sworn in as mayor of his Bay Area city, he invited our dad to attend the swearing-in ceremony and to help administer the oath of office. Nick declined to drive down for it, skipping the event.

In my midthirties I came back to California after a long stretch of living in London. Like a salmon, I sometimes joked, coming home to spawn. I got married, to a man, and had children (though not in that order) and took on what looked like a fairly regular life, some distance from the problems of abnormality. Our small wedding gathered the four parents and stepparents and a few other friends and family members and their kids at a house in Big Sur, where my lifelong cellist friend played Bach after we spoke our idiosyncratic homemade vows and became, in a phrase I'd scarcely ever been in the same room as, "husband and wife." Instead of a band and dancing after, we had an improv comedy group doing sketches, improvisation seeming well-matched to the spirit of what we were doing, a ceremony that had included a small ritual for my stepson and his year-old half brother, our son. During some lull in the long day, my dad pulled aside my new husband, a man he liked a lot—they made each other laugh—to murmur in his ear: "Welcome to the ball and chain, old man."

The first letter Nick sent me after my marriage was addressed to "Mrs. Sedge Thomson." After that, there were letters to Sylvia

Thomson, Sylvia Thompson, Sylvia Thomson Brownrigg, and Sylvia Brownrigg-Thomson; every now and then a Sylvia Brownrigg slipped into the mix. I did not correct him, but my replies always had BROWN-RIGG penned in the envelope's top left corner. My younger self would probably have vocally challenged my dad's sexist assumptions, but I found the sequence funny and even poignant. There was no aisle in the place where we got married, and God knows I did not think anyone was in a position to "give me away," least of all Nick. Nonetheless, after that event an old-world dad surfaced, one who thought his married daughter would take on the name of someone else. He was, after all, the eldest son of Mrs. Harry Batten, who had cycled through five names in her life, including Mrs. Edmund Engel, Mrs. John Burnham, and, many long years before, Mrs. Gawen Brownrigg. Née von Borosini. In Albuquerque, some of my grandmother's countless belongings were monogrammed with LvBB.

I never argued the name issue with my dad. I was done arguing with him about anything. And he did not press the point or bring it up in conversation. Our communication was in the form of a silent exchange on the envelopes we sent back and forth to each other. It wasn't that our relation was superficial, but there was plenty we were not going to talk about, ever. I had little kids, a stepson, a complicated family life, and was still trying to hold on to the writer—the Brownrigg—I had become, before motherhood.

I kept my name, of course. It never occurred to me to do otherwise. I am still a Brownrigg.

12.

OBLIQUELY PANTING PROSE

+

IN THE EARLY 2000S, AFTER OUR SON WAS BORN AND BEFORE
our daughter had been, an English actor and bibliophile named Neil
Pearson came to my husband's and my house in Berkeley. Pearson was
researching a book about the publisher at Obelisk Press, Jack Kahane;
the life sketch in the book was titled "A Very British Pornographer."
Some might dispute the forceful word *pornographer*, but Kahane did
sail close to the winds of censorship, frequently tagging his editions
with the tantalizing warning "Not to be imported into Great Britain or
U.S.A.," while targeting Anglophone readers in Paris who might seek
erotically charged writings. The Parisian publisher had brought out
Star Against Star in 1935, around the time of Henry Miller's *Tropic of
Cancer*, the latter adorned by a blurb from T. S. Eliot. "My only feeling
against it," Jack Kahane wrote to Gawen on accepting his novel, after
praising its "perceptiveness and good writing," was that "it may be considered too purely a restatement of the case disposed of, probably once
and for all, by the WELL OF LONELINESS."

Neil Pearson was the first person I had ever met with an independent interest in Gawen Brownrigg. It had caught Pearson's eye that
I was a writer, too. A friend of his at Macmillan, Peter Straus, was
the English editor of my most recent novel—*Pages for You*, also a love
story about two women, a parallel we jokingly acknowledged. Apart
from telling Pearson what it was like to discover and read *Star Against
Star* at college, though, I did not have my own stories or lore about my

grandfather to contribute. In fact, the information went the other way: Pearson was diligent and thorough, a completist about Kahane's authors no matter their broader importance, and he went to the trouble of finding a publicity questionnaire Gawen had filled out for Knopf in 1937, ahead of their bringing out *Portrait in a Windscreen* (the novel published in England as *Later Than You Think*). Since Kahane did not publish Gawen's second novel, it was all the more surprising that Pearson had unearthed this document.

He also interviewed Lucia by telephone. She advised him to call her in the morning: "Earlier in the day I may growl; by afternoon I bark, and in the evening I'm likely to bite." My grandmother was near the end of her long life, but she had stuck to the story about her first husband, and Pearson duly included it in his brief biographical remarks about Gawen in his study of Obelisk and Jack Kahane. I liked Pearson when I met him—he was funny and affable as we sat in my chaotic Berkeley kitchen chatting while my toddler son played nearby—but it was startling later to read his account, the only contemporary remarks anyone had published about my grandfather.

After a somewhat sneering summary of *Star Against Star* ("Sex does happen in the book, but it's either sex of the 'that night, they were as one' variety, or else sex described in a miasma of obliquely panting prose"), Pearson provided a similarly dismissive description of *Later Than You Think*. He concludes:

> It's unlikely that Gawen Brownrigg ever saw the book in print, as by 1938 he was living in Nairobi. There, according to his widow (to whom I spoke more than sixty years later), he was "writing a book on the effect of pills." He died of an overdose on 8 August 1938, aged 27, leaving everything—minus one dollar—to a girl in Nairobi of whom his family had never heard. The dollar he left to his son.

PERSUADED BY LUCIA'S recollection, Neil Pearson had written Gawen off as a bounder—a heartless father and a hack.

What I could not tell this pleasant English visitor in 2004 was that Gawen had certainly seen the London edition of the book in print.

Copies reached him in Kenya, where his mother, Beatrice, had also sent clippings of some of the English reviews; they were not wholly complimentary, but the vividness of his racing scenes was uniformly admired: "a quite astonishingly brilliant account of a great motor-race," "the motor racing in it is excellent and authentic," "And when the voices die down and he comes to describe a motor-race he can write very well indeed."

Nor was I able to fill in the backstory of this book's publication, as summarized by a British paper:

> A first novel which was published by Michael Joseph this week has had a rather unusual history.
>
> Over a year ago *Portrait in a Windscreen,* by Gawen Brown-rigg, was accepted for publication by another publisher, was set up, printed and bound, and was nearing its publishing date when a director of the firm read it, thought it unsuitable for publication by his firm, and ordered the whole edition to be scrapped. Only a few copies survived, and one of them came into the hands of the American publisher, Mrs. Alfred Knopf, when she was in this country looking for books to publish. She read *Portrait in a Windscreen,* was impressed by it, and mentioned it to Michael Joseph. Mr. Joseph read it, was equally impressed, and determined to publish it himself. The novel has now been printed for the second time and awaits the verdict of the critics and public.

Pearson might have been amused to see the reference to Gawen's "first novel"—which erases the prior existence of *Star Against Star,* showing how faint a mark Gawen's Obelisk fiction had left on the wider world—and to learn that there were moral qualms about his racing novel, too.

And if, as Beatrice had intended, we had been able to read everything she included in her dense and loving work on Gawen, including that clipping, I could have given Neil Pearson a fuller biography. I might have described that "girl in Nairobi," of whom his family was in fact well aware, as an American in Kenya, daughter of a consular officer, who enjoyed her romance with Gawen until it was discovered that his

British divorce had not yet been finalized, causing her parents to force her to break off relations. This might not have altered Pearson's opinion of my grandfather's fiction, but it would have of the man.

Like Brownriggs before and since, Beatrice was a great believer in writing letters. She knew they could build a world. And she wanted those who came later to know that among her son's other qualities—his humor, affection, playfulness, and filial loyalty—Gawen had been perfectly normal.

That was how she saw it.

13.

NOW WHAT?

✦

I WAS WORRIED BUT NOT SHOCKED, NO ONE WHO KNEW him was, when I heard of my dad's diagnosis with liver cancer. Such news might have come sooner if he had not quit drinking for that earlier period, after his old friend's intervention. Still, my dad's serious illness knocked the wind out of me. You can know someone is mortal and still be stunned by the reminder. The revelation happens every day: parents are not eternal.

The great thing about the liver as an organ, though, is that it is regenerative. Not everything is. Nick had surgery in San Francisco to remove the diseased portion, and we waited to see how he would recover. It was the start of the child-parent reversal of caregiving that middle age delivers; it's just a little different when your parent never gave you much care in the first place. Mike and I visited the hospital, sought out entertainment for him in the long dull hours in the ward (an iPad, whose workings defeated Nick, though Valerie tried to help him), and learned about his severe reaction to morphine, which meant they had to tether him at night in case he wandered. I had the feeling my brother and I were finding a way of redressing an old imbalance. Being the kinds of adult son and daughter we wanted our dad to have was how we filled in our sketchy family picture.

The irony extended to one day's turnaround of our old custody meetings at Denny's, frequent site of tense handings-off that forever colored the feelings my brother and I had about that benign chain of diners. One early morning some months after his initial recovery, I met Valerie and Nick at a coffee shop in Boonville in the Anderson Valley so that I could take my dad the rest of the way to San Francisco for a follow-up medical appointment, sparing my stepmother another four-hour drive. In the afternoon I would return him to her at a place near Healdsburg.

After a short spell in the Pacific Heights waiting room, during which I silently tried to become comfortable in my unfamiliar role, I went in with my dad to the plush office. Nick had slowed down some but was still tall and broad and basically mobile. For the appointment, and to absorb the verdict whatever it might be, he wore blue jeans and a tucked-in, button-down cotton shirt—his most formal look.

This skilled surgeon had excised a cancerous third of my dad's liver, but the patient had come through remarkably well. The doctor issued a cautiously optimistic report. Dressed in an elegant suit, sitting behind a wide desk, he spoke in a clipped Iraqi accent. He had a sense of humor and was bullshit-averse, which made the two men a good match. My dad knew he owed his life to this surgeon. He liked and trusted him.

"But . . . Nick." The doctor's face grew serious. He leaned forward. "Things look good now, but—you cannot drink again."

"I know." Nick sat, hands planted on knees, subdued. He looked away.

"No." The doctor waited for his patient's gaze to return, to ensure eye contact. "Nick: you cannot drink anymore. Ever."

"All right, I know. I know." A scolded child.

The doctor looked at me to check that I had witnessed this moment, and I nodded, as if the daughter in the room could have any impact on what happened. No one could make my dad do a single thing he didn't want to do.

But he stuck with it, for a while. For the second time in his life, Nick took alcohol out of his days and nights and let his body restore itself, as it did. The experience had highlighted the reality of his own end, though, which led Nick to ask Mike and me to join him for that lunch in Healdsburg, to talk about his will. We gave him something, a lost object, and it might have been important to him, but he elected to put it away for later. He turned eighty in December 2012, when

Mike and I and our families traveled to meet him and Valerie for a celebratory meal together. Beforehand, I experienced a random attack of severe back spasms, my body registering some hesitation (on an earlier visit once, I had strange sudden chest pains), but I popped painkillers and shook it off. Nick's grandchildren, six of them, sat up and down the length of the table, while he was the jovial, snowy-headed patriarch at its head, content though also, as he confessed in letters after, rather amazed. "I think of things that probably a great deal of people do when they reach 80," he wrote. "I mean, you can sort of sigh and think, Thank God I got this far—now what?"

Nick was fully conscious and still himself when he stored that package in a cupboard in his and Valerie's Fort Bragg home. At times, my regret about my dad's not seeing all this family material until so late in his life has made me clench my teeth and wring my hands, like someone in a cartoon of wincing disappointment. *But he could have . . . ! But what if he'd . . . ?* You just want to rewrite the damned thing and have him find out sooner.

Gradually, though, I have come to recognize that our dad's delay was a matter of choice, not a tragic mistake. He was, against appearances, the author of his own family story; and in his version, he kept his father, Gawen, a closed book. In the first years after we gave the package to our dad, Nick was not suffering such memory loss that he forgot it was there. Besides, Valerie kept reminding him.

He preferred not to find out.

I can't pretend not to know the impulse to take a letter you have received and put it away for later. I do know it. There were, especially as his faculties slipped, cards or letters from Nick I did not open right away. They were painful to read. Not because they weren't still funny, friendly, at times touching; rather *because* they were. I learned that my brother had a habit in those later years of doing the same. We put the cards away for later. It baffled others, but Mike and I shared this species of reluctance. You know you'll get to it eventually, but just—not *yet*. Not now. This is not the moment.

You turn away from remaking the connection. It is self-protective.

Someone is trying to reach you—they have something to say to you, to convey to you. But you are not sure you're ready for their voice, and that contact. You don't necessarily want to be touched. To be touched is to open yourself to caring, and in turn to being disappointed. Disappointment is such an undignified wound. Less poetic than the big dramas of betrayal, abandonment, heartbreak. (It's *Death of a Salesman* rather than *Lear*.) Disappointment is not easily healed, and there's no real form of catharsis for it, though there are the obvious ways to numb it out, anesthetize it. We have all tried those.

I think of this when I picture Nick putting Beatrice's offering in a cupboard for some distant, possibly never-arriving date. I sympathize with his act. Of course he did not know what was in that package. It might be safer not to know, and never to find out. He had made it this far in his life. He was fine. What good could come from opening it now?

14.

WHEN YOU ARE OLD ENOUGH TO WISH TO KNOW SOMETHING ABOUT YOUR FATHER

✦

SHE HAD A LOT TO SAY, MY GREAT-GRANDMOTHER. Beatrice.

We have all been reminded in the past few years what it's like to have to stay inside for months, to be quick and careful when venturing outside. We've inhabited silent battle zones with unseen antagonists. During the pandemic, and especially in cities, people learned to make up interior entertainments, to find occupation for otherwise anxious minds. It was not so dissimilar for Beatrice Brownrigg, who from 1939 onward got through the war in a flat in Westminster, in the center of London. She had to sell and abruptly leave the family's house in the country. From rooms at a hotel and apartments called St. Ermin's, where on a different floor Britain's Secret Intelligence Service, also known as MI6, held clandestine meetings, Beatrice Brownrigg got to work on her lockdown project: producing a scrapbook in remembrance of her late son, Gawen.

> Hi Syl, Do you remember that package that you received from your [other] grandfather's house a few years ago?? Well, when Mike was here he suggested we open it. Luckily I remembered where we put it. Inside the package was a "Book for Nicholas" written by his English grandmother Beatrice in 1939, to be delivered to Nick after 1952 at which time Nick would have been 20+. Mike will tell you as much as he can, it started out with a letter to Nick to let him know

THE WHOLE STAGGERING MYSTERY   65

how much his English family (and his father) loved him, how they were a family of love for each other, how they might not survive the war. It's a history of Gawen, his books, his marriage, his death, but we only read the cover letter so to speak. So, I guess I want to thank you for retrieving this, it means SO much to Nick at this stage of his life and it makes me want to punch Lucia in the nose:) There's lots more, it is beautifully put together and I can't wait for you to see it. So thanks to you and Mike for this very valuable and revealing document, it's the stuff of novels!

Anyway, I'm sure Mike will be in touch with you about it . . . Love to everyone . . . XXX

My stepmother's email is from a year of seismic changes in both countries I consider home. It was 2016; Britain voted to retreat from Europe, and an American election set the country on a dangerous, winding road away from democracy. For the intrepid Brownrigg party, however, 2016 was a year that restored a special relationship, like the one said to exist between Britain and the United States. I gained another English relative in addition to my grandfather: Beatrice Brownrigg, a woman who was intelligent, perceptive—and grief-struck.

By temperament, I have always leaned into melancholy. A reviewer of my first novel said that I seemed comfortable with the "somber hues" of human emotions, and the phrase became a running joke between my husband and me, a shorthand for my chronic attraction to stories of separation, misunderstanding, death. "Somber hues," he'd wryly note, if I started dwelling on some mournful detail. Much of the scrapbook my great-grandmother created was shaded in somber hues. But Beatrice's fortitude, her determined positivity in the face of her losses, moved me, not least because she was trying to channel it into something of use for someone else—for her grandson, Nicholas. I thought of my own sweet son when I read about the bond between Beatrice and Gawen. ("No son could be more loving to his mother, or more tender and anxious if she was in trouble or pain than your father was to me," she wrote to Nicholas.) This was a new experience: a feeling of affinity with one of my relations.

What Valerie and Mike—and, from a distance, Nick—found inside the thick outer wrapping was a large black scrapbook carefully prepared and labeled: it contained envelopes filled with correspondence, clippings, photographs, telegrams, obituaries, and reviews. At the start of the whole was the document my stepmother called "the cover letter" from Beatrice. She seemed to stand outside herself and watch her own production. She used the third person.

```
A memoir about her son Gawen,
written as a letter to Nicholas by his Grandmother
Beatrice Brownrigg


LONDON. December, 1939


My very dear Grandson,
    When you are old enough to wish to know something
about your Father as we knew him I shall be an old
woman, if I live as long as that; so while my memory
is clear and I am still close to the events about
which I write, I am going to tell you that which will
be of value to you to know.
    This is war time, and no one can foresee from day
to day whether I shall be among the survivors or not.
    Juliet knows all that I know and will perhaps
fill in the gaps which I perhaps have not been able
to fill.
```

My dad had a portrait of his aunt Juliet, a soft, hazy oil of a pale face in a gold oval frame; it was the only Brownrigg-related item he ever displayed, though he never spoke of his aunt. It is clear from letters that Gawen and his older sister were close. In the photographs of Gawen and Lucia's Somerset wedding, she is a serious, white-clad figure. When it came to my writing a book for children, I borrowed Juliet's name for my pseudonym, and I have a picture of her, too, near my desk.

```
    Your parents were married on 10th of September,
1931. We strongly opposed the marriage because Gawen
was much too young and had too little money, but
```

```
Lucia's Mother wished for the marriage and she made
it possible by giving Lucia a sufficient allowance.
    . . .
    In May, 1932, Gawen was seriously ill and it was
considered advisable that he should spend some time
in an equable climate where great care could be given
to his health, so Gawen and Lucia went to Pasadena
for a year and lived with her parents.
    On December 22, 1932, you were born, and you can
read of your birth from Gawen's letter to me.
    June, 1933. You all returned to England, and went
to live in London.
```

Though written and intended for Nicholas, Beatrice's account of her son's life and work and marriage turned into a collective reading endeavor. My dad was unable to make sense of the words himself, but three of us—this time Valerie, Mike, and I—read different passages aloud to him. There were parts we attended to closely, guided by our reactions to their revelations, and other parts we may have skim-read, especially on first encounter, when the memoir-writer ventured into the tangled issues about Gawen's estate, the custodial arrangements for Nicholas, and convolutions of the British divorce courts in the 1930s. (Who knew our grandmother had been a bigamist, in legal English eyes?) Beatrice also discussed carefully the brief history of Gawen's literary career, spending no more than half a sentence on *Star Against Star* and considerably more detail on *Later Than You Think*. All these lengthy excursions, along with details of the inquest after Gawen's death, were in support of Beatrice's main thesis: that Gawen had loved and looked out for Nicholas, and planned a future for him—despite the split from the boy's mother, Lucia. At the heart of her argument was her conviction that Gawen had died of natural causes, and had not taken his own life. Her son would not, she believed, have chosen to leave them all behind. To Gawen's lawyer, Joynson-Hicks, who tried to help the family with Nairobi bureaucracy in the wake of Gawen's death, Beatrice wrote, with touching confidence: "There was certainly nothing *morbid* about Gawen, as you know." What first caught my own eye, given conversations I had had with my grandmother, were Beatrice's descriptions of Gawen's marriage, the first in a series of two Brownrigg marriages, one per generation, that ended swiftly in divorce. It was hard for me not to read this account through the lens of Nick and Linda's short, unhappy union.

> In character Lucia and Gawen were totally different; beyond their mutual sex attraction there was nothing to keep them together.
>
> . . .
>
> Lucia was half-American, half-Austrian, and her character was altogether opposite. She was violently jealous with an uncontrollable temper, and both Gawen and you as a baby experienced the effect of this. She had no guide except her impulses and desires; she was in some ways completely uncivilized, and more forlorn spiritually than any young creature I have ever known. She was well educated and had plenty of book learning and the undigested knowledge that is superficially acquired by travelling. Unwisely spoilt by her Mother and unwisely bullied by her Father, she had no poise and no sense of responsibility or moral obligations.
>
> Lucia's habits were those of a sloven which dismayed her Mother as well as it shocked and dismayed Gawen and his family, especially when these habits were tolerated in the nursery and in the neglect of your welfare and health.

"A sloven": my brother and I could reduce each other to tears of laughter with tales of our grandmother's Hacienda del Lago—another name for her Albuquerque home, after the pond (which wasn't much of a *lago*) created on the grounds in the 1940s. There was the time the city required Lucia to drain that pond, where she kept geese and ducks and eventually toxic algae, so she wouldn't poison her neighbors. That none of Lucia's guests ever perished from botulism is a matter for genuine wonder. My grandmother went to sleep with plates of food on her bed, often shared with her dog, and the adobe itself was thick with alternating layers of clutter, valuables, and dirt, a unique European-southwestern squalor. (The library, housed in a separate building, had a distinct and separate order.) Beatrice's 1939 observation about Lucia remained accurate right till the end. On a bad day, assessing my own domestic environment, when the stacks of papers are perilously high and the kitchen countertops crowded with bottles and spices, I worry about having the sloven's blood running through my veins.

> In October, 1936, Lucia went to Reno to qualify for a Reno divorce. I imagine because she ardently wished to marry John Burnham.
>
> Before there was time for mutual discussions, and without informing Gawen of her intention, Lucia married John Burnham on 8th December, 1936. This action still left her English marriage legally intact, and she rendered herself liable to imprisonment for bigamy which is a criminal offence in any country where English Law is in being.
>
> In 1937 Gawen instituted divorce proceedings. The difficulties and delays, owing to distance and differences in international law, and the long correspondence between the solicitors on both sides, created a painfully protracted business for Gawen. Although his case was complete before he left England for East Africa, the abnormally congested condition of the English Divorce Court in the first half of 1938 further delayed the hearing of the case.
>
> Before the Court could give him his Decree Absolute and his freedom--the same freedom which Lucia had had for a year and eight months--Gawen suddenly died of heart failure.

This leads into the many long pages Beatrice devotes to establishing that Gawen always suffered from a weak heart, which was the cause, she firmly believes, of his untimely death.

Now I shall end this letter to you, my very dear Grandson, with two things I wish you to always remember.

Firstly, you must never judge either of your parents.

When they married in September, 1931, Gawen was less than 21 years of age and Lucia was less than 20. They married when they were much too young for the responsibilities of marriage. The first cause of estrangement leading to the Separation of October, 1935, was the incompatibility of their temperaments, tastes, habits and ideals; and the final cause leading to the definite break between them was your Mother's Reno divorce and immediate marriage to John Burnham. [In 1936.]

Secondly. You must never think that your Father's family willingly surrendered you as a child to your Mother because they were indifferent to you.

If your Father had lived he would have arranged to share you with your Mother; and your Grandfather and I looked forward with happy expectation to making White Waltham an English home for you.

After your Grandfather's death in February, 1939, the house and land and contents of the house had to be sold because everything belonged to you and also to your Aunt Juliet by the terms of a Settlement made by your great-Grandmother.

IT WAS NOT until I absorbed more thoroughly the contents of Beatrice's scrapbook—which included obituaries published in the British newspapers of Sir Douglas Brownrigg, her husband, as well as short notices about Gawen—that I fully understood the sequence of Beatrice's losses. Six short months after their son died in Kenya, Beatrice's husband died in France. Douglas was buried, as he had asked to be, at sea. Consequent on his death, Beatrice had to sell their home and move.

The loss of your English home made it undesirable to bring you to England even if your Mother had

wished you to come to me. Your Father wished you to
be brought up in England after you were seven years
old, but this wish cannot be carried into effect at
present; apart from the changes in the circumstances
which we hoped would be yours, there is the present
dangerous and disturbed condition of Europe.

I have requested through your sponsor, your
Great-Uncle Hubert, that the Court should permit
your Mother to keep you with her for the next five
years.

This is plainly her moral right, and the longing
that is both Juliet's and mine to have you live with
us has no claim for consideration in opposition to
any wish of your Mother to keep you in California
during your childhood.

I should like you to know that I had a great pity
and a real affection for your Mother and I often
think that she regrets as I do that her wayward
nature prevented a better understanding between us
before she left England in October, 1935. I know she
sympathises with the sadness I feel at this separation from you, and knows how much I appreciate her
thoughtfulness and kindness in writing about you.

*I think of you with love, and pray
that every blessing in life may be yours.*

Your loving grandmother
Beatrice Brownrigg

She did survive the war. Beatrice died in 1952, having survived not
only the death of her son and her husband but also that of her daughter,
Juliet, in 1947. Beatrice got through the Blitz, and postwar rationing;
Clement Attlee's Labour government and the death of King George
VI. Her life ended the same year that Elizabeth II took the throne. But
she never got to see her grandson, Nicholas, again.

People in my generation, whatever you want to call us, the tail end of the Boomers or the start of Gen X, are the bridge between those in the past who wrote and kept letters—Beatrice, Gawen, and Nick, and myself, too, shoeboxes full from friends and beloveds—and people now whose messages will die on the vine or, more accurately, in the cloud. My kids and I communicate often, but frequently from a distance as they make their way into college and adulthood. When we are apart we speak via FaceTime or WhatsApp, trademarked means of interaction. We send plenty of texts and pictures. I don't, however, sit down and write them for an hour or two, sharing my reflections, descriptions of what's around me, notes on what I'm reading, romantic or practical advice. At best I might thumb-type a few such thoughts in a message on my phone. If my children ever wonder, in years ahead, what I thought about anything, they won't be able to go back and find out. They'll just have to remember. We'll see how that goes.

Then again, letters are not always reliable, either. They can sustain a connection, yes: allow you to hear a voice, understand someone's inner workings, bring someone long gone back to life again.

They can also get lost or go astray. In Hardy's *Tess of the d'Urbervilles*, a book I broke my heart over as a somber-hued teen when assigned to read it at school and for my O-level exams, Tess writes a crucial confessional letter to her soon-to-be-husband, Angel Clare, so that he can marry her with full knowledge of what had befallen her in the past. She believes he loves and accepts her anyway, a serene, beautiful moment of relief—until she discovers, too late, that her letter never reached Angel: it slipped under the mat and remained unseen. This small accident sets in motion a series of tragic events and prevents the two from fulfilling their deep love for one another. Their happiness is destroyed. Tess tried to write the truth, but the writing did not reach him.

This plot point has always haunted me. It is as though I were waiting for decades to become aware of the parallel accident in our family. The near miss, the might-have-been. I think of the fate of Beatrice's heartfelt missive to her grandson, lost for fifty years, as Hardyesque. Even if my dad ended up living most of his life in the redwoods of Northern California, you could say he stayed English at his core.

15.

GENTLEMAN FARMER

✦

OF ALL THE THINGS THAT BEATRICE DWELLS ON IN HER many pages in the thick black scrapbook, nothing takes up more of her energy and concern than how Gawen died. That is her passionate proof. She does not want anyone, ever, to believe it was suicide.

The life story hinges on the death story. My dad closed out his days on California's north coast, where he and Valerie had been living for nearly twenty years, though in his last months she sometimes found Nick downstairs in the morning with his bags packed, telling his wife he wanted to go home. (Did he mean the Circle C? Or someplace earlier?) From their windswept house perched on the dunes' edge, they could daily watch the drama of the Pacific, its weathers and tides, at a point just before the shoreline curves around in a half-moon up to a wild, wooded stretch of land known as the Lost Coast.

Living with his failing mind, the chaos and confusion that went with the gradual erosion of the man who had been her companion, took its toll on my stepmother, though she cared for him lovingly throughout. My brother and I took turns driving the four hours up, helping her sort out caregivers, taking our dad off for lunch or breakfast to give her a break. We kept conversation going as well as we could with Nick, and though he made less and less sense, he continued to like to laugh and stayed curious about the world. Even as his language diminished, his speech retained its distinctive rhythms, his humor strangely intact. A few days before the end, my brother and I were there together with our dad, telling him we loved him, holding his hand.

To feel the weight of someone's death, you have to feel the weight of their life. This must be obvious to people schooled in their family's history, who can recite the names of distant relatives, what they did and how they are remembered. But if you're self-taught in these matters, you work out each step on your own. Like looking at ruins and imagining the shape of the buildings that sheltered those old lives—it's easier to do if there's a panel handy with a diagrammed reconstruction. I used to love playing around ruins when I was small; they were one of my favorite things about England, more than the still-whole castles or cathedrals. We lived not far from Minster Lovell, pretty riverside remnants of a fifteenth-century manor hall, and took visitors there when they came through Oxford. The melancholic romance was everywhere in the broken stones, the emptied windows, the roofless rooms. The echoes around the abandoned dovecote. It was right there in the word *ruins*.

In 2018, a few days after my dad's death, I was talking on the phone with my stepmother. She had to deal with the various administrative aspects of a spouse's passing, including a query from the funeral home about how to describe her late husband's occupation. It was a line to be filled in, and Valerie wondered what I would suggest.

"I thought about 'writer' . . . ," she said, though added she did not feel that would really be accurate. "Then I considered something like 'investor.'"

This surprised me, as it seemed even less apt. Then again, I had spoken with my father about finances precisely never, apart from hearing about his will at that one lunch in Healdsburg. My stepmother could see the humor in her uncertainty; we both could, and I imagine Nick would have, too—younger, mentally sound Nick.

Valerie laughed. "I finally decided on 'gentleman farmer.'"

So on some county form, that is what Nicholas Brownrigg did for a living. He was a gentleman farmer.

Sometimes the story unfolds almost too neatly, with a symmetry you would not risk in a novel. Philip's illness, a different cancer, suddenly became acute a few months after Nick died. Another handoff. And the back-and-forth between countries that had characterized my stepfather's largely happy relationship with my mother continued: his first months of treatment were in California, dealing with the American health-care system, before he got strong enough to fly to London. (On a wheelchaired outing by the southern edge of San Francisco Bay, when he was quite frail, I asked Philip if he'd like to return to the United Kingdom if it became possible. He replied, "Of course.") From the Cotswolds village they had settled in after Philip retired from his academic post, trips were made to doctors in Oxford, coincidentally in the suburban neighborhood where we used to live, near the roller-skating sidewalks and the former football grounds. One sad afternoon, after sitting with them both while Philip received the worst, terminal news from his trusted doctor, I took a long, solitary walk past the house where he and my mother first met in 1971, and where we then all lived together the following year, a period that encompassed the Watergate hearings, and Monty Python on television, and our school performance of *Joseph and the Amazing Technicolor Dreamcoat*, whose songs I could still sing, if I had to. I'll likely be crooning Tim Rice's lyrics about Joseph's dreamcoat long in the future, when I can no longer remember what I ate for breakfast.

Philip remained resilient throughout painful episodes and hospital stays, maintaining his solicitous manners and characteristic wit to the end. "Dying is boring" was one of his late, succinct pronouncements. His four nieces, warm and generous women, were frequently on hand to advise and help, liaising with the synagogue when it came time to make the last arrangements. He died in August 2019.

One late-summer day, we gathered in the Jewish section of the Oxford cemetery. It was the first time I had been around an open grave since the one I had dug for Sab at the top of the short hill by our house in Los Altos. Philip had chosen to be buried near his brother, an eminent classics scholar, not far from the final resting place of Isaiah Berlin and a somewhat greater distance from Tolkien's. On a cool, sunny afternoon, surrounded by English relatives and friends, Michael and I spoke about the man who had raised us, taken care of us, celebrated our milestones, consoled us over disappointments; who had, we both felt, modeled for us how to live, and what was right. Under a spreading cypress tree, we read part of the Kaddish in English and Hebrew before the pallbearers lowered his narrow coffin into the ground. Then we each took turns scattering shovels of Oxford earth over the wooden box, and afterward a few of us added a ritual handful from Israel.

Nick had been cremated the year before, without ceremony, very soon after he died. It took months for us to gather in a small family group to remember him—my brother's family and mine, and Nick's two half brothers, the "Brosies," as he called them, whom, in keeping with Brownrigg ways, my children were meeting for the first time. It was an unstructured, informal afternoon, a conversation mostly, with some music, some jokes. A Kerouac reading here, a boogie-woogie recording there. Later, we all went out to dinner together in Mendocino and drank good wine, something we all agreed Nick would have wanted us to do.

Our dad had not wanted a service. There was no burial, and so there is no grave.

PART TWO

✦

A Death in Nairobi

I was almost you once, and that's why I have allowed myself to make up this world to talk with you.

—YIYUN LI, *Where Reasons End*

1.

WHERE REASONS END

✦

IN YIYUN LI'S WRENCHING, BEAUTIFUL NOVEL *WHERE Reasons End*, the narrator has a long dialogue with her teenage son after he has died by suicide. (As Li's own son did, in high school.) The narrator has herself known depression, so she feels she can understand his act, yet in describing how their surviving family has dealt with and responded to the young man's death—the rituals, the outpourings of love and support from their community—it is as if she is hoping to amass enough evidence to get her son to change his mind, retroactively. As though she might still be able to talk him out of it.

Suicide is an acid and dramatic word, and the act's looming shape tends to overshadow the other facets of a person's character. Plath, Hemingway, Woolf: you have to find the poems and the novels on the other side of the mark left by their ending, and not be so distracted by the way they quit that you fail to take in their life's work. The life story hinges on the death story.

That thick black scrapbook rested in an archival box on my standing desk, a desk I rarely stood at, though my daughter, keener on healthy habits, used to do her homework there some evenings. She once had a math tutor who, upright at a whiteboard scribbling puzzles and equations, chided, "Sitting is the new smoking, you know."

My dad was a big smoker in the era when the cigarette's image was evolving from cool to carcinogenic. I hated the smell of his smoke and quietly fantasized about getting him to stop. (I was not brave enough to try.) There were still cigarette ads on TV then, like the one that had grinning men or women, a black smear under one eye, speaking their cheerful slogan: "Us Tareyton smokers would rather fight than switch." It was confusing to think someone might throw a punch to defend their cigarette brand, though I did know my dad to be loyal to his red-boxed Winstons. In his unpublished novel *Moebius Curve*, Nick's alter ego was called Winston. I wonder if it was after the cigarettes or Britain's wartime prime minister, but by the time I read it, the manuscript's author was no longer around to ask.

I sat at a regular desk to work, a black-and-white photograph of Gawen on a nearby surface, though not so close that I felt he was watching me. Not quite an adult, he is seventeen or eighteen, dressed formally in a suit, tie, pocket square. He is half smiling, and there is warmth in his eyes under thick dark brows not unlike my son's; a tidy line parts his slick, wavy dark hair. When I had reading to do, I took to the beat-up IKEA couch by the window that looked out over the garden, to wonder at Gawen's frothy early love letters to Lucia or pore over the grimmer details from the Nairobi inquest after his death. That upstairs room, vacated now after a house fire, was where I began to get to know my grandfather. He was sweeter than I expected, and younger; less self-confident, more self-aware. "I know that I'm much too concerned with other people's opinions of me—people who don't matter a damn in my life," he confessed in an author information form he filled out for Knopf, the one Neil Pearson found and sent me. I recognized this feeling. (Pearson comments, dryly: "Quite how many books Brownrigg thought this would help his publisher shift is unclear.") This self-description comes shortly after Gawen's response to the questionnaire's prompt "Brief Summary of Principal Occupations," here in its entirety: "Office boy in a London stockbroker's office (1930 and 31); literary editor in the publishing firm of Arthur Barker Ltd (1932-35). Since then, writing novels with conspicuous lack of success and occasional reviewing."

At the beginning I thought this was a father-son story. Reading and taking in the contents of the scrapbook, I wanted to restore Gawen to Nick, as if in giving my dad back his own father, I might at the same time bring back Nick to myself. I imagined a tale of two fathers, though the remaining one died before I finished it.

But the women kept edging into the account. I became more and more aware that this rich trove of papers was a curated one, Beatrice Brownrigg burnishing the picture of her late son. The scrapbook did not make Gawen a saint—as presented, he was a man with frailties and flaws—but she allowed strategic omissions. (What mother doesn't, telling you about their kid?) Along the way, I discovered I had a surprising other source for new dimensions of Gawen, some that complemented Beatrice's narrative and others that complicated it. Lucia had kept all the letters her first husband wrote to her, as well as some he received while they were married: correspondence about *Star Against Star* from editors apologizing that the lesbian subject matter was too risqué, or a kind note from Vita Sackville-West cautioning Gawen against reputational damage if he published it. From the letters Lucia kept, it was clear that Vita and Harold Nicholson were friendly acquaintances of the young couple, and Gawen must have pursued the connection for help with his career. Lucia had a collector's instinct and a hoarder's habit, and the two together gave me another inheritance of printed matter, enough further material about Gawen to counter Lucia's own slanderous dismissal of her first husband. Her fourth, Harry Batten, had long since died when I met her, and she was done with husbands altogether, but she held on to her Gawen archive—whether or not she consciously knew it. The sorting task was mine.

I did worry, as anyone with posh English relatives is bound to, about my grandfather turning out to be someone I did not much like, after these new discoveries. It would be a horrible irony to exhume a grandparent only to feel I should have let him stay buried. In our contemporary era of reckonings and reparations, it was all too likely that I would find a Brit of empire days to have blots of character or attitude. And I *have* had moments of blood-shuddering, when Gawen's background hampers his empathy or narrows his perceptions and I feel implicated in his prejudices; or I hear phrases or tones of voice that make me cringe. I can only hope he might have changed, if he had aged. (God only knows what any future grandchildren of mine would think of my old letters if they read them.) Flaws and frailties, again, though of a different kind from the ones his mother noted.

Mostly, though, I like Gawen. I have sympathy for him. Sometimes he is like any writer friend, alternating pride in his latest novel with self-deprecation about its chances, trying to be levelheaded about reviews (the ones clipped from British newspapers by his mother and sent to him in Kenya) while imagining his next, better book waiting around the corner. My grandfather can sound like a sweet little boy when writing to his parents—"Darling Mums and Daddy" begins the letter he sent home about the birth of his son, Nicholas—and elsewhere just like a young man in his mid to later twenties, the age my stepson is as I write this, trying to figure out his way in the world. In one touching moment we hear Gawen warmed by the first sincere literary encouragement from his own remote father, in a segment of correspondence Beatrice thought to include: "Before I close this over-long letter," Gawen wrote, "I should like to tell you that there was one thing in your letter which gave me more pleasure than anything I've heard from you for a very long time, and that was your wish to see me succeed as a writer. This is the first time that you have expressed such a wish personally to me, and it becomes for me not only a great occasion in my life, but a potent incentive to get on with the job."

At times I sense the depression waiting in the wings for Gawen. I have known moments like those, picturing all that would be made easier by my absence. Writing fictional scenes with a suicidal character is something Gawen did, and I have done it, too. We each wrote novels, his second, my first, with protagonists tempted by the possibility of seeking their own end; his is vivid and convincing. His Val imagines having to get fished out of the Thames; mine stands by an open window on a high floor in a city apartment. I'd not yet read his when I wrote my own.

There was another worry, too, which occurred to me only when I was knee-deep in the writing of this book. What if it went the other way as I read all these pages about Gawen? What if I started, perversely, to miss my grandfather?

It was the beginning of new reasons for sadness. Not just for what Nick had lost, but for what I had, my brother had, too. I joined the long queue of people who could only wish Gawen Brownrigg had lived many more years.

2.

CONDOLENCES

✦

YOU HAVE TO WRITE PEOPLE AFTER SOMEONE THEY LOVE has died. My mother taught me this. For the most part she has not been a parent to impart life lessons, but this is an important imperative she conveyed to me along the way. *Write people after someone they love has died.* It makes a difference to the ones left behind.

When a friend of mine lost his beloved wife of twenty-nine years after a short illness, he was flooded with cards and letters. (Mine was one.) He is a writer, and a lot of their friends were writers, and doubtless many of those letters were beautifully written. In a time of no relief and only pain, when he wondered how he would go on without her, these expressions of sympathy gave him some solace. He sorted the collection into three categories: the ones he read then threw away; the ones he kept; and the ones he kept but separately, a small number that said something to him in a way that helped. He reread those periodically, for a long while after she died.

There is grief's egotism—why did this happen to me, to *me?*—and then there is grief's selflessness, too, when all the bereaved wants is for everyone to say or write or post how remarkable was that person they have lost. "I know you loved her and I'm glad you did," my friend wrote in response to one of my first, probably emailed, condolences. After the initial raw shock, the necessary silent aftermath of the ending, he came to relish anecdotes people told about his wife. He enjoyed learning new things about her. It kept her vibrant, as though she were still changing; she was not frozen, like a marble statue.

Sometimes I have been with Gawen in this story, and sometimes with his mother. It took me months to read everything in the scrapbook she made. It became my own lockdown project, rereading and absorbing letters and documents in my room upstairs, as my understanding constantly shifted, while my daughter, downstairs, attended high school on a laptop. From my perch in Berkeley I tried to make sense of Gawen's end in Nairobi, as filtered through the sensibility and editorial decisions of his mother.

Beatrice included a selection of condolence notes she and Douglas received in order to give Nicholas a sense of how people wrote about and remembered his father. Her son.

Dear Sir,

Please permit one who is a complete stranger to you, but who knew Gawen well, to send his sympathies with you on your son's most untimely demise. I first met him in 1933 and last saw him not long before he went to East Africa.

He was a most lovable fellow, who, to character, added great personal charm.

But many will have written to say that. Perhaps, however, you may like to know that he would probably have made a big—a distinguished—name as a writer, for he had an exquisite sense of style and a most perceptive understanding of people . . .

He is deeply mourned by his friends, who admired him, not only for the qualities I have mentioned, but for the courage he showed in a matter that wounded him profoundly.

Believe me, Sir, to be
Yours faithfully,
Eric Partridge

My dear Lady Brownrigg,

I can't say all that I'd like to, the whole thing is so terrible. I didn't hear about it until two days ago and haven't recovered from the shock yet. You see, I too loved Gawen.

There seems to be only one consolation in his death, and that is that he will miss all the futility & heartbreaks of life—he was so good and kind.

It must be terrible for you. I wish this was a more adequate letter to let you know how deeply I sympathise and feel for you. When Gawen died something of me died with him & yet I believe he is still with us now.

I cannot write any more but please believe me he is so much happier now. May I come and see you a little later on?

All my feelings are for you, he did adore you so.

Yours with love
Bettie Browning

Dear Lady Brownrigg,

I have been meaning and wishing to write to you for some time now. Just after Gawen's death, I didn't feel I could somehow. Gawen was my best friend out in Kenya and I miss him more than I can say. In the office where we had adjoining rooms he used to wander in and out when there wasn't much to do, and talk to me. We used to criticize each other's work, and sometimes tease one another about it. Mummy will have told you, how he used to come round and visit us often and talk about his thoughts and the things he wished for. I felt I knew him so well because in great many ways we felt the same about things, and so I was fond of him as I might be of a brother. He very often talked to me of you with great affection and understanding so I know that the feeling between you must be much the same as between my mother and myself—and so I know too what a great loss you must feel—not only for a dear son, but for a friend and a companion. Perhaps one day, when you feel you can think of him without that sense of irreparable loss which even I feel in a degree which must be so much less than yours, you will write to me about him.

When he signed a copy of his book for me he wrote in addition: "with a lively sense of friendship, affection and gratitude that we can find so much to laugh at together." That sums up better than anything I can say our friendship. I was certainly touched that he should put it so, and now I am doubly grateful.

from Sybil Weir, his colleague at *The East African Standard*

"Lady B" darling. There is absolutely nothing to say on an occasion such as this. You are all in my thoughts the whole time. I know what I feel, which must be quite infinitesimal, as he adored you, above all else.

As always, Betty [Lampson, the
mother of Juliet's first husband]

And there are others, from his boss at *The East African Standard*, tasked with the administration issues of Gawen's death; from an earlier coworker at a London publishing firm; and even, to my shock when I came across it, from Lucia. They did what such notes do, try to comfort with memories and snapshots of the loved one. For the ones who came after, who never knew Gawen, these helped break the ice he had been encased in. Gradually, my grandfather was warmed back to life.

There was also a transcript of a radio obituary broadcast in Nairobi:

```
OPENING REMARKS IN "A TALK ON BOOKS" BY A.W. Devas
Jones
BROADCAST FROM CABLE & WIRELESS STATION 7. L.O. Nairobi
On Wednesday Evening the 10th, August, 1938.


     Some months ago I reviewed through this micro-
phone a book called "Portrait in a Windscreen" by
Gawen Brownrigg, who was the Sports Editor of the
East African Standard.
     It was only on Thursday last that I was talking
to him in Nairobi asking whether he had any news
about another book of his we had been talking about.
     To-night I wish to pay tribute to his memory as
a fellow journalist for, as most of you will know,
```

he died on Monday last at so early an age that one
might almost say that he had hardly had time to live.

Out here in Kenya it is so seldom that we have a
real contact with a living author, and now he has
gone from us. When I reviewed his book on the wireless, I said that I would look forward with great
pleasure to his future work, but that is not to be.
I would just like to add that having met and talked
to him dozens of times, I found him to be a fellow
of infinite charm to whom the strangeness of East
Africa was all so new that he had not yet found the
tempo of what we may call our rather strange way of
doing most things, so entirely different from any
other parts of the world I know.

Farewell Gawen Brownrigg!

3.

THE KIPLING TOUCH

✦

KENYA HAD NOT BEEN AN OBVIOUS CHOICE.

Gawen's family had no history in that part of the world. The Brown-riggs were in no way insular, but outside of Europe their experience had been in Asia—Japan, Malaysia, Ceylon. Otherwise the only African connection was Gawen's father having, early in his career, "seen some fighting in the Soudan [sic]."

Evelyn Waugh exerted an influence, from a distance. Gawen, an admirer of Waugh's work, would have read about Waugh's adventures in the East African countries then called Abyssinia and Tanganyika, whose borders had been drawn by European powers during the nineteenth century's Scramble for Africa. From his time in the region, Waugh produced newspaper columns and books, including the 1930s novels *Black Mischief* and *Scoop*—the latter a great, stinging satire of hapless Western war correspondents in a fictional African nation, which retains an eerie currency and is frequently mentioned on "best novels of the century" lists. Gawen was enough of a fan that he had his own fictional character Val reading Waugh's (mostly) England-set novel of marital betrayal, *A Handful of Dust*, on the evening his protagonist contemplates suicide. "Funny that the title should be prophetic," Val muses darkly.

A word on the Waughs. In their few London years together, Gawen and Lucia socialized with Evelyn and Alec, especially Alec, who remained lifelong friends with Lucia. Perhaps more than friends, we'll never know, though my dad occasionally muttered jokes about Alec Waugh being his real father. (On his second honeymoon, Nick traveled with Valerie as well as Lucia—who doesn't bring their mother along on their honeymoon?—to Morocco, where they met up with Alec Waugh. At the beach, to Lucia's irritation, the incorrigible Alec spent more time ogling Valerie in her swimsuit than he did Lucia.) I believe Evelyn Waugh's travels in East Africa helped Gawen decide to go to Kenya, along with his desire to get as far from the scene of his failed marriage as possible. When a family friend of the Brownriggs offered my grandfather an opportunity at *The East African Standard*, in Kenya, he leapt.

The move took courage. His decision was a roll of the dice, the kind people often make in their twenties when other things have not panned out, and an outlier opportunity arises. He wrote of his news to Lucia, who was Mrs. John Burnham by then. There was still a layer of unreality between himself and the place he was going.

White Waltham, Berkshire
13th October. 1937

Dear Lucia,

Please excuse the typewritten letter, but I am forced to practice on one of these infernal machines as one of the prerequisites for my new job.

I've suddenly had a series of truly amazing breaks after everything had been going wrong with heartbreaking consistency for the last year.

To begin with, I've landed the post of Sports Editor on the East African Standard. It's the largest newspaper in East Africa. I start at a salary of £500 a year, rising £50 a year with a four year contract. Passage paid there and back, and all club subscriptions paid by the newspaper. I sail for Mombasa on November 25th. And arrive in Nairobi on December 21st.

To me, it's all very exciting, not a little frightening, but, nevertheless an eminently suitable solution to nearly all my outstanding problems. Moreover, I've an idea that it may not be at all a bad life. My boss, whom I met through the most incredible series of flukes, is the most charming man one could hope to meet. I can't think of anyone easier to work for.

The odd thing about it all is this: since last June, I've been in negotiation with Desmond F. about a job at Cassells. The same day that I get my contract from the E.A.S., I am called up by Desmond confirming the Cassells job. I had to turn it down for reasons of money. It's nice to feel oneself wanted all of a sudden. (In a business way, of course.)

Mrs. Burnham must have replied warmly to her ex-husband's October news, as the next missive Gawen sends her, while he is preparing to go, is more cheerful—and more honest about what he is leaving behind.

November 11, 1937

My Dear,

I was so happy to get your nice letter and all your good wishes. Four years is, as you say, a long time, but not, after all, a life-time. I feel, at the moment, rather as I did just before I first went to my prep. school; not having the faintest idea of what to expect and wanting desperately to make a good impression. Almost worse than meeting in-laws for the first time!

. . .

Well, you seem to be having a pretty good time. I'm truly glad. You sound happy and contented. I've forgotten how that feels—if, indeed, I ever knew. And, look, while I think of it, be a dear and don't keep asking me about whether I'm in love or if I've found someone I want to marry, etc. etc.; there isn't any answer . . . now. I've been through bloody hell these last few months and I don't awfully want to be reminded of it. An impoverished and undivorced young man can't do much with elderly parents, who are utterly on the make, and open one's letters and slander one and—oh well . . . I'll tell you the whole sad story one day. I hope, from the bottom of my heart that you realise just how lucky you've been. Do you wonder that I'm glad I got this break that takes me right out of this country?

Enough of my troubles.

I sail on the 3d. December on the good ship UBENA. Oddly enough, it is of the Deutsche-Ost-Afrika-Linie. In other words, it's the good old HAPAG [a Hamburg shipping company]. So I shall have all the familiar accoutrements . . . ab und zu, and round-about with a hey-nonny-nonny and militarisches music . . . Vrightfully cherman.

Now, to be serious for a moment. I have appointed my uncle Hubert as deputy-guardian of Nicholas, while I'm away. He's a very reasonable person—the only one of my appalling relatives who shows any signs of humanity. It is a pure formality, and if there should arise any question of moment during my absence, he has instructions to cable to me for authority to act on my behalf.

Here is a copy of my book; and, since you flattered my always easily susceptible vanity, a press photograph. Will you look upon this as a birthday present for your twenty-sixth anniversary.

I was so thrilled to hear that Brocks have lovely cuff-links. I was always appreciative of their wares. I have not lost my tastes for barbaric splendour, and if you would like to send me some, let me hasten to give you my address in Africa. It is;—

> c/o The East African Standard,
> P.O. Box 671,
> Nairobi,
> Kenya,
> British East Africa.

So now you've no excuse. I should like a pair with lots of diamonds and/or emeralds to wear when I go to Government House. You see what I mean . . . . ? All I can say is that it's terribly sweet of you and I don't deserve it. (A smile and an eyebrow-lift here, please.)

Well, I must stop now. I've got to do three articles on the Book Show for "my" paper. (Still can't believe I'm a reporter!) It doesn't look like it by my typing, either, but I am.

Love from,
Gawen

P.S. The Book Show isn't what it used to be. Much too formal and pompous and dull, these days! GEB

Gawen was aiming for, and inclined to, friendship with his not-quite-yet ex-wife. (Not, as would prove crucial, by British law, that is.) He was not trying to win Lucia back; his letters, after she married John Burnham, were open and curious about her new life—"I didn't know you were interested in horse racing!"—but he was self-conscious about being unattached and wanted her to know he was still charming and a good catch, perhaps soon to be a better one as his prospects improved.

And Gawen had not forgotten their son.

> White Waltham House,
> Maidenhead, Berks.
> 28th November

Dear Lucia,

Will you buy something for Nicholas with the enclosed? I don't know what he'd like, but how's about something in the way of livestock?

I'm having a feverish time packing up all my belongings—but it's all rather exciting . . .

Well, I hope you all have a fröhliche xmas and a glückliches New Year.

> Affectionately,
> Gawen

4.

WILD AND WOOLLY PEOPLE

+

THE WORLD MY GRANDFATHER WAS ENTERING WOULD REQUIRE an element of role-play, and a robustness that did not come naturally to him. When a bookish character in Anthony Powell's seminal novel series, *A Dance to the Music of Time*, prepares to leave boarding school and join his (alcoholic) father in East Africa, he says with some dread, "I imagine everyone in Kenya will be terribly hearty and wear shorts and drink sun-downers and all that sort of thing." This was the kind of Englishman attracted to East Africa, a place where, as an American reviewer of Waugh wrote in 1932, "charming British settlers are trying to live the life of country gentlemen as it is no longer possible to live in England." Vast amounts of drinking feature in nearly every story about the British settlers in Kenya (whereas heroin, only in some of them). The large staff at one Englishman's thousand-acre farm included a servant whose sole job was pouring whiskey sodas.

Certainly, Gawen felt the social difference soon after the ship he traveled on docked at Mombasa. "There are so many wild and woolly people out here," he wrote to his mother, before he journeyed by small plane to Nairobi. Within a few months, his novelist's fingers were twitching: "I shall write an epic book about Kenya one of these days. There's an amazing amount of copy—all it needs is sorting, and with tact." Gawen knew the backstories of some people he was meeting from newspapers' gossip pages he had read growing up—they were among the society celebrities of their day. Lady Idina Sackville, the subject of

Frances Osborne's *The Bolter* (Osborne is Idina's great-granddaughter), was a louche hostess in Kenya along with her third husband, Josslyn Hay, later known by his title, Lord Erroll. The couple had notorious parties and a spouse-swapping friendship with a glamorous French American pair, Count Frédéric de Janzé and his wife, Alice, a beautiful and unstable American heiress. Alice became famous in 1927 for shooting her English lover at Paris's Gare du Nord (an incident Fitzgerald borrowed for a scene in his novel *Tender Is the Night*), then shooting herself. Thanks to the skill of French surgeons, both survived. A French judge, persuaded that it was a "crime of passion," acquitted Alice and released her with a suspended sentence and a fine. Later, divorced from her French husband, she persuaded the man she had shot, Raymund de Trafford, to marry her.

In letters Gawen refers to Alice, with whom he was becoming friends, as "the one who shot Raymund at the Gare du Nord":

> I've made great friends with Alice de Trafford who is really an angel and extremely intelligent. Someone with whom I can talk books and be "cosmopolitan" with! I'm only sorry she doesn't live in Nairobi, but up in the Happy Valley at Gilgil at the foot of the Aberdares. One of these days I suppose I shall get a weekend off, something I have yet to achieve after three months working 6½ days a week.

Gawen's mother, in reconstructing her son's brief Nairobi life in the scrapbook, underplays his encounter with Alice and other members of her set. The Happy Valley was a name given to an area within the Wanjohi Valley, several hours' drive from the capital up a steep, rough road—like Ukiah's Low Gap Road, but more so. Nairobi, where Gawen lived and worked, was the center of colonial government and the site of various social clubs, tiered by class, as was the British way: different places for higher officials than for whites who worked as policemen or railwaymen, and the exclusive Muthaiga Club for the landowners or "settlers." This infamous spot, with its pink clubhouse, was favored by the Happy Valleyers, and a place Gawen frequented, enjoying its golf courses and tennis courts. During race weeks the Muthaiga Club was especially packed, horse racing having been one of Britain's earliest sporting imports; the first such race in Kenya was held in 1897 to celebrate Queen Victoria's jubilee. Gawen's job at *The East African Standard* was to cover sporting events near and far, writing under the journalistic pseudonym "Reflex."

It was a different culture from the Raj, Britain's imperial project in India. White Europeans were relatively recent arrivals on the African continent: whereas Britain's East India Company launched its first voyage in 1601, the Imperial British East Africa Company formed only in 1888, coexisting with a German counterpart that occupied the area later known as Tanzania. The Danish baroness Karen Blixen, who wrote under the name Isak Dinesen, came to Kenya just after the First World War, in an early wave of European immigrants who were "almost all themselves country-bred and open air people," as she described herself and her fellows, "themselves untamed, with fresh hearts." This description would not fit Gawen Brownrigg. In Blixen's telling, these early settlers lived more harmoniously with the native Africans, and however wishful the author's picture is, she certainly was more engaged with these cultures than many others were, establishing schools for her farmworkers and alert to religious differences among various tribal groups. There still exists a Nairobi district, Karen, named for her; and in 1963, the Danish government gifted Blixen's old house at the edge of the Ngong Hills to independent Kenya's new government. It has been transformed into the Karen Blixen Museum, a popular tourist attraction.

Dinesen's famous book *Out of Africa*, on which the film was based, has an epigraph taken from Herodotus: *Equitare, Arcum tendere, Veritatem dicere*, "To ride, To shoot, To tell the truth."

I do not believe my grandfather was adept at any one of those things.

5.

END OF EMPIRE

✦

IT IS EASY TO DISAPPEAR DOWN A RABBIT HOLE, READING about the British in East Africa. I've done it. The warrens are deep.

As with other geographies of empire, the tone of accounts has been changing, as new narrators take up the telling. The history of Kenya Colony has curdled, in even the white British imagination, from something colorful—the bold, remarkable accomplishment of constructing a six-hundred-mile railway from Mombasa up to the edge of Lake Victoria; the antics of aristocrat settlers who got up to naughty high jinks on their upcountry farms—to a shameful nightmare, emblematic of the violence underlying other imperialist takeovers. Stories of high-born people having sex parties and shooting up heroin, inventing cocktails with hilarious names, and keeping cheetah cubs as pets have generally lost their appeal. Bestselling books profiling the intertanglings of the Happy Valley set and bearing jaunty titles like *The Bolter* or James Fox's *White Mischief* have ceded ground to academic accounts of the very bloody winding down of Britain's colonial venture in the 1950s: *Imperial Reckoning: The Untold Story of Britain's Gulag in Kenya* by Caroline Elkins or *Histories of the Hanged: The Dirty War in Kenya and the End of Empire* by David Anderson.

Hollywood won't be making any more star-studded costume dramas set in colonial Kenya anytime soon. It is all but impossible to pause nostalgically in the thirties, when my grandfather lived and worked in Nairobi, without being aware of what was to come a decade or two later. The Mau Mau Uprising—or "rebellion," as the British called the movement of predominantly Kikuyu fighters against British colonial powers—led to the colonial government's declaring an eight-year-long state of emergency in 1952, a justification for the creation of concentration camps and other repressive policies in the fierce effort to retain control.

Reverberations of this struggle continue into the twenty-first century, and not just within East Africa but also in post-empire Britain. There was the blaggard Boris Johnson throwing jibes at Barack Obama, saying the American president nurtured an "ancestral dislike of the British empire" based on the experiences of his Kenyan father and grandfather; there was Johnson's silence when the UK's Conservative government, in 2013, paid out nearly twenty million pounds in compensation to surviving Kenyan victims of British torture. The then foreign secretary William Hague made a remarkable speech of acknowledgment in the Houses of Parliament: "The British government recognizes that Kenyans were subjected to torture and other forms of ill-treatment at the hands of the colonial administration." Using careful statecraft language, Hague avoided the verb *apologize*, though he deemed *regret* safe. "The British government sincerely regrets that these abuses took place," he said, "and that they marred Kenya's progress to independence."

Gawen Brownrigg did not live to see any of this, and I can't know what he would have thought if he had. He did not even get to experience the scandal and excitement of the murder of his acquaintance Josslyn Hay, Lord Erroll, in 1941, the never-solved crime at the heart of *White Mischief* (both the book and the subsequent film), and a mystery that made global headlines even when the world was in the throes of another war, as did the inconclusive but salacious trial of the main suspect, Jock Delves Broughton. Sixty years on, sleuths were still puzzling over the story of the slain Lord Erroll, found shot dead in his car, with at least one writer convinced that the cavalier womanizer was killed in a jealous passion by Gawen's friend Alice de Janzé. Not long afterward, de Janzé killed her beloved dog and then herself—both with lethal doses of Nembutal, the same drug Gawen had used, though Alice also turned a gun on herself, to remove any chance of failure. She died with an armful of flowers at her up-country home, the one my grandfather had hoped to visit.

Gawen was amused and perhaps lightly shocked by the goings-on of this "set" in Kenya. To his mother he wrote with some disapproval about the sexual mores of certain men and women, "bounders" or "trollops" as he called them, respectively, but he was not untouched by some of the individuals' glamour or charisma—and besides, letters home to parents are always going to err on the side of propriety. It has struck me, reading about Alice de Janzé, that in her educated eccentricity, love of exotic animals, and boldness in travel, she prefigures the woman Lucia became in later life. Both were American heiresses, and both had a reckless selfishness that may have come in part from their wealth and erratic upbringings. Lucia would probably have kept a pet lion cub, if she could.

As for the racial politics of his new situation, although Gawen read and enjoyed Elspeth Huxley's history of the colony's early European settlers—called, because this seemed unobjectionable to English publishers in 1935, *White Man's Country*—he did apparently share Evelyn Waugh's stated skepticism about "the indefensible and inexplicable assumption of superiority by the Anglo-Saxon race." My grandfather wrote home, a month after he arrived in Nairobi, aware that he was going against the grain of most of those around him, "Personally, and no doubt quite wrongly, I do not feel that I am in my own country or that the presence of white people here is an inestimable blessing."

I can go so far with my grandfather, and no further. I don't pretend to find in him an enlightened attitude about the colonial complexities that made up his world, but I also don't comfortably wear the fashionable moral smugness that goes with judging those who came before us. I cannot predict how my grandfather would have changed or evolved as the country around him did. He learned Swahili and communicated in it with his African servant (who was Maasai), and I believe that by temperament he was resistant to imperial bombast. However, he seemed more prejudicial about the many Indians he encountered in his sportswriting gig, which was to include cricket and polo. Indians in Kenya then outnumbered Europeans by about two to one, according to some estimates. Much of that South Asian population had originally been brought over as laborers by Britain in order to build the railway.

My stories begin with Gawen's end, and what followed from his end. The people are real, the details factual, the thoughts of those around him knowable only through imagining. Beyond that, the reasons give out and, like Yiyun Li, I'm making up worlds. These family stories come from all I've read in the scrapbook, the letters, and the novels, and extending out from there the works of many others who wrote then and have written since about East Africa. Including, of course, writers from African countries.

Kenya's great writer in exile Ngũgĩ wa Thiong'o was born in 1938, the year my grandfather died. Ngũgĩ was a teenager during the Great Emergency, and he lost a brother to the British during the Mau Mau period (a name he rejects for that movement). His masterworks about the devastation wrought by British colonialism in his country are written both as fiction (from 1964's *Weep Not, Child* to *Wizard of the Crow* in 2006) and memoir, both in English and, from the 1970s on, in his native Kikuyu. One of Ngũgĩ's most influential works, *Decolonising the Mind: The Politics of Language in African Literature*, expresses the author's deeply held view on the importance of reclaiming and writing in African languages, though paradoxically this act of literary rebellion contributed to his yearlong imprisonment in Kenya in the late 1970s. After teaching for many years at UC Irvine in Southern California, Ngũgĩ received the 2022 PEN/Nabokov Award for Achievement in International Literature (and his name comes up annually as a potential winner of the Nobel). Several of Ngũgĩ's adult children are now writers and professors in the United States and elsewhere, the storytelling continuing, in various forms. I have not met them, but it's good to know there are families where a tradition of writing books can be openly shared.

In *Birth of a Dream Weaver*, Ngũgĩ writes:

> "Kenya was the land of black people," we sang in opposition to the European settlers' claims that Kenya was the White Highlands. Their claims had been given literary immortality in the work of Elspeth Huxley. The colonial state sided with the literary, but the oral was the voice of a people, and even after the state banned [the freedom fighters'] songs and poetry, song and dance inspired defiance in those herded in barbed-wire trucks into concentration camps. They sang:
> *Deport us to concentration camps*
> *Or lock us up in prisons*
> *Or exile us on remote islands*
> *We shall never cease to struggle for freedom*
> *Kenya is the land of black people*

The Standard

✦

THE MANAGING DIRECTOR WAS STILL AT HOME MONDAY morning when he received word that one of the paper's writers had died in the night. Captain Anderson was urgently asked to come to the compound where the man had lived, to help prevent scandal or confusion.

It was a harder errand than it would have been had Anderson left from the offices of *The Standard*. There, suited and groomed, he would already have had on a public, outward-looking face, no skin or tenderness exposed. As it was, in his shirt sleeves and surrounded by the pleasant dust of domestic life—Claude Anderson was not one of those men for whom young children were a strangeness and annoyance, but rather one who found the continuous motion of his wife and daughters a comfort—he felt caught out. Guilty, almost. He thought briefly of his time in the King's African Rifles years earlier, how in the barracks a common currency between soldiers and officers was the readiness to meet death. It was in the fabric of the service; you did maneuvers at the edges of oblivion. Anderson had been a young man himself then and not yet a father; by now he had got out of the pragmatic habit of dealing with a life's abrupt end. Receiving this news at his Nairobi home, the bustle of breakfast at his back, Anderson had a baffled instant when the words and information made no sense.

Mr. Brownrigg found dead in his rooms. Require identification of and instructions for deceased.

This came from the proprietor of the Salisbury Hotel, a cluster of low-lying buildings at the western edge of the growing city, who had sent a driver to deliver the message to the young man's employer and then wait to return with him. Anderson found a tie, jacket, hat, the ritual giving him moments to collect himself. He could see the dapper journalist in his mind, working with concentration and some self-consciousness. Absently, Anderson donned his jacket. It was cool but would be warmer later. The Kenyan sun had intentions for that August day, as it had intentions every day, outside of the rainy season. His wife came to see him off with a murmur of sympathy. The scent of her in their brief embrace stayed with the director as he braced to perform his duties.

An anxious atmosphere permeated the Salisbury's foyer when he got there, an oil-and-water mix of hecticness and hesitation. A stern young policeman stood by the broad doorway as if on the watch for something, though unsure of the nature of the threat. The squat South African at the front desk had a feral, caged expression, as though he would rather have been out hunting than cleaning up after this sort of mess. He had come to Kenya, Anderson imagined, as South Africans now did, to help expand the British enterprise in the colony. It was a time of growth for the white population. *Settlers welcome.* Running a hotel for European residents of Nairobi must have seemed a promising endeavor, relatively. This event was unfortunate. People dying at your new establishment was not good for business.

"Mr. Brownrigg is in the rooms across the courtyard." He was unable to feign sympathy or smother his disgust, as if Brownrigg were a selfish guest who had carelessly damaged his rooms, something the unruly British upper classes were known occasionally to do. "His boy found him, about an hour ago, as he was preparing to bring him breakfast. The police have asked him to stay here, though they have already taken his statement."

Anderson thanked the man and proceeded in an innocent yellowish light across a tidy sanded courtyard whose borders were brightened by flowering bushes. Young Brownrigg had been pleased to have secured such a place for himself, recently, after moving from a more central hotel, right by *The Standard*. Calmer out here; lonelier, possibly, too. He had only lately arrived in Kenya, altogether—Christmastime. Eight or so months ago. *He had just started to settle in.* The sentence kept returning to Anderson's mind that morning, as if he were typing it up himself. Anderson wasn't a writer, never had been one. Still, sometimes the stories wrote themselves.

Seeing Brownrigg's lifeless body made the thing real. The Englishman's skin was a pale gray, the color of stationery, and he was lying on his back, quite straight. He looked younger than when Anderson had last seen him, finishing a piece previewing the week's races. Glancing at Gawen Brownrigg at his typewriter while he joked with a colleague, Anderson had had the satisfied thought, *He is getting the measure of this work now.* It pleased the managing director to think this. He had not been at all sure of the man when he started; Nairobi might be too much for him. He seemed so thoroughly a Londoner.

Here, motionless, in his bed and clothed in pajamas—a flicker of blue silk was visible at his neck—Gawen Brownrigg looked like a boy, not a man, and Anderson felt he was intruding on something quite private, an interior moment. He had had that sensation before, dealing with casualties during the war. Captain Anderson had once been quite capable of and familiar with the handling of dead bodies, sorting out where they needed to be moved and how to honor them, record the details, get word back to HQ.

A policeman stood just outside the bedroom, apparently guarding the hallway through to the living quarters, where there must be personal effects. The other boy, the Masai servant who had found the Englishman, was there in the corner and standing still, preternaturally so. The only flickers of movement were in his eyes, which watched Anderson closely without appearing to. They had that art. M'changi—Anderson had learned the boy's name—knew this was a dangerous situation for him. He feared he would be blamed. It was not Anderson's responsibility to comfort the African, nor would the servant likely accept such reassurance, yet Anderson made a point to convey his swift conviction that Brownrigg had died hours earlier. Long before M'changi arrived.

"In his sleep," Anderson gestured. "He must have been sleeping."

The constable grunted agreement. Anderson repeated the sentence in Swahili, to no visible response from the African, then pulled the sheet from the English boy's stiffening hands and over as much of his face as he could. The key thing was to shield Brownrigg's eyes. They were closed, but needed to be covered.

It did not explain anything, of course. What took him in his sleep?

"The coroner will be here soon," the constable said. "After his examination, he'll arrange transport to the morgue."

A man in his forties, as Anderson was, the constable had a thick ginger mustache over a resolute mouth, and an air of keeping chaos at bay. He seemed familiar to Anderson, but it took a moment to place him. Then the scene returned: a long June night at the Muthaiga Club, when there had been trouble. Someone had to be thrown out; it happened rarely at the Muthaiga, as you could get away with practically anything there, but on occasion a guest went too far. The offender had been not just drunk but scathingly insulting, at volume, about the wrong man's wife—the recently acquired second or third wife of a prominent landowner. That set felt they made the rules on who was a fair target for abuse: they could insult or cheat on their own spouses, and flamboyantly did, but if someone outside their circle tried the same trick, the outrage was absolute. No matter that the landowner was drunk, too, roaringly so. His prideful anger must be met, and satisfied.

The man to be thrown out was a Scot, like Hume the policeman, and Anderson wondered if a superior had deliberately chosen that match. If so, it was a wise move: the unruly guest quieted on hearing the tones of voice he knew from home. Hume used his advantage, and the scene calmed. *We all have our tribes:* Anderson had the thought often in Nairobi. At certain breaking points—birth, death, marriage, violence—like does better with like. It was just a fact about human beings. In daily life the mixing of peoples and their habits was fine; it was interesting. It was why one chose to live in Kenya. Without that starting conviction, a person should return to the motherland, on the next boat from Mombasa.

This young man, for instance. Here before Anderson lay a dead man of his own kind, more or less (Anderson had lived in Kenya since he was a boy), and it was up to him to inform the poor fellow's parents in England, see that after the postmortem the proper thing happened to the body, then carry out the family's wishes, as well as he could, from several continents away. Beyond the practical matters, Anderson's task was to shape the story to be told to the wider world. There would be a proliferation of accounts, shaped by gossip and hearsay—it was inevitable and he could do little about it—but he could exert control over what appeared in print, in the pages of his paper, *The East African Standard*.

How did Brownrigg die? Hume told Anderson that empty pill vials had been found in a wastepaper basket in the other room. That was why the Scotsman was guarding that area. He had seen the medication name. "Nembutal," he said, with a slight creasing of his ginger brows.

Anderson pressed his lips tighter, as if to seal them shut. He knew about Nembutal. Sleeping pills, potentially dangerous ones. So suicide, then, in all likelihood? The managing director folded his arms, as if to contain the thought. Oh, he had to tread very carefully. He knew this. Anderson would not pronounce the word aloud. Even as a speculation, in passing, it would be nearly impossible to retract.

Suicide was a scent that never left a room, once the bottle was unstoppered.

BROWNRIGG WAS AN unprepossessing young man. Anderson had met him soon after he arrived, at one of the many New Year's Eve parties that took 1937 into 1938, one champagne-flowing gala following another at that time of year in Nairobi, among the upper echelons. Mervyn Hill, the Englishman who had offered Gawen Brownrigg the job of sports correspondent for *The Standard*, introduced him to Claude. Hill and Claude Anderson had together come up with the contract for this position, a commitment of four years. They hoped not to have to fire a writer for debauched incompetence, as they lately had Brownrigg's predecessor. (Drink was a hazard of life in Kenya, like sleeping sickness, but one had to build up an immunity, learn how not to get swallowed by it.) Training people took time, and they wanted their investment to count.

Elegant, well-mannered, but quiet, Brownrigg carried a furtive half smile and that lack of self-assertion which could come off as arrogance, as though the man were unsure whether to squander his wit on people who wouldn't appreciate it. *So Mervyn Hill saw this cautious fellow as a sportswriter?* was Anderson's first thought, even on shaking Gawen Brownrigg's delicate hand, for he hadn't the jocular muscularity one associated with someone traipsing around after rugby players, racehorses, cricket matches. There was quite a lot of ground, physical ground, to be covered in order to take in the colony's range of sporting events. Brownrigg was, however, confident on the subject of golf, including his own game, and similarly on tennis; and he seemed eager to prove himself. On the crossing, he said, he had been reading histories of Kenya, which distinguished him from any number of others who arrived in the country, planning simply to take what they could get. As if sensing Anderson's nascent skepticism, Brownrigg mentioned that his second novel was to be published in the spring, and it contained several scenes set in the world of car racing, one of his own passions, which he felt conveyed the excitement of moving at such speeds around the track, of which he had some experience. The managing director appeared interested and tried not to show, by his expression, that penning a novel, while all to the good in London, did not necessarily correlate to the skills required for a journalist at *The Standard*. Still, perhaps this young writer would have a way with description, or the ability to bring some of the athletes or jockeys to life, in a brief newspaper sketch. Brownrigg had chosen the pseudonym for his pieces, he told Anderson: "Reflex."

After those first social encounters, he met Gawen Brownrigg primarily in print. The man worked hard; Tom Dando, the editor working with him directly, assured Anderson of that. Long days, a willingness to take on unexpected assignments. He had filled in for someone— Rogers probably, that man was always falling ill—on a piece about army exercises, which required an overnight trip out into the bush, from which the newcomer had returned in good humor and with the requisite tale of a long night listening to a lion scratching outside his tent. He had a nice line in self-deprecating jokes about his fear. And if some of the sportswriting was bland or clichéd, at other times Reflex had a way of putting across the excitement of a match, or an inherent comedy in the failed hopes of the spectators. He had written an article about a show in Nairobi of new motor cars so detailed and vivid that Dando urged it to go on the paper's front page, below the fold; and so it did. This was in July sometime. Brownrigg had been finding his feet; he had been honing his voice. *He had just started to settle in.* Had he lived, he would have come into his own.

What a waste it was. A waste of the young man himself, who might have done things, taken a place in this peculiar but not trivial society, and for *The Standard*, too, Anderson could not help thinking. The newspaper did not have unlimited resources. They would not, again, hire from England. Anderson did not blame Mervyn Hill for this tragic death, of course—there was no way to imagine or predict such an outcome—but the managing director did plan to revert to his original thought that someone local would be the better choice for this beat.

Anderson had the driver leave him at one end of Government Road so that he might walk some distance with his thoughts before reaching the post office. It was two hours earlier in England. He must get the telegram off to the parents now, before a day could properly begin without them knowing how their world had shattered. Sir Douglas and Lady someone—he had the names, he'd made sure he had the family information before he had left Brownrigg's rooms, where the boy's marbled self awaited removal.

Anderson hesitated outside the building. But it had to be done, simply. Part of the job. The high-ceilinged post office was not yet busy. Anderson composed the words at a side counter first before approaching the spectacled man behind the glass. He did not want to pen these brief, difficult phrases in front of someone else.

REGRET ANNOUNCE should come first. Twenty years before, during the war, telegrams were known harbingers of doom, and everyone up and down Britain dreaded receiving one. But in the 1920s and now '30s the form had relaxed into a medium often conveying train arrival times or celebratory greetings. So it was crucial that regret came right at the top. *This is bad news. Brace yourself.* That must be conveyed in the first blink of an eye. The stomach would harden against the worst. *YOUR SON DIED IN SLEEP.* Let them understand it was not violent. They might otherwise imagine barbarity in Kenya; there were of course those in England with such prejudices, and Anderson did not know the Brownriggs or how they thought. *LAST NIGHT.* You are learning this, Anderson was telling them, nearly as soon as I did. *ANDERSON*—though he realized that, especially in shock, they might not recall who he was, so he added *STANDARD.*

There. That was all that was needed, initially. *REGRET ANNOUNCE*

YOUR SON DIED IN SLEEP LAST NIGHT. ANDERSON STAN-DARD. Speed was the important thing. Later he would send a letter with softness and flourishes, but for now they simply needed the unadorned information.

Anderson gave thanks in his prayers, nearly every day, that he was in newspapers now and no longer in the business of war. There was talk of another European war brewing; many of the sharpest minds around him felt it was all but unavoidable, but he preferred for the moment not to believe it. God had been merciful to him, as Claude Anderson was well aware. He felt blessed. He *was* blessed. He longed for the evening, when he could go back to the house knowing his daughters were safe in their beds.

As he walked out into the brightening sunlight, Anderson thought of two people, miles away, in the gray of England, who would within the hour read his just-composed words.

He could only hope the Brownriggs' faith would offer them some solace.

THE OFFICES WERE next.

Again, the importance of getting the story out first, the right one. The rule applied within *The Standard* as well as outside it. Anderson asked Dando to help him alert as many souls as possible in the building: there was to be a general meeting, ten o'clock, in editorial.

"What's happened?" Dando asked.

Anderson liked Tom Dando and trusted him, but he knew that news to be delivered at once to all must be delivered at once to all. Whispers and rumors undermined everything: authority, decorum. This was one of the minor graces Anderson was in a position to bestow upon Brownrigg, in death: an avoidance of slippage.

"I've an announcement to make." Anderson knew Dando had been a friend to Brownrigg, a sort of big-brother figure, encouraging the younger man, spurring him on when his spirits flagged. Dando would take the news hard. "It won't take long. We need as many there as possible, though whoever can't make it will be informed by a circular my secretary will send round this afternoon."

Soon a few dozen mostly men had pooled in an open space near the glass entrance doors on the first floor. Some chairs and side tables scattered about made it an informal conversational space, where writers sometimes broke for tea or a cool drink, away from the incessant typewriters. Two women were seated, leaning forward apprehensively. A couple of the men, in shirt sleeves, smoked; others stood with jacketed arms folded. The wariness on most faces told Anderson that their concern was self-protective. They imagined workplace changes, perhaps some belt-tightening due to the tax evasion scandal Anderson had to sort out earlier in the summer, bad behavior by one of the London stakeholders. An unenlightening situation, though not fatal for the paper. Or perhaps the employees guessed at unwelcome political news, which might affect their safety. He must fix and narrow the scope of the news immediately. *REGRET ANNOUNCE . . .*The managing director cleared his throat, then took a breath. The town crier.

"I have sad news to deliver. One of our colleagues has died, suddenly, overnight."

Heads swiveled, to see who among them was absent.

"It's Gawen Brownrigg, I'm afraid—our young sports man."

"Oh!" Sybil Weir, that game girl in a pale, sturdy dress, stood up abruptly rather than fainting downward, in her shock at the sound of her friend's name. *"No!"* She covered her mouth with her hand.

Dando moved to put an arm around her. His own brow folded down, his eyes dulled. Elsewhere, murmurs of shock.

"He came by to visit us just last night!" Sybil gasped as if there were not enough air in the room. "He tried to visit Mother and me—we weren't yet back from the country—I was going to rib him about it when I saw him today . . ."

"How?" Dando lifted his head toward Anderson. "How did he die?" A muttered chiming in came from a writer on the crime beat.

"There is no foul play suspected."

Some who hardly knew Brownrigg made small restless movements. There were coughs and mumbles of dismay. It was uncomfortable news, but they met it with a combination of indifference and relief. They were newspapermen; he was new and not one of theirs. Unfortunate, but they had work to get on with.

"Then how did he die?" Dando pressed.

"In his sleep." Anderson fanned his hands out before him the way you might calm a classroom of children or quiet an orchestra. The managing director knew how unsatisfactory the answer was, though also that it was a phrase you might write in an obituary if you were trying to be discreet. Having dispatched the telegram to Sir Douglas and Lady Beatrice—Anderson knew her name now, Brownrigg's mother—he reminded himself that in this case, son of a baronet, it was especially crucial not to ride roughshod. "It is very sad. And unexpected," he added, superfluously. "I have informed the family." Indeed, he reflected, the governor would have to be told as well. "Tom, Sybil, as you knew Mr. Brownrigg best, perhaps you could write the notice for the paper? We'll have it in tomorrow's edition."

Sybil was crying now, though shielding her eyes from the others' view.

Dando, still comforting Sybil, nodded. "Of course. We'll write it." In a lower voice directed to his boss: "Drink later?"

"Good idea." Anderson would be ready for one, end of the day. In the interim, he must ensure that the body was in the coroner's safe hands, and discover whether he had had any reply from the blighted, distant parents.

THERE WERE THOSE who came here to escape, and those who came here to build. The builders fared better, on the whole, in Anderson's experience. They might have to teach themselves how to raise cattle or grow coffee, but at least they arrived with fewer illusions and less lurid fantasies. They expected life in Kenya to be hard, and it was. "Mosquitoes, madness, and making do," as someone had put it. They carried on. That man who ran the hotel, for instance: this death of a new resident would be awkward, but he could not allow it to slow him down. Anderson himself came from a family of builders. His father had brought *The Standard* to Nairobi, along with another family, the Mayers. The conviction they had, the perseverance and also the sense of the newspaper's necessity, ran in his blood.

The escapers were more obvious out in society, and had slanted the way others told the narrative about Kenya. Englishmen sent here in some disgrace by exasperated parents, dispatched because they had botched their place at home; women with fallen marriages behind them, like Thoroughbreds who had trotted away from the cross-country course, unable to make the clearances. Different from the English citizens who went to India: the men of the Raj tended to be sober and bureaucratic, the women less inclined toward adulterous adventure. There was not, as far as Anderson knew, an equivalent in India of the Happy Valley, nor of the louche joke, said to circulate at fashionable parties in London: "Are you married, or do you live in Kenya?"

The men and women who came to British East Africa were often from a hunting set, priding themselves on their athleticism, their lack of squeamishness, their ability to hold their drink. (The holding did not always . . . hold.) They had bravado, and an aggressive impatience toward those who could not keep up. Contemptuous of convention—when it suited them, that is, in matters of marital habits or clothes or pets—but fiercely attached nonetheless to a social order that placed their settler status far above others who lived here. He had not known this breed of Briton to evince much interest in the distinctions among the region's tribal groups, or pay attention to which Indians were Muslims and which Hindus. These English were largely godless. Their own Christianity was understated, a cultural ritual like having tea. The belief they had was in themselves.

Anderson had not known Brownrigg well enough to be sure, but he sensed that the fellow was an escaper. He had come from some species of trouble—a failed marriage, that was it. Common enough. He was not physically robust, and had an interior glance that did not align with the usual jovial Kenyan arrival. It was not a good country for quiet sorts: Anderson, who liked nothing better than a peaceful evening at home with his wife and children, had been made aware of his own inadequacy in that aspect.

In his office, dictating letters to his secretary, Anderson looked out the window at the foot and motor traffic, allowing his thoughts to wander roughly along on the verge, while his words traveled their paved and smoother route. He recalled something else Brownrigg told him at that gala. Mervyn Hill had taken a small plane to Mombasa to meet and collect Brownrigg off the boat from Port Said. Hill knew the parents from previous colonial posts, which explained why he stretched to such favors. He flew back with the new recruit to spare him the long rail journey. Anderson's view was that the train from Mombasa to Nairobi invaluably prepared a newcomer for what lay ahead, in addition to being itself an essential element in the colony's history. Anderson's father used to say that Nairobi would still be nothing but a swamp with a few scattered shacks, were it not for the railway.

"It was astonishing to see the herds of giraffes and elephants from the air," Brownrigg had said to Anderson that evening. The recollection brought him to life. "This may sound strange, but the open land reminded me of California."

"California! You've been."

"Yes, I used to live there, with my wife. It's where our son was born."

So he had already escaped once before! A man eager to shed England.

"What was it like?" Anderson asked, to be polite. "Orange groves, film stars, millionaires?"

"A change, certainly, from gray old England." Gawen smiled. "But good for one's health. I'd had lung trouble in London."

And other kinds of trouble, too? Anderson wondered.

"The air's very dry and pure in Southern California. Like here, I should imagine."

"Until the rains come." Anderson checked himself from saying more. Why discourage the young man? He could experience the transformation for himself in March, when the skies opened. "I'm sure you'll settle in well here."

"People have been so kind. I'm grateful for the opportunity."

"Have you met Sybil Weir?" Anderson deftly directed Brownrigg toward another young writer, a good-natured girl who did not take herself too seriously. The best sort. "We call her our 'social editress.' Sybil will show you the ropes. She's a hardened newspaperman, aren't you, Sybil?"

"Thanks to you and Tom I am." The tall, rangy girl laughed, with all her teeth. Her fair hair was curled around her ear, where she retucked it, just to make sure.

She shook Brownrigg's hand, understanding that Claude was handing him off to her. It was a relief to have people one could count on.

The news would have shattered her, Anderson reflected. The young woman's affections ran deep. There she was, spending her days noting the comings and goings of the social set, their scandals and peccadilloes, and yet in herself Sybil was a person of sound heart, neither flighty nor skittish, feet planted on the ground. She might have had a steadying influence on Brownrigg. Perhaps she had tried to. Anderson turned from the window to face his secretary. Miss Allen's lined, sensible visage reassured him, her coral lipstick applied as ever just to the outer part of her lips, as if more would be wasteful. Patiently she waited, fingers readied on the lettered keys. He must focus on the task at hand. He would not be able to complete all the administrative duties this death placed before him if he allowed himself to wander off into sentiment.

THEY CHOSE THE Norfolk Hotel, end of day, to meet. Anderson preferred it to the braying tones and jocular pink of the Muthaiga Club, where in any case too many likely listeners would be close at hand. Not that anonymity was possible at the Norfolk—it was not possible anywhere in Nairobi, among Europeans—but Anderson felt freer there. The place had gone out of fashion, which suited him.

Dando was already seated in a wicker-backed chair near the window up on the first floor. He was slightly disheveled, his chin shadowed and his disordered hair pushed back every few moments with a heavy hand. His greeting was perfunctory. He had ordered a drink and made fair headway on it. Anderson did his best to catch up.

"I had the hell of a time drying up Sybil," Dando began. "She found the news difficult to accept. She kept repeating that he had tried to visit her and her mother that evening, as though if they'd been home—the night might have gone differently."

Anderson shook his head. All those might-have-beens, after a tragedy. "Well, thank you for filing the death notice," he said. Did just what it needed to, in a few spare details. They would publish something longer in a few days. Devas Jones, the man with the local radio program, had what he needed to broadcast a small in memoriam. "In love with Brownrigg, was she—Sybil?"

"No." Dando drank his second whiskey soda. "They were friends.

Like brother and sister, she said, and I believe her. They made each other laugh."

"I don't remember him as much of a joker."

"He had to warm up. He could be quite sharp, and sly, once he was at ease. It was beginning to come up in his work, especially longer pieces. He was improving."

"I thought so, too. That racing story was fine."

Dando leaned in across the table. "He had designs on someone else, Claude." Lowered his voice. "He had confided in Sybil about it. And in me, as a matter of fact."

Anderson frowned. "Do you know who it was?"

"Elenore Talbot-Smith. The American consul's daughter."

"Don't know her. But perhaps, in that case, it's less likely . . ." He let that sentence end without its end, as he saw Brownrigg's pajamaed corpse again in his mind. The bloodless face. Lips pursed and slightly open, though breathless. "That family will be distraught at the news, then, if he had declared himself to her. Had it got that far?"

"Well—yes." Dando looked around the bar for likely eavesdroppers before continuing. "But the parents had insisted she break off the engagement."

"He was engaged! I don't recall hearing that."

"Gawen had given the young woman a ring; the parents made her give it back."

"Good lord. Why?"

Dando required another draft of whiskey. "Because he was not 'free,' technically. Legal complications with his divorce. It was tied up in the English courts."

Anderson's frown deepened. He had hoped to stay on point here, keep the writer's death story simple. He'd no wish to further complicate it. "Why on earth did the man propose, then—if he wasn't divorced?"

"Fair question. I think, in part, he was eager to catch up with his ex-wife."

Anderson shook his head. Tom Dando was making *The Standard*'s sportswriter sound more and more like one of the local English, the Happy Valleyers. This was just the sort of thing that lot got up to: competitive adultery. Competitive remarriage.

He sighed. "Explain?"

"She had already remarried! His former wife, that is. In America. She got herself an American divorce, as Americans do, and a new American husband. With whom Brownrigg's little boy—*their* little boy—lives, in California. While he still had a job to get the divorce finalized in England, with sparing cooperation from *her*. The man felt it was rather unfair. With some reason."

"And yet didn't you just tell me this Talbot-Smith was American?"

"She is."

"I'd have thought Brownrigg would have had enough of Americans."

"Yes. I more or less told him that, Claude. A few days ago, when he came to me in some distress about the whole situation, I told him"—Tom Dando lowered his voice further—"the Talbot-Smiths were not worth bothering with and he should just be patient, and wait until he was well and truly in the clear, and meet someone then. I believe his mother wrote him the same thing."

Anderson absorbed the implications. If he had the sense of being intrusive before, standing in the Salisbury Hotel in the bedroom of his employee, noting the color of the silk at the dead man's neck, this set of revelations made Anderson feel practically squalid, like a voyeur. He screwed up his mouth as if at a bad taste. "All right," he muttered. "Still. This unhappy episode needn't concern us, surely, Tom?"

Dando looked surprised, as if his boss were missing something rather obvious. "My worry is that the family will want to make something of it."

"Of what, precisely?"

"Of the way he died." His voice by now a whisper. Tom Dando shared Anderson's sense of the need to keep a fence up around this subject.

"How do you mean 'make something'?" The conversation was making the managing director unhappier by the minute. He began to feel the need to smoke a pipe.

"I hope I'm wrong. But they strike me, in what has already gone on, as people rather drawn to—*drama*. I've no way of knowing if it's the mother more than the father, or indeed if it is the girl herself. But there was a level of exhibitionism about the engagement's end that troubled me."

"The risk of hiring a novelist to write one's sports pages . . ." Anderson had never been fully convinced of Brownrigg's qualifications for the post.

"Perhaps."

Anderson realized that Tom Dando had been genuinely fond of his younger colleague. He reminded himself that it did not do to speak ill of the dead. At this hour the previous evening, Gawen Brownrigg was still alive. Mixing himself a gin and tonic, perhaps. Staring at his vials of pills.

"Much will depend on the coroner's report." Anderson stayed on the solid ground of what would certainly happen, rather than what might happen. Speculation did not have much place in newspapers, as he conceived them. "With luck there will be enough ambiguity that we can simply stay with that line. *Tragically, the young journalist died in his sleep.*"

Dando nodded, hearing the phrase he had dutifully written in the notice, though Anderson could see he was unconvinced.

"What would be in it, Tom, for that family to make any of their story public?"

"Two things." Dando held out a couple of inky fingers on his left hand to count them off.

It was an editorial moment. Dando was structuring the story. As new facts came in, narratives changed, of course, but the managing director might have to impress on Tom again that none of this version, whatever he was about to say, must be allowed into print.

"One: never underestimate, Claude, the pull for Americans of a British title. The parents knew their daughter was ever so close to a union with a future baronet. Don't imagine they were not eager to leap at that chance. Hence the showy return of Brownrigg's ring: they were keen not to look desperate. As if they were digging. Not for gold, of course—but for lineage. Still, they might like it known that their girl had had that chance."

Anderson remained impassive. "What's the second thing?"

The bitter smile of Dando's first point faded, suddenly, to a thin, serious grimace of his wide mouth. He folded his arms and turned his gaze away from his boss, out past the balcony that edged the Norfolk's upper veranda. The two men had remained inside so that their voices wouldn't carry.

"I spoke to Mervyn Hill earlier. He was quite distraught—he was fond of Brownrigg, too, as you know." Dando continued speaking out toward the view of early-evening Nairobi. "I must tell you, Claude, that a few days ago Gawen asked Hill a personal favor. He said it was not significant, that it wouldn't commit Hill to anything, it was just a business matter." He paused. "Hill gave me permission to tell you this, by the way."

Anderson's brows lifted above his spectacles. "All right, Tom. You've built the suspense well." He was not sure he wished to hear what would follow. "What was the favor?"

"To act as a witness." For a moment, Tom Dando's eyes seemed to moisten. "Gawen was signing a new version of his will."

THERE WAS MORE, but Claude stopped Dando soon after to say that he must get home to his family. Tom, unmarried, waved his boss away with a muted wistfulness. It was true that Jean counted on Claude's being back to dine with her, and it was also true that exhaustion had struck Anderson like the heat that struck one on a drive up-country. Anderson imagined the tangle that awaited him in the week ahead as this death became known. There would be so many opportunities to trip and cause injury. How innocent he felt he was at the beginning of this Monday. Before he had had to *regret announce*.

One reason Claude Anderson had flourished in his position at *The Standard* was that by temperament he was not a man tempted by gossip—of which, as the managing director of a newspaper, especially one in British Kenya, he was presented with a bottomless supply. The people who thrived on gossip were those who enjoyed having an edge over others, the sense of status raised by possessing information others lacked, which could be doled out to the favored, like money or privileges. Anderson had no need for such jostling. He was precisely as high as he wanted to be, and no higher than he ought to be. His placement suited him. He enjoyed the invitations he received, and had no wish for further social reach or adventure.

Perhaps the fever behind such chattering and maneuvering was all the more frenzied for expatriates far from home. At times they minded that distance a great deal, felt they had to make their own noise that might carry. Or their isolation made them amplify matters that were fundamentally minor. Europeans who had been born here, or came young, as Claude had, were less drawn to the costume dramas of outlandish socialites. He took in the tales when others felt compelled to share them—putting in his hours at the Muthaiga Club, out of professional duty—but he did not often gratify the teller with his reaction. "Even-Handerson" was one wag's nickname for him: he tried not to take sides. And he did not pass along what he had been told.

With one exception. He always talked to his wife.

He and Jean sat down in the narrow, windowed room off the more public reception rooms, where they preferred to eat when it was just the two of them, as it gave them a modicum of privacy. Jean saw the weight of the day on him; Claude carried it in his shoulders and on his pulled-down mouth. He did not deliberately exaggerate his expression, though the anticipated warmth of his wife's sympathy, which had hastened his return home, perhaps allowed him to let worry run loose across his features, like a mouse scurrying across a kitchen floor.

She waited until the cook, Njoki, had finished doling out the evening's boiled beef and potatoes, smothered with a kind of thick, muscular green not known in England. "Thank you, Njoki. This is everything for now." She waited a beat, a first good bite, then asked him, "The journalist's death—it was difficult?"

Anderson nodded. Jean's voice was so calming, sweet yet firm, like the primary school teacher she once was. She made everything seem containable. His taut muscles eased slightly. "A shock, of course. Most everyone at the paper was very sad."

"Not violent, I hope . . ." Her tone rose with some anxiety.

"No, no. As peaceful as could be. He died in his sleep. As I wrote the family earlier today, he looked serene, like a marble statue."

She shuddered. "You said he was young."

"Twenty-seven."

"Married?"

"Divorced. That is—in the final stages of divorce. His ex-wife is in America."

"How terrible for his parents." It was like Jean, to go to them first. She was quiet for a moment, communing in her imagination with those English unknowns. "They'll want to know, of course, whether it was . . . an accident."

His wife's tact was another trait he appreciated.

"We'll wait for the coroner's report. The Brownriggs sent a telegram by return with questions, of course, few of which I can yet answer."

"Perhaps it's as well he was divorced . . . So no children?"

"A little boy."

Jean yelped then in pain, as if she had just stepped on a nail. Njoki came rushing in from the kitchen, followed by the maid, who had been having her own supper. Jean's cry had been frightening, an animal sound. She put her hand up in apology to them both.

"I'm sorry, Njoki, Mumbi. There was just—"

"Mrs. Anderson had some bad news," Claude offered.

"Mem is all right?"

"Thank you, Njoki. I'm fine." She smiled. "The stew is delicious tonight. But not to worry."

The two women, satisfied by her assurances, retreated.

Claude unspooled some details about the office to fill the air with an ordinary conversational tone for a few minutes. Then he lowered his voice and returned to the other subject. An unknown child, a couple of continents away in California. Jean tended to share Claude's general indifference to America. "It was the wrong kind of colony," his late stepfather, the co-proprietor of *The Standard*, used to joke. "Too much land to govern, and settlers too big for their britches." He had always made a point of his reverence for the king, and frowned on any rebellious talk.

"The parents," Claude said, "mentioned him already, in their first reply. Their grandson, that is. They are anxious to know what will be said about Gawen's death. Or written. For his son's sake, as they put it."

"Though they also meant for their own. You reassured them that the paper would be discreet, surely?"

"Of course. 'Sparing of detail' I wrote. But the coroner's report will say—whatever it will say. I can't influence that."

"No."

"And it will get out."

Jean reached out her hand, open palmed, and he placed his on hers. Delicate hands, she had.

She was silent for a moment, lost in reflection. Then, after a sigh, she murmured: "O, that this too too solid flesh would melt . . ."

Back in England, when Claude was courting her, they had gone to *Hamlet* together. After they were engaged Jean told him that her friends had teased her about that choice—*Not very romantic, is it!* But the outing *had* been romantic for the couple, discovering that the play was a touchstone for them both. Listening side by side to Hamlet's haunted words, verses they each knew by heart, brought them closer. He had not been bold enough to hold her hand then, but he had thought about it.

"Yes, that came to my mind, too." He stroked Jean's fingers. They were so warm. "Though this prince's flesh did not thaw. Nor resolve itself unto a dew."

At last Claude allowed himself, with Jean nearby, to consider the possibility that Brownrigg's act had been intended. That he had really wanted this end. "Self-slaughter," in Hamlet's violent phrase.

"In fact, I doubt it will resolve anything at all." Claude felt like a disappointed parent, tempted to chide the young man, as if his ghost were with them at the table. The managing director was sympathetic, up to a point, but also impatient, always, with those who lacked consideration for others. "Someone might have told him," he added, wishing Tom Dando had, "that death can be like that. Creating more problems than it solves."

Though not for Brownrigg. Not for their former writer. That person, *The Standard*'s brief employee, had forever left any earthly concerns behind.

Shottesbrooke

✦

WELCOME, BROTHER.

I have been waiting for you.

It seems unfair to have a brother you never got to meet in life. Did you feel that way? I could have teased and belittled you, mostly with affection—tousled your hair, tackled you to the ground, taught you how to throw or catch. To wrestle and whistle and fight; to play useful tricks, like how to hide sweets for later. You could have had an older brother to clear the path ahead for you, as a boy and then a man, my example encouraging you or else showing you what not to do. Heroes are helpful, but errant elders can be even more so, offering warnings or cautionary tales.

Instead you had a ghost, a name to remember in your prayers, and sad parents. Not that you saw them openly speak their sadness, certainly not our father, for whom cheerfulness was a personal creed, like honor or decent grooming. You were close enough to our mother, though, that you knew her grief over me had never left her, even if she hid it about her person, a tucked-away handkerchief. She might as well have worn a locket around her neck with a keepsake of my hair, and perhaps she did, in earlier days.

Sorry, old chap! Couldn't help it. I "fell asleep at Portsmouth," as the pretty plaque in the Shottesbrooke church, black Gothic script on a brass plate, lightly puts it, "aged 3½ years." I never woke up.

You know what that's like. It must run in the family.

"God called a little child unto Him," the plaque adds piously, on our mother's insistence. It dulled their pain a small amount to think so. To say so, in public. Our father's name is on the plaque, too. Our mother goes unmentioned. His initials and mine are picked out in blood red. You read the lines often when you went to church there on Sundays, as a boy. I was flattered by your attention.

Forgive me for asking this, but were you aware of the date when you retired that August evening in Nairobi? I'm not asking what your plans were, brother. It would intrude on you to demand an answer, and some thoughts shouldn't be shared, even with siblings. I am just wondering whether you knew, in the back of your disordered mind if not the front of it, that you would die on my birthday? Don't think our mother did not notice. I would have been thirty-four that day, had I lived. You were twenty-seven and a half. Our mother kept an unwritten calendar of me in her mind, in which I got older just like anybody else. We are both on it now. Aging invisibly.

Robert Cecil. Robert, for our pre-Victorian relative awarded the baronetcy for his doings in Kandy, as that island nation was then called, in the name of our king; and Cecil, for our mother's father, himself an upstanding colonial administrator in Ceylon, a place eventually reborn as Sri Lanka. (Your granddaughter sees our mother's maiden name, Clementi-Smith, in the Sri Lankan memoir *Running in the Family* by Michael Ondaatje. So many loops and recursions in our story.) The geographic echo was not a coincidence, as I expect you know: it strengthened the union between our parents, Douglas and Beatrice. Their families knew each other broadly, if not personally, and all seemed well after they were married and I was born. Everyone was confident that I, a sturdy heir, would heft the Brownrigg name onto whatever plinth next awaited it. I was only a little boy, brother, I could not yet even read, but I was funny and strong and I would have done just what they wanted: become a naval officer, as our father had. When I came of age I would have proved myself to be brave and patriotic and good with my men.

You were never that sort. We were different that way. When the Royal Air Force turned you down for service due to your weak health, you expressed disappointment for the sake of our father, though that masked some relief. You did love to fly: you loved the speed and exhilaration and self-erasure in it, as with racing cars; both were an escape from self-consciousness. (Drugs offer the same, as you learned. Your son learns it, too.) But being in a troop of other men and following orders or giving them was not something you could ever quite picture yourself doing. (I say it would have been good for you!) Our mother was relieved, too. Her nerves jangled at any possible danger for you. You knew each other well enough to sense how the other felt about it, though that harmony went unacknowledged. You were aware of her fears.

My death had been sudden. We lived in Portsmouth then, one of the world's great naval ports, and at three I loved being taken by our father to see the harbor bristling with its ships. Holding my chubby hand in his, he would lean down to point them out and name them with true delight, as though they were his personal friends. The Captain, as he was then, felt happiest by the sea, and discussing maritime history; the salted vessels brought him to life, and he told me stories of his adventures and famous others'. Did you know, brother, that Nelson left from Portsmouth on his way to fight the Battle of Trafalgar? Maybe our father told you that, too. Did you ever think of Portsmouth and of your brother lost there when you passed by Nelson's Column in Trafalgar Square, on your way to meet some fashionable person at the bar at the Savoy, on the Strand?

My dying was abrupt and cruel. It shocked them both. Our mother urged her husband to help them quit Portsmouth as soon as possible. She never returned. Months passed and she fell pregnant again; all you can do is to carry on, as the doctors told her. I didn't mind, of course; I did not think of it as an attempt to replace me, and in any case why shouldn't they? I needed replacing. During her second pregnancy, our mother nurtured any number of superstitions mixed in with the optimism our father insisted on, but she wisely kept them from him, her quiet efforts to appease the gods, really her one true God, so that He might not call the next little child unto Him, too. In her prayers, our mother was clear with God that she was not still fighting my death, that she had accepted His will. I have no idea if God believed her. I wouldn't have.

Did you ever wonder why our sister, Juliet, born the next year, 1908, always had an unseen weight pressing down on her, as though there were lead in her fingers and toes, and draped across her sloping feminine shoulders? I believe it was the dread our mother could not shake as she carried Juliet that she passed down to our sister (who will join us, after the Second World War is over, childless, gone before she turns forty). Our mother admired our father's blustery insistence on good humor and did her best to match him, but she bled sadness into her subsequent children nonetheless. You may question me on this, brother, but after I fell asleep at Portsmouth I'm not sure that Juliet, the child who followed, ever stood a chance.

You did, though. You had possibilities. Born on January 15, four years after my death, nearly to the day. I don't have to tell you our mother noticed that first coincidence, too. It confirmed a belief she never spoke aloud that God had, in His mercy, given you to them as a form of compensation for His having taken me.

She allowed herself hope, with you.

TOKIO, 1911. THAT is where you entered the fray, brother, after our father accepted a two-year post as naval attaché to Japan and China, and the family shook off English gloom to look outward, embark on a new adventure, with a fair young girl and another baby on the way. A son was born, the next baronet as they imagined you to be. Your first breaths were of a Pacific-inflected air, and when taken out in your pram into Tokio streets, your tiny ears took in sounds of Japanese voices and the curved cries of the gulls. You were too young when our family returned to Britain to have distinct memories of Japan, but I think you never felt truly at home in this country. You were always looking for an elsewhere. If Juliet had melancholy bred into her, seeded in you was an urge to leave. It made sense that you would marry an American, live for a while in California, take a journalistic post in Nairobi after your divorce. You hoped to discover a place where you felt you belonged. At the end you thought it might be Kenya, but you did not stay around long enough to find out for sure.

Thirty years I have been waiting for you, though time is different for us than for the ones we leave behind. You'll get used to this. Thirty years of your busy earthly days jumble along here, chopped and changed as time moves now forward and now back, not the simple directional sequence it appears to the living. There are simultaneities. They allow us to read ahead, so we can see how the plot thickens. Brother, your son grows up. He will have children, and they will. On we'll go, the

Brownriggs, in spite of the thread seeming frayed and nearly snapped, for some years after you died.

The period of the Great War, for instance: out there, in the place of bodies and breath, it was a four-year saga, but here an unboundaried blur of blood and mud and crowds of corpses joining us from battered theaters of war in Western Europe and Russia. (So many Russians.) That is the word we English use, and there are times when the carnage does seem staged by some artless dramatist who can't craft a resolution to the conflict he's set up and so just slaughters all his characters. Poison gas and relentless artillery and a flu epidemic afterward that cleared off millions more who had somehow to that point survived. It was a catastrophic purging of the young, and it scarred a generation. Parents lucky enough to have children the wrong age, like ours, could sit out the war at home, daily thankful their boys did not have to don a uniform. Our mother's patriotism ran deep and strong, unmixed with anxiety, and telegram deliveries did not cause heart-pounding dread. Lady B, as her friends called her, worked on a military biography to be published after the war, a portrait of a courageous nineteenth-century English general, which she dedicated to "Our Glorious Armies, 1914–1918."

I said Douglas and Beatrice sat out the war "at home," but of course our father was rarely at home in Berkshire with all of you. While you were at White Waltham learning how to read, Sir Douglas was mostly in Westminster, appointed the naval censor for the length of the war, lodging conveniently near the red-brick Admiralty buildings, working long days and nights among the governors of war, the gods of war, whatever you want to call those lofty Englishmen who distantly directed the battles their countrymen fought and, in our father's case, filtered the information given to the British public about those battles. It is a theme in this family—deciding how to shape the story. You were not the only one who took on that task, you know.

Our father ensured that newspaper articles and radio broadcasts on the setbacks and progress of the war revealed no details that could aid the enemy, or alternatively depress British morale. Later he was awarded a promotion in rank for this work, and from then on the Captain was the Rear Admiral, or "the Rear A," as he called himself for a joke. He removed telltale marks from a U-boat photograph, excised mentions of specific offensives, coordinated with the American military when they eventually joined their forces with ours. His creed of cheerfulness became a professional obligation: there needed to be a degree of truth in what was communicated, but not too much. At points Sir Douglas tried to engage writers, including Joseph Conrad and H. G. Wells, to assist in the production of stirring national narratives, and afterward, writing alongside his wife, he produced his own jovial autobiography about his wartime work, *Indiscretions of the Naval Censor.* As if our father were ever indiscreet, outside of champagne-and-whiskey-enhanced exchanges at his club! Even about Churchill, whose importance in the next war the Rear A did not live to see, his anecdotes were complimentary, the lightest of jibes about the man's cigars and brandy more than offset by praise for Churchill's brilliance. The book's title was the kind of joke against oneself at which our father excelled; you know it well, boasts disguised as self-deprecations—he did it equally at private dinners and at naval functions all his life. It is the English style and admirable, I think, preferable to the bald-faced bragging of other military cultures in countries more willing to admit the ruthlessness required for victory. Not everyone agrees. Some see it as distinctive of our national hypocrisy.

You never had an ease with that manner, did you? Another reason, perhaps, you left. Self-deprecation, yes, but the swagger beneath it, never. You were not one who could command a table's attention with your tales, make others laugh and want to follow you, as our father was. You lacked the loudness and the confidence, the knack with a punch line. It took you time to work out where your own art lay.

Then you learned. Finally, at a distance from home, you found a different way of telling stories.

YOU WROTE. IT's nothing I would have done.

Not very manly, is it? That is, plenty of men do it but not really our sort. Not novels, I mean, brother. What possessed you to want to write novels?

When we speak to each other, you may tell me, *There are a few reasons. I'll name some.* Evelyn Waugh. Somerset Maugham. A man who sees the antics of privileged interwar Englishmen and women and writes raucous fictions about them. That's Waugh, whose "burlesque," as you called his style in a half-apologetic letter to our mother, you adore. You claim to know all his books by heart. (The antics of Waugh's characters are very much not to Lady B's taste.) You don't have the icy distance that satire like Waugh's requires, though, so that will not be your medium. A deeper ambition of yours is to be a writer like Maugham: European in sensibility, cool and detached in tone, naturalistic in content.

You weren't sure of your place. (Anywhere.) You were spoiled, as you freely said of yourself, and so were others around you and the people they wrote about. Champagne in Paris, roulette in Monte Carlo, schnapps in the Alps. Your granddaughter, someone you can't fathom existing, comes of age when a chic set of American writers canvas similar excesses—of money, alcohol, cocaine. Look how careless we are, in our self-destruction! You may shake your heads, but our novels will sell. *Bright Young Things* in your era, *Bright Lights, Big City* in hers; two sharp young men capturing the glitter of their peers and the debauchery of their many, many parties. In England, after the crash, when you left the university after a scant year and the soberer thirties dawned, you wanted to find your own corner of a world to draw. If you were going to become a novelist, could you do something that had not been done?

You had that question on your mind when on summer travels you met that vivacious Austrian American girl, Lucia von Borosini, and were smitten. Hooked. Heady days of romance in Austria and France, a secret engagement, were followed by a separation when she returned to California, and your desire heated into fever. Your first literary outpouring was the torrent of near-daily love letters to your "darling baby." From your sedate English home in Maidenhead, the volume of words you wrote to your fiancée persuaded you that she was worthy of them. It's an easy mistake in love, one people make every single day, confusing their own adoring with the reality of the adored. And you wrote well! You convinced yourself and her both.

How proud you look in the wedding photographs, brother, by the pretty church in Somerset. (There is so much not to envy the living for, but that gathering gave me a twinge for all I missed.) You finally had her. Your bride gives her open, strong-toothed smile—even young and happy, Lucia has an air of insatiability about her, the way some men do.

In your face, I see a man who has arrived where he wants to be. In hers, someone who has found her setting-off point.

After the marriage, you and she lived in London less than a year before your ill health and your new wife's inability to manage an English household drove you out of the country. You set sail for her America, a journey on which your normally solid wife had bouts of seasickness, signs understood once you arrived in Pasadena as the start of her pregnancy. It was on that tumultuous crossing that the idea for a book came to you. Travel can provide that spark. Disillusionment, too. Unhappiness broadens the imagination. The scales were falling from your eyes, as the cliché goes—not being an author, I'm not too proud to use clichés. If lust had blinded you to Lucia's qualities, you were beginning to make out the shape of them. Now, as you sailed, you sensed the wrong moves of your own heart, which opened you to understanding the same in others. You were getting ready to write.

Your heart, brother. I'll tread lightly when speaking about your heart, given your end. In 1932, your lungs were the worry; you'd had pneumonia in London, and unknown to you our worried mother wrote ahead to Lucia's parents to request, politely but firmly, that you be well fed and looked after in California, for the sake of your health. As if you were a schoolboy. Was she being fussily intrusive, haunted still by my early death, or having a flutter of maternal premonition about yours?

Something crept into your imagination, on the journey. Someone you met on board, perhaps, or stories Lucia told you of her years at school in Switzerland. I can't try to pry apart the workings of your creative urge; that is as private a place as thoughts of suicide. An image or a line catches someone's attention and becomes the start of something. It's alchemy. All I know is that you went from writing, at age nineteen, to your Californian fiancée—

> I don't think I ever told you that my sister went back to her old school . . . as a games instructor . . . just for one term, and . . . came home, absolutely disgusted with the whole thing, because she said that nearly all the other instructors were lesbians, and never left her alone for a single minute. Pretty revolting, isn't it, darling.

—to sitting down at a desk in Pasadena, two scant years later, and dreaming up the passionate, doomed relationship between Dorcas and Consuelo. Your two women were real to you, and their love was real to you, too. You did not deliberately choose an outlandish subject, but when the characters arrived, the defiance it took to write them attracted you. No one would want you to bring those two women to life, least of all our parents. You would do it anyway.

Some rebels are noisy and exhibitionist, making scenes. Others who want attention disappear, theatrically, so everyone has to go looking for them. But for someone like you, close to our mother and with deep empathy for her, it was impossible to enact such flamboyant dramas. You never wanted to hurt her. She suffered from the loss of her first child—me, brother—and that unforgotten grief made her hover and fret over you, always. You walked a line in your short life (if not as short as mine) between the need to leave our parents so you could breathe, become a person in your own right, and the compassionate sense that you should stay close. If not to him—the salty old dog was fine, he hadn't a tenth of our mother's sentiment—then certainly to her. She was often lonely and she relied on you, brother, your understanding and love, to sustain her. Whatever else can be said of your heart, whether the physical organ with its possible congenital weakness or the metaphorical one that made its lavish errors—I agree with others that your filial affection ran deep, was one of your best and truest traits. You loved our mother, were kind and considerate to her. And from my placeless place here I can say that, in time, what made you a good son would have made you a good father to Nicholas. Not that he'll ever know that. If only someone could tell him.

Writing allows for the quiet, offstage rebellion. I think that's why you chose it. No one need know till the book comes out what you have been up to, into what risky or risqué territories your mind has traveled. You thought this more than once in California as you composed romantic scenes between Dorcas and Consuelo. You looked so proper and professional as you worked at your desk in filtered Pasadena sunlight, filling your notebook with your tidy handwriting, yet how these pages would astonish anyone who read them! Fortunately, Lucia, so unrespecting of privacy in other ways, was too involved with her own pleasures and pursuits—socializing, shopping, reading—to peer over your shoulder at yours. You had the pages to yourself. There, you could return to Europe, wander round Paris and London and a pretty country house in Berkshire as you wove together memories and inventions. Writing gave you another exhilaration, a blissful loss of self. (If only it had remained your main addiction.) Lucia was pleased you were writing, it made you an even better accessory than your future title did, and she felt it reflected well on her, to the extent that she thought about it. Mostly she was having fun out on the courts, and with friends. It was a point of pride with your wife that she was playing tennis up to a few days before giving birth to your son.

You wrote. I wouldn't have. Brother! You dared. Our parents were never going to be pleased by this first book of yours, once they discovered the nature of the story. Not least the early heated sections about Dorcas and her upbringing. "The incest-plus-sapphism theme between the mother and the daughter would cause every bishop in the Church of England to turn as pale as his lawn sleeves," is how Vita Nicholson, or Sackville-West, as readers know her, put it in her letter, though the muse of Virginia Woolf's *Orlando* gentled her comment to you by bemoaning the "present infantile condition of the English conscience." Our parents were right there with Vita's imagined bishops in their dismay. If you aimed to be a writer, not a military man, and if you chose to write novels rather than history or biography . . . did you have to choose sexual deviance as your fictional subject?

You were braced for that reaction, or thought you were, but you underestimated the depth of your own discomfort at their recoil. It shook you. Still, you had a completed manuscript. Living back in London with your wife and baby boy, you ignored Vita's advice and that of a few English editors, to shelve this work and produce something more palatable. You did what you could to see that the book made its way into print. As it eventually did, in Paris, thanks to Jack Kahane.

You had wanted our mother to understand, or to be proud of you for *Star Against Star*. Yes, somewhere within you were still that boy. It was another improbable dream you had to abandon.

FRIENDS WOULD HAVE helped. A few did, men you encountered in the publishing world. But mostly you turned for consolation to women, and over a few tumultuous years you discovered that the woman you had married was not and could not be a friend to you. By the time you fully understood this, the tie between you was all but broken, and Lucia was taking Nicholas back to California, without you. The chubby-legged future baronet toddled about, gaining admirers on the crossing. He'll be in his twenties the next time he's in England.

In the same year they left, 1935, your first book sank and vanished, like a torpedoed battleship.

This happens with some books. Philosophers have set a puzzle about whether a sound is made by a tree falling in the forest if there is no one to hear it, but there is a sadder question, about a man pouring out a story to which no one listens. Does his story make a sound? Does he?

As I said, brother, I think the RAF would have been easier on you. No matter what their doctors said, your health might have improved with the hard training and activity, and the company of men. As it was, blocked from service, your wife and child gone, you turned to work on your second novel, willing yourself not to be discouraged by the failure of your first. I am proud of you for your determination not to be faint-hearted. (There's that heart again.) Big brothers can admire younger brothers, too, you know. I'd have pounded you on the back, if I could have. You didn't give up.

Which comes first, the novel-writing or the breakdown? Do people like you write to exorcise their demons, or does writing rather keep the demons close, fray the spirit, addle the brain? You see what I mean about the unmanliness of the business. You worked so hard on your second novel that you could hardly sleep or stay calm, and your mental state disintegrated. Eventually, our mother had the modern idea that you should consult a "nerve specialist," and the family GP, Dr. Wilson, made a referral. She wasn't so modern as to have read Sigmund Freud, but as a parent, she could see that you needed help. A couple of short years later in his homespun laboratory, this same Dr. Wilson will perform experiments with the solubility of Nembutal, to help our parents determine whether you could have died by overdose.

There is always a prescribing doctor somewhere in these stories, isn't there? "I have ventured to put him on 'nembutal', and he reports that it is working well," writes the psychiatrist Hugh Crichton-Miller to Wilson, who will sympathetically return this letter to Lady B after your death;

she keeps the grim souvenir to include in her book of memories about you. "I do not think there is any reason to stop his indulgence in this narcotic in the immediate future. Let him carry on until he feels that it is entirely unnecessary." Why do doctors ever feel that day will come, when their drug won't seem necessary to a troubled patient? Crichton-Miller is not alarmed by your case: he finds you delightful, sympathizes with your grim marital situation, and locates the kernel of your problem to be having two personality sides at war: "excessive aggressiveness or power urge, or virility—call it what you like" on the one hand, versus on the other "a creative side, literary, musical, artistic," which he also deems feminine. He jokes that you "would do well as a prize-fighter or lumber-jack!" The line moves a shiver through me. I am not untouchable in my cold bed, you know. I see your adult son, a father himself though taking a page from your book and living at a distance from his children; he is older than you or I ever were, a man in his forties, tramping through a forest in Northern California. Chainsaw in hand, he prepares to fell trees. Unknowingly satisfying Crichton-Miller's ghost as he goes.

For you, the solution to your problem seemed to be moving to Kenya. Empire was grinding down by then, though still operational across every continent (excepting Antarctica). Our island nation had given up trampling its way about the globe, claiming countries as its own and insisting that countless foreign peoples recognize the British sovereign. But the maps were still colored by an imperial hand, and British-born governors wielded real power over lands far from their own. Nearly a quarter of the human population was under our thumb. I was three when I died, brother, an age when a child feels the right to grab on to things and call them "Mine!" My life approach might have been modeled on that of the recently departed Queen Victoria. If I had lived, I would have been, like our father, a loyal unquestioner of the imperial venture, but your temperament, and the times, gave you an innate skepticism on all that. You wrote as much to Lucia before your departure, when your new job as a "newspaper-man" was secured:

> So here I go to the colonies, all set to be "far-flung," a staunch supporter of the British Raj, whatever that may mean, and full of the Kipling touch etc. etc. This must make you smile, yes-no?

YOU COULD NOT take on colonial swagger with a straight face. If you had stuck with it—life, I mean, but also Nairobi, and your post at *The East African Standard*—you would have had to work out your attitude toward Africa and Africans. The British Raj, whatever that may have meant, and whether or not you had the "Kipling touch."

Nice to hear you joking with your ex-wife, though. She had remarried, so your letters to her were now addressed to Mrs. John Burnham, and you tended to include civil lines about her life with her new husband. It freed you not to expect much from Lucia anymore. You preferred wry amiability to bitterness. There were still details to be sorted, practical ones as you tried to secure your own English divorce (ironic, but one still needs an ex-spouse's cooperation to quit them, legally; Lucia, with the help of Nevada's Wild West laws, had got quite the head start on you) and dealt with the leftover chattels of your life together. You wrote to her, while considerately checking whether Lucia wanted anything, that none of your former household's furniture was of interest to you, as you planned never to live in London again. Whether this was an optimistic sentiment or a pessimistic one is hard to say.

And Nicholas, your son, would always connect the two of you. One day, you imagined in a playful missive you sent Mrs. Burnham before you left for Kenya, you and she would be cheering on your grown-up boy, as he played American football for some California university: "I shall be expecting to do some long distance rooting for him in the Rose Bowl game soon (Brownrigg, Brownrigg, rah rah, rah—yea, BROWNRIGG!!!)" This urge to turn a failed marriage into an affectionate friendship skips a generation—your granddaughter will have it, too. It was easier to forgive once you let go of any hope that marriage might make your life worthwhile, that a wife, or a lover, could rescue you, keep you anchored.

We are getting back to dark waters, brother. To where my words to you began.

Love won't save you. Our mother tried to tell you that. But heartbreak should not kill you, either.

I don't believe it did.

I can't say I'm sorry to have missed all that you had. Growing up, falling in love, falling out of love, suffering despair. Being scrutinized for the despair. Being medicated for it.

There is an advantage to ducking out early, before adult anxieties strike. As a child, I had fears, thunderstorms, the choking fire that broke out one day in the kitchens, a vicious dog we used to pass on the way to the harbor that growled loud and low from behind a stone wall. It leapt up and threatened but could not jump over. I was too young for torment, though, and our parents' hearts were lighter then, so I felt no shadow of it from them.

You wrote of the feeling. It is no wonder the inquest in Nairobi will quote from your work. You were your own posthumous witness.

The man you dreamed up, your Val in *Later Than You Think*, is a dark-haired, self-indulgent young man with a taste for fast racing cars and a potent love for a married, older woman. In the course of the narrative, Val loses any sense of his own life's value. After a last, affectionate but thwarted exchange, his lover, Camilla, sends him away.

> "You've got to make something of your life. That matters."
> Val walked back to his flat in a mood of curious fatalism. For perhaps the first time in his life he knew, clearly, that he really did not mind if he died or if he lived.

Val stays up in his flat, smoking and drinking, contemplating suicide by taking something he calls Alanol or by jumping out of the window.

Finally, some pages later, he hits on a definitive method, and one which he is confident will disguise his intentions:

> He would go up in the new machine [a small plane], take it up to ten thousand feet, then put it into a dive. From that height, he should strike old mother earth at a speed of about five hundred and sixty miles an hour.

Oh, brother. You should not have written about this if you did not want your own death to be haunted by any number of living ghouls. To fall asleep, as you did that August evening, with a new will freshly made and witnessed, empty pill vials left in the wastebasket, was to invite in crowds to guess and condemn. You would not have wanted that.

Your second novel testifies against you, the coroner using it to argue that this writing, though of a year or more earlier, proves something about your state of mind. Our mother writes from England in an exasperated rebuttal of this argument (she calls it "sheer nonsense" in her point-by-point refutation): "Every adult person is fully aware of endless 'methods of self-destruction'"—as though any fool knows that people keep a suicide plan to hand, just in case. Perhaps even stoic, stalwart Lady B does.

You could have learned from me, brother. My end was so much simpler.

I just fell asleep.

I left no evidence.

I WOULD LIKE to curl up with you. That's all.

Sleep in parallel curves, as pairs of dogs do. Nearby and companionable.

You could come lie near me here, brother, where I am in my stone English bed—rather than so far away, in a mismarked grave in Nairobi. Think of it: our father lies full fathom five, somewhere in the Atlantic off the west coast of France. You out in Kenya. Our mother is left with only me to visit. She prays for all of us, of course, but this church, St. John the Baptist at Shottesbrooke, is the only physical place where she can remember and commune with her vanishing family of Brownriggs. Juliet joins her on occasion, though our sister is unreligious and never recovers, really, from the loss of you. When she goes, after the war, Juliet's burial is elsewhere. After Juliet, all is silence with our mother. She lives on five years after our sister. No more words come from her for the others. She said all she had to say.

I have missed you, brother. Strange to say of one you never knew, or have known only from an omniscient distance. I have watched and listened to you as you lived. Taken notes. Noticed turns your life took, contemplated your significant changes of direction. Read you. Thought of you. Scorned you. Loved you.

I may have always seen how your story would end, but I was still interested in trying to understand it. "The unendurable rustle of the wings of time"—another phrase from your second novel. When you read back through, that one struck you, alternately, as profound or empty. You could not decide which. That was true of your feelings about existence in general: it had meaning or it hadn't, you were not confident to say.

I have been waiting for you. At last you're here, and I am no longer alone.

St. Ermin's

✦

OFTEN, ON A DARK MORNING, SHE DID NOT KNOW WHERE she was. The room smelled different, and there were strange sounds, of machines and of strangers. It took time to place herself.

Westminster.

That was it. After a few moments, she remembered.

The name meant the government, steely gray buildings of the civil service as well as the modestly named Houses of Parliament, blackened gold structures with serrated edges that looked more like a university or a castle than a place where gentlemen met in corridors and chambers to decide the policies of the nation. And Westminster was the noble abbey, too, the majestic, saint-filled sanctuary dedicated to monarchy but allowing a corner for Shakespeare and Dickens and other authors whose works gave voice to the country. Kipling, who lately was given a memorial slab. *It's good of the church to remind visitors that writers matter, too,* Beatrice's son had once joked to her there, in a low voice. *We can't all be kings and queens.* She winced at the memory.

Westminster was also a neighborhood, if you could call it that, the part of London where Beatrice had moved just as the war was start-ing. She had become a city dweller, residing close to Britain's centers of power—Buckingham Palace was also a twenty-minute walk away— and every day that dawned was a new reminder of the fact. She was in her latter sixties now, and her mind had not caught up with reality. She was not at home, surrounded by modest countryside and the reassuring markers of the known and remembered. She had abruptly had to sell their Berkshire house, White Waltham, and now lived at St. Ermin's in a faceless suite of several rooms, where all around her was cold, sterile, artificial. Like a stage set for a play she did not audition for, something modern and bleak. She slept poorly. Her lungs hurt.

On a clouded, threatening afternoon in October 1939, Beatrice forced herself to go to the park after lunch. She had had a heavy, solitary meal at the restaurant—a tough, grayish chop with soggy roast potatoes, followed by a poor job of a trifle; over, too, was familiar food, eating what she preferred at her own well-worn table—and the urge was strong to retreat to her rooms and sink into a stupor of reading. But if Jim, as she called her late husband, were here, he'd have told her to walk, and so she walked. Beatrice promised her husband she would make one complete circuit around St. James: over the bridge, up a lane of unleaving plane trees, round by the willows and the tiny island at the end. *That's right, old girl. Keep yourself moving.* Throughout their married life, Jim had distrusted stillness. For better or for worse. For richer or for poorer.

It challenged her, the constant traffic of cars and buses. *Cleaner than horses, anyway!* Jim would have said. *They don't leave dung heaps lying about.* The problem was not so much the noise, though there was that, but the unexpected strain of having to pay constant attention while she walked. On the streets, anything could be coming at you at any time.

The park offered relief. Within it, at least the only possible collisions were with other people. It was good to see the life and normalcy there, as though within its wrought-iron borders the world had not yet changed, and a holiday of forgetting was on offer. Young couples took afternoon strolls, solitary men made purposeful strides toward their offices, coots scooted across the water with their syncopated Morse-code movements. There was only one group of men in uniform. On the other side of the pond, Beatrice saw two women leaning in to conversation with one another, while the boy in their wake kicked at fallen yellow leaves. He might be the same age as her grandson. Since Beatrice had last seen him, Nicholas had turned into a proper boy. Letters from Lucia told her so. He would be seven this December, a thought that caused an ache in her, somewhere not far from where her heavy lunch had lodged. Her grandson was growing up. *Give me the child at seven and I will show you the man.* Still, that was a task Beatrice could set herself, to find and send Nicholas something for his birthday and for Christmas. She should do it early, given the post's uncertainties now. Los Angeles seemed farther away than ever, the fictional city where the child lived. One was encouraged to think of America as an ally in these days. Beatrice was not so certain.

Sometimes she made a push over to the river, or even visited the abbey if she had the energy for exaltation, but this afternoon Beatrice felt once round the park was enough. A chill was coming into the air, and she had not brought gloves. She made her way back to Caxton Street, where turning into the short drive that led to the three-sided, six-story mansion block of St. Ermin's gave her that day's involuntary startle. She was still getting accustomed to having the same home as a hundred others, as if they were all guests at a hotel, as indeed some were since part of the building did operate as a hotel. Transience, that was the sensation. It was in the nature of wartime, and of life after crisis.

Beatrice watched a black taxicab pull up by St. Ermin's revolving doors, and out climbed a frowning, bowler-hatted gentleman who used a cane but irritably waved off a suited doorman's offer of assistance. She did not recognize the man, not specifically, though as a species he was familiar enough, the reddened cheeks, impatient mouth; he might have been a colleague of her late husband's, or someone who had known her father in Malaysia or Ceylon. Perhaps she had met this man during an earlier, innocent time at White Waltham. Or perhaps she had never met the man. There was no way of knowing, Beatrice felt, as his bulky, charcoal-coated form vanished into the foyer of St. Ermin's and she held back, walking slowly in her own knee-length woolen wrapping so that she would not have to encounter him inside. Her ambition was for the man to have removed to wherever he was meant to be by the time she entered the building. She hoped never to have to learn, one way or another, whether this was someone she knew.

Beatrice won a solitary ride in the lift upstairs. Relief. Returning to her flat along the carpeted corridor, she unlocked the dull beige door and entered the sparsely furnished sitting room, where, without even removing her coat, she sat, unreasonably tired. She had kept back a few items from White Waltham before disposing of the rest at the sale—a desk, two Regency chairs that had belonged to her father, and a jade-green walnut settee, where she rested now, though stiff and upright, as though awaiting her next direction. A half hour's walk should not have emptied her so; it never used to at home, when she took the dogs out. She missed the dogs, but they had to go too, their two dear terriers, to the farmer where the family used to get their eggs. (She could not have kept them in the city.) Beatrice gazed around the place, blankly. What might revive her? The view out one window was of an undifferentiated, to her, mass of entities, smoke-colored and brown and blocking of light; on the other side, the bustle of the drive, its endless coming and going and coming. Both prospects made her shudder. As though there were no clear way forward. *Don't be morbid*, she told herself sternly. The word made her think of her son, again. Had he felt that way?

Beatrice pushed the thought far from her. She stood, removed her coat, hung it in the hall closet. She forced herself to settle at her desk. There were letters in need of writing. Death had brought with it a long queue of lawyers, shuffling like mourners, awaiting their turn. Where before she had had family, it sometimes seemed to Beatrice, now she had lawyers.

There was plenty of work to do. Beatrice must simply put her head down and do it.

YOU BUILD SOMETHING, only for the world to unbuild it.

Children.

The family.

Their home.

Beatrice had been a good reader all her life, but she still found the run of events illegible. She could not find its meaning.

THE WAR WAS here. The new one. It had arrived in England on the third of September, more or less when Beatrice took up residence where Douglas had largely lived during the last one. There was a symmetry in this: twenty-five years before, Beatrice had been educating their children at White Waltham—she had scarcely breathed un-til Gawen turned four, passing the age their first child, Robert, had reached—while Douglas was here in SW1, working long days and nights at the Admiralty, offering his wartime service. And now here was she, Beatrice, near the beating heart (don't think about hearts) of the British government as it made a new round of plans and preparations, readying to send another generation of husbands and sons to war. She sometimes had the brief bitter thought that she needn't worry: her own were already dead.

In October of 1939, London had not yet darkened. In the air was a sense of determination, excitement even. Few were fighting yet, the terms of engagement were uncertain, and Britain took satisfaction in proving to itself how sensible and orderly it could be, sending city children away on trains to stay more safely in the countryside, swapping out khaki and steel helmets for the troops guarding the palace rather than the traditional red and black, ensuring that citizens carried gas masks with them in case of attack. Air raid sirens rang out from time to time, and people practiced going into bomb shelters, but calmly, making jokes even. The sirens were, so far, false alarms. There was scarcely any fear in most people Beatrice knew, though nerves were taut and alert as everyone waited for news. When would the war properly start?

She wished she could speak with Jim. (The nickname came from her husband's early naval days, being easier to wield than *Douglas*, now reserved for official occasions. When Beatrice missed the man she talked with, that was Jim.) He would have helped her manage expectations, judge the correct measure of precautions, offer reassurance if she needed it or else a brisk "Buck up, Beats," if she was not showing enough mettle. He'd have had an opinion about whether the need to carry a gas mask around was real or "a piece of show," and of course even now he'd have had access to better information, which she, like everyone, craved. For nearly forty years Beatrice had depended on Jim for conversation about world affairs; it was the greatest territory they shared. Lady B never understood women who did not speak with their husbands about politics. Hers was astute and knowledgeable, canny on foreign powers' interactions, familiar with government's gear shifts during war. The two years the couple spent in the Far East had been among their happiest together, Beatrice having given birth to their second son there, yet always alert for discussions about Jim's work and the region's politics. Beatrice was a mother of young children but also a well-read person of the world, and Jim had never been a man to see the two as contradictory. He took his wife's opinions seriously. She had helped him, that way. They had helped each other.

Now here she was walking Westminster streets without the link she once had to its inner workings. She had enjoyed, no reason to deny it, her husband's previous proximity to prime ministers and their advisers. There had been thrilling moments during the last war when her husband returned home with stories he told his wife in confidence, reports on naval maneuverings around Argentina, for instance, or in the Dardanelles, which must remain secret for the conflict's duration. Beatrice was proud of Jim's trust in her discretion. It was well founded, and in truth she had no female friend who would even have been interested. She found that most local conversations went along the lines of which families had lost sons in which battles, and various recent engagements that had had to be mournfully canceled.

Now the country was alert again with terms and urgencies submerged for two decades, but in a changed, modern Britain, Beatrice felt unmoored. She had no haven at home and no trusted voice to hand nearby. There was the BBC, of course, she forced herself to try to share the expanding fondness for its news, but she was by nature a reader of reports, not a listener to them. She recalled the night a few years earlier when Gawen and Juliet stayed up late together at White Waltham, sitting beside the wireless as it issued hushed bulletins on the slow dying of George V. Then the household was appropriately serious, but later Gawen used to mimic that night's somber voice intoning: "This is London. The King's Life is moving peacefully towards its close. Signed, Frederic William, Dawson of Penn." He liked to exaggerate irreverently the ponderousness of the announcement. It made Juliet laugh.

To Beatrice, the BBC was impersonal, and it could not replace having one's own private announcer, as she had for so long. Having to absorb all the changes of '39 without being able to talk them through with the man she had relied on her entire adult life rattled her, left her almost shaky on her feet. Perhaps this was why she tired more easily. Beatrice knew widows who said they spoke to their husbands still, and found it a comfort, but when she broke the silence in the St. Ermin's flat by saying, "Today, *The Times* reports that Chamberlain will send troops to Poland, and I'm not sure whether to view that as good news or bad," or "A man in the restaurant at St. Ermin's stated for all to hear that France was more vulnerable than we realized, that we must not assume they will hold against the Germans," she felt foolish, as though she were acting in an amateur drama.

In my view, Beats . . . She could hear the start of an opinion, but after that the air was silent. Had been, since Valentine's Day. Another moment of Beatrice being given notice that altered her life, though this one by telephone, from the British consulate in southern France, rather than the telegram at the door that told them of Gawen. "I'm very sorry to tell you, Lady Brownrigg," said the scratchy-sounding official, "that your husband has had a heart attack in Cannes. Sir Douglas will not survive. Please accept our deepest condolences." The pause. "We'll need your advice on the arrangements."

All the arrangements. Such a deceptively businesslike word.

BOOKS, OF COURSE, she had made sure to bring with her. Her late husband's voice was there, if anywhere, in his fair and jocular account of the war years and the work he did during them. If Beatrice wanted his companionship, she could simply pull him off the shelf, and so, after she had finished her letters, she did.

Indiscretions of the Naval Censor: she had teased Jim about his proposed title, but he insisted, shrewdly, "It will make the thing sound a bit more interesting. Can you imagine, Beats, how many tedious volumes there will be on display at Hatchard's called *My Important War Years, and How Important I Was in Them?*" They had been writing their books at the same time, another period of companionable harmony, in the wake of the national peace. Beatrice's was a biography, including many letters, of Sir John Moore, the general whose heroic death on the battlefield in A Coruña, Spain, was memorialized in a famous poem ("Slowly and sadly we laid him down / From the field of his fame fresh and gory . . ."). Sir Douglas liked to say to friends that the Brownriggs were operating a cottage industry in the production of military history, and joked that there was a race on between himself and Beatrice. "And may the better man win." That her husband's book ended up being finished and published first was, Beatrice felt, probably best for marital relations.

A few years before, she had written a small book about prayer, for children, a volume called *The Well of Life*. Neither she nor Jim counted that as serious writing, though this past year she found herself finding and consulting it. She intended it for her own children, especially Gawen, who even when he was young could get overwhelmed by the clamor in his mind. Prayer would, his mother hoped, help steady him through those moments.

When Gawen was grown, and Jim expressed dismay at their son's professional decision to turn toward writing, Beatrice put it to her husband: What else might either of them have expected, given that both his parents were producing books while he was growing up?

She picked up the *Indiscretions* now, and Jim's amiable voice poured into her inner ear. Gawen had his skepticisms about his father—he liked to call him the Salty Dog under his breath, when Sir Douglas embarked on one of his familiar anecdotes from that time—and Beatrice indulged her son by smiling at his mostly mild rebellions; but she felt, too, that Gawen did not fully appreciate both how important Sir Douglas's work had been and how genuine was his modesty. Her husband had bluster, of course he did, but also a sense of proportion. About himself and others. Perhaps it was that sense more than anything that Beatrice found herself missing in these strange, solitary days. Gawen—beloved, troubled, affectionate Gawen—had not always been able to muster that equanimity, that balance. A sense of proportion. It was, finally, her son's fatal flaw. She would never have uttered the opinion to anyone, not even to Juliet. But in her mother's heart she believed that was the difficulty that had held him back.

Beatrice continued reading, on the settee, trying to find her own balance. On she read, through radio communiques and stories about Churchill and the mournful names of the navy's own sunken ships, the darkly celebratory lists of the sunken Germans'. But how far away this earlier war seemed to Beatrice, its failures and its triumphs. How hard it was to concentrate on Jim's account.

It was the sound of him she missed.

BEATRICE WALKED LATER to the abbey, for solace and to hear evensong. Yes, it was a place for coronations and funerals, but daily it was open for ordinary people and their worship, and she needed to hear voices. Singing in praise and celebration. And warning, too, of course. The war was in every clergyman's thoughts and words. Beatrice arrived at the arched doorway early in order to have her own private, subdued communion first, before the service.

She sat on a dark wooden pew listening to rustlings of preparation, bodies moving around the organ that waited, overhead, to send its throaty chords into the religious air. Far above that music chamber a late, watery light angled through the highest stained-glass windows. Wrapped in her wool and her incomprehension, Beatrice gazed up into that weakening glow and made her best attempt to find order in her story.

You build something, over years, only for the world to unbuild it. The thought would not leave her mind. Surely it was the world, not God, knocking it down? An impersonal unbuilding of all that you had spent your life trying to shelter, to keep safe.

Children.

The family.

Their home.

It couldn't be God wreaking this havoc. If it were, Beatrice would be obliged to change the tenor of her faith. Hers was not a vengeful God, smiting his disappointing children. She thought of the line Claude Anderson, Gawen's employer, had written to her toward the end of the previous year's agitated autumn: "However inscrutable may be the workings of Providence the purposes are directed by a compassionate spirit." He was trying to get Beatrice to stop fighting.

His expression echoed her own belief. It was not in Beatrice's nature—she was repelled by self-pity—to feel herself singled out or victimized; she was no English Job. Then again it was hard not to look for a pattern or reason in her sentence of serial disasters. Beatrice thought of sins she might have unknowingly committed. Perhaps she had taken part in some grand moral error, and these were her punishments. The last was the most literal unbuilding: emptying out and selling the house where she had lived for twenty years and raised their children. "Why not call your house Walt Whitman outright, & have done with it?"

ran Vita Sackville-West's joke to Gawen in a letter, a line shared with his mother as much to show off his brush with that literary set as for the joke itself. White Waltham was the place the family had moved after their little boy Robert died, and a sanctuary for Beatrice. *Safe as houses.* Jim used to use that phrase in the rare talks they had about financial matters. "Not to worry, Beats," he'd say of some investment he was making. "It's safe as houses." How comforting that had been. As though her husband knew solidity when he saw it. Now she wondered: What had mortared their family construction? Something strong enough? Safe enough?

The vaulted stone roof so far overhead made Beatrice all too aware of her own smallness. There were mysteries beyond understanding, she knew that perfectly well; it was nothing but typical human pride to imagine that she, Beatrice Brownrigg, could comprehend the purpose of these abrupt losses and dislocations. She thought of her little book on the importance of prayer. There were times, now, when she felt as though she were the same innocent age as the children for whom she had intended her words.

> Take an object—a watch—a book—look at it steadily, notice its shape, its colour, think from what materials it was made, of its use. Take a flower, think of where it grew, of its colour, of all its wonderful beauty and perfect finish. Think steadily, and think of nothing else for two minutes, then five minutes, then longer. If you do this during any idle moments this control of your mind becomes so much a habit of mind that you will be able to concentrate at will on any object, or any idea, and anywhere, even in noisy crowded places. You will then have learned to possess your own mind instead of having it invaded by all the loose and wandering thoughts of the outside world.

She gazed at the stone ceiling overhead. Beatrice made herself focus on it.

"Wait in silence, thinking only of the Presence of God within you," she had written elsewhere. "Then your Divine Nature will rise into your region of self-consciousness, and you will find that crooked things become straight, rough ways will become smooth, worries will cease, and patience, courage and a quiet mind will be yours."

Sometimes in writing, a wisdom surfaced you did not know you had. Sometimes, she knew now, you were writing, unsuspectingly, for your future self. In her short book, she instructed the young on the value of meditation; of remaining calm, avoiding agitation; and of reflecting, of course, on God, and on the meaning of crucifixion: "Each one of us, in a spiritual sense, must be crucified . . . our hearts—the symbol of love—pierced as with a spear, that our self-will may surrender its existence to the Will of God." As she wrote, she had had Robert's still-recent death in her pained imagination. She had not conceived of the further tests ahead.

Surrender. That was what she must attempt, every day, to do.

Besides, it had not all been unbuilt. *Proportion, old girl!*

She still had Juliet. They were not close; the connection between Beatrice and her daughter had never been the strong, rope-thick bond she had with her son. Juliet was hard to reach in her second marriage, and she had a susceptibility—to drink—of which Beatrice was aware but about which she would never speak. But there was a friendliness between them. They did not argue. And they had lost the same men, Juliet her brother followed by her father. Juliet hoped to find a place with the Red Cross, the ambulance service, to be sent somewhere far away to work. That might be good for her. For them both: give Beatrice a sense that someone in the Brownrigg family was still helping the country in its war.

And there was Nicholas.

The Englishwoman sitting with bowed head, all but invisible to those around her, allowed herself a memory of her grandson's round, plump-cheeked face at two years old, when he came to live with them at White Waltham. She felt the boy's satisfying weight on her lap when she sat at a table showing him a picture book about ducks, his doughy arm pointing to things on the page. He is a strong one, this one, the nanny they had brought in said to Lady B. She had believed it. On he grew, in Los Angeles, stronger, bigger every day. A proper boy now.

Evening gathered, and other bodies settled on the pews around her in the high and narrow quire. The white-robed choristers got ready to send their voices up into the abbey's atmosphere, its stern and silvered grace. One was tempted, on hearing their lofty purity, to call them cherubic, but to look at them was to see an array of quite ordinary boys, in a variety of sizes and complexions and degrees of seriousness.

They only became angels when they sang.

They gave her an idea.

IT WAS DURING one of the sung psalms. The rhythmed, chanting tones lulled Beatrice's thoughts, freed them. Loosened something.

She could write to him.

To *Nicholas*. Not to his mother, Lucia, as she had been, regularly, in a friendly way though also in a deliberate, stealthy effort to keep the connection between them warm. With a shudder, Beatrice could imagine the risks of its cooling. She depended entirely now, in a terrible way, on her erratic former daughter-in-law.

But how could she write all that was in her heart about Gawen to a boy of six, turning seven? There were undoubtedly adult elements in what she wanted to communicate about her son. Her writing would have to be not for her grandson as the boy he was now. She would write rather to the man he would become. A future Nicholas. *Give me a child until seven and I will show you the man.*

This gave Beatrice a purpose. Something to salvage out of this rubble. And she could tell the story as clear-sightedly as possible; she need not soften every detail. She could describe the son she had known and loved—Nicholas's father. It would be a kind of memoir of Gawen, for the boy who had to grow up without him. A gift for Nicholas, though it would comfort the giver, too.

It must take the form of a letter.

She sat up, even with her eyes still cast down. As her back straightened against the wooden pew, Beatrice's breaths grew deeper. She felt herself taking in air, her mind becoming more alert and even, a novel feeling in these days, that slight twitch of anticipation. Of eagerness. Because of all the things she missed about her son—they were countless, a year on, the pain was unblunted—on some dim days what she missed more than anything was being able to write to him. With Jim, she wished she could speak: touch her husband's clothed arm, hear the genial gruffness of his voice, feel the reassurance of his presence. With her son the loss was a sharper, more specific blade. She wanted to write him. Her words were all stopped up. It felt, at times, like choking. *Let me write him!* she had once even murmured that, madly, in a prayer, but she knew the illogic of the plea and that it was foolish to trouble God with it.

She had got used to Gawen's being far away during different spells, when he was traveling in Germany or living in California; he was in his twenties, after all, and she knew, she had a mother's awareness, that being at home at White Waltham dampened her son's spirit after a while, hampered him. He had been better off far from them, and they had been better off, mother and son, writing to each other. Of course she would do anything to hear Gawen's voice again, but the lack she felt every morning, especially in the mornings, was of the young man to whom she could pour out her impressions. Her descriptions and reflections on the people she met and the places she visited; literary commentary, social musings, gossip. (These were the elements of life that didn't interest Jim; she rarely wrote to Gawen about politics.) Writing to someone you loved inspired you to notice the world more closely, catch entertaining details for them, find moments in a day or a journey that would bring them some light. You could send light all that way, yes all the way to Kenya even, in a letter. Gawen always apologized in his replies that he hadn't the time to write back as much as he'd have liked, he was working so hard, but of course Beatrice did not mind, as she told her son every time in her own letters. She did not expect a prompt reply, just wanted to keep him company in Nairobi as he built up his new life, and though she left this unmentioned it gave her company, too, to write him. When she sat at the desk and reread what she had written before folding up the pages and sending them, she saw that in reminding Gawen of the cloistered Maidenhead world he had left behind, she was perhaps helping to underline for her son all the reasons he had left. Well, if so, that was not such a bad thing for him, either. *Walt Whitman.* Why had they not simply called the house that, and had done with it? Gawen could tell that Bloomsbury joke to his new friends in Kenya.

He did reply eventually, with accounts of the unruly people he was meeting and descriptions of the extraordinary world he found himself in, dropping names of famous exiles he was confident his mother would have heard of, whose notoriety she would shake her head over. That mad woman who had shot a man at the Gare du Nord, not the sort of story Beatrice had time for, but she remembered reading of it in *The Times'* back pages. Both parents had been wary of that element of society their son would find in Kenya, but they trusted he would find his way, and his letters home would help him do that. Beatrice encouraged Gawen about the value of trying out scenes in letters. They were often rough drafts of future fictions. If Gawen meant to write an epic book about Kenya one day, as he had written to her, then it could only help him to produce sketches in his correspondence.

She had kept them all, every letter her son had sent her. She had gathered them in a wooden tray on the edge of her desk, even before he died. It was as if she had a maternal instinct to keep his words all together, in case she would need them later.

What she had not anticipated was the return of her own letters to him. They came back in a thick and unbearable box of Gawen's personal effects, one of several that the unfailingly kind Claude Anderson at *The East Africa Standard* arranged to have sent home to England. Like a grim sequel to the telegram's arrival that August, was the unforgettable presentation of the boxes that came two months later, Mr. Reynolds carrying them into the drawing room, brightly stamped with Kenya's rendition of the king and colorful, as though they contained early Christmas presents. The contents seemed to Beatrice like nothing so much as a monument to futility: her son's clothes and his watch; books about Kenya and some novels, including those she had sent him; and letters—hers, those from Douglas, and those from Juliet. (The latter were brief; it was not her daughter's best medium. As Juliet said, "You three are the writers. I'm the chatterer.") The detritus of eight months lived abroad. Transience, again.

Beatrice began the very next morning.

My very dear Grandson,
    When you are old enough to wish to know something about your Father as we knew him I shall be an old woman, if I live as long as that; so while my memory is clear and I am still close to the events

about which I write, I am going to tell you that which will be of value to you to know.

In the mornings, by long habit, Beatrice sat at her desk to write letters, and to read them. Mornings were for sharing her thoughts with someone at a distance—the place where loved ones so often were. At home, at White Waltham, her desk had stood before a window that looked out into the garden, and so her thoughts often wandered over the lawn and into its textured herbaceous borders, sometimes up into the thick greened limbs of the mulberry tree while she composed her thoughts. She loved the peace of those hours at her desk, quietly conversing with people elsewhere. It was such an assumption in her life that Beatrice could scarcely have put it into words: how many of her relations with others were formed out of the letters that flowed between them. If asked, she might have said those were the best exchanges one could have.

And so she devoted her mornings, that first autumn of the new war, to writing Nicholas the story of his father's shortened life.

Afternoons she feared, still. Afternoons were when she needed Jim's voice telling her to buck up, as Beatrice turned to all the rest she had to do. Letters to lawyers. The constant sorting out of estate issues. Correspondence with the men at the bank, who had impressed on her how very different her circumstances were and would be, going forward.

A year earlier there had been an endless stream of terrible letters, during the harrowing period after Gawen's death. To the magistrate in Nairobi, to his editor in Nairobi, to a legal adviser Sir Douglas engaged in Nairobi—all those people to whom Beatrice wrote, with frantic determination, in order to prove that her son had died by natural causes. Not suicide. His heart had stopped. He had a weak heart, and it had stopped. Months she spent trying to ensure that that was what went into the official register of Gawen's death. Beatrice had made an unshakable commitment to that project, for her grandson's sake, until finally the back-and-forth and all their distress over it began to take a toll on her husband's health, and Dr. Wilson, their family doctor—who had helpfully attempted to prove, right there in Reading, that Nembutal could not have acted on the young Englishman as the Nairobi coroner claimed—recommended that for the sake of Sir Douglas's well-being, they accept the final determination of accidental death, death by misadventure. Beatrice wanted *natural causes.* The people in Nairobi would not let her have it.

But in her writing, she could shape the story as she saw it. Mornings now would be hers, to narrate the life of her darling boy to that other darling boy, who would one day, in an unseeable postwar future, sit down somewhere comfortable, and read her words.

THE WAR GOES on. The work grows.

And grows.

Beatrice found, in writing the memoir of Gawen, that she had so much material about him. She made up her mind and frequently changed it on what to include, but certain documents made it in entire. She retyped the will Gawen wrote and signed before he left for Kenya, to establish that he meant to leave everything for his son Nicholas, as well as the assessment of the nerve specialist, Dr. Crichton-Miller, from 1937, a description she found herself often thinking of, after rereading it in the light of her son's death.

> He would do well as a prize-fighter or lumber-jack! There are plenty of men about for whom the sole problem of adjustment is the appropriate expression and sublimation of aggressivity. I have told him to punch a ball or fell trees! but then we come to the other side which creates incompatibility.
>
> It is this feminine and creative side of him which is so badly crushed by his power side, except and unless his power is being suitably used.

She knew she must be careful about reading, and rereading. Jim had often told her, especially in the lightless days after they lost Robert, that there was no use in replaying the past; one simply had to move forward into what was next. *Keep moving, Beats, old girl. Don't let yourself become stuck.*

Yet she found going back through the missives strangely soothing.

And not just Gawen's to her, as one might expect, but hers to him. Someone who cared about Gawen Brownrigg would want to know how his mother had tried to guide him in the last romance of his life—wouldn't they? Wouldn't Gawen's son, one day, when he had grown up, want to know what Beatrice had written about the woman in Nairobi her son felt he loved, whose rejection had caused him such disappointment? She pored over she sheets of her words with the inevitable question of whether she might have been more persuasive, more helpful to her son. She did not feel she could have been. Was she too harsh? Not at all. Gawen had once told her he appreciated how well she knew him, his flaws as well as his virtues. She told herself (*Now, Jim, you see, this is why it helps to look it over again, for reassurance*) that she had expressed as much as a mother could, in the circumstances. In a letter Beatrice had written in this very building, at a time before she suspected it would become her permanent and only home.

And when she was unaware that this was the last letter she'd write him.

St Ermin's 30 July 1938

My darling boy—

I was considerably shaken by your letter of 23 July, & answered in a hurry to assure you of all my sympathy & understanding—but I felt bound to ask you to accept the difficult situation in a reasonable manner. I know in these crises you feel they are more important to you than the same crises (those of love & marriage) are to other people—but of course this is not so—& there are other valuable & important aspects of life that matter in the long run quite as much.

You are the superlative Egoist—during your emotional experiences—it would have been infinitely wiser & kinder to have left Jerree [Miss Talbot-Smith] out of an intimate friendship with you when you first felt attracted sexually & so upset her life—but I know it is too late to look backwards. I am not sweeping all prospect of a marriage with Jerree aside, you are not a child, nor am I in any position to interfere or arrange your

life for you—but I am deeply concerned with your happiness &
ultimate satisfaction.

I know your complex character & the needs of that character better than anyone—& I have absolutely no doubt in
my mind that because of its complexity (half-poet, half-prize
fighter!) it is essential to you to avoid the bitter struggle to keep
love alive in a marriage where poverty would first dim & then
extinguish all romance. You are a very difficult person with
whom to live—nervous—sensitive—highly strung—impatient
with the smallest discomfort in your home. Your nature de-
mands the champagne standard, & when custom had blunted
or numbed the sweet intimacies of passion & you found you had
only the tepid barley-water standard your married life would
become intolerable. It can only be an appalling captivity to you
without enough money to permit a sense of space & freedom—
you quoted the married life of the Waughs as the comfortable
married life—money which allows of pleasant separations &
so prevents a sense of blighting domesticity is essential to your
happiness in a marriage. I feel this profoundly. You say you like
"the married state", but you have a good deal of the "wild ass of
the desert" in your blood—as has your Father—& a good deal
of conscious individuality—as has your Mother—& the combination of these characteristics in your composition do not make
the prize husband & father!

Do read this to Jerree—& endeavor to be perfectly honest
with her—with so young & inexperienced a girl there is danger of a cloud of blindness enveloping you both from mutual
flattered vanity. Now you think each other wonderful—but you
are merely young—not wonderful—& are looking at a mirage
instead of realizing the desert, but the mirage will fade & the
desert remain.

Take life quietly, learn wisdom & have faith in God until
such a time you are free in every way (released from Lucia &
financially at ease) to consider that terrifyingly long & close relationship of marriage, before you enter upon its hard conditions.

Talk to your old Priest—darling boy—it is often a great solace to talk openly to one who is not biased by prejudice, & pray for patience—courage & a quiet mind. & work conscientiously to prove your value & keep the life of your heart & emotions in a water tight compartment—out of sight from curious eyes—

All my love always, darling boy—

Ever your very loving

Mum

It grew into a book.

Yes, it became a book, the project for Nicholas. That way it could contain multitudes: not just her memoir, but the elements that went into the memoir. Gawen's letters. His death certificate. The wording from the October inquest. The reviews of his book, *Later Than You Think*.

The war goes on. She maintains her correspondence with Lucia, who launches into her third marriage, with Edmund Engel, quickly producing two further sons. (Poor Burnham, Beatrice has no idea what happened to him.) Lucia and her expanding family move to New Mexico, a place that means nothing to Beatrice. Her eldest son, Nicholas turns ten, eleven, as the war goes on: a boy whom Beatrice once imagined returning to England at age twelve for his schooling, will stay in America. Lucia sends him to boarding school in California.

Beatrice is losing Lucia, she feels it, and so she decides to add other material to her scrapbook: letters to and from Lucia's parents, showing that they worried over Lucia's behavior, too. Beatrice begins to feel the oxygen taken away from her, her ability to breathe life into the story of her son Gawen, who becomes further and further away, more and more dead, with every passing year. While his son, Nicholas, grows on and grows on, without him.

For if Beatrice loses Lucia, she loses Nicholas. The war becomes frightening and ugly, and Beatrice slowly accepts the fact, in her flat in St. Ermin's, that she is losing her grandson. That she will recover him, that he will recover her, only through this book she is making for him. He'll receive it when he is twenty-one, in 1953. It feels a lifetime away, and indeed it is all too likely she won't live to see the date herself.

Anyone who has written history, though, is capable of taking the long view. Beatrice wrote about the history of the Kandian throne, for her children to know more about their Brownrigg family, and she wrote about Sir John Moore for the same reason. The scrapbook is of a piece with the work she did in younger days, more optimistic days. This one is for her grandson, Nicholas. He carries the title, after all. He is the fifth baronet. Perhaps one day he'll return to England; perhaps he'll marry in England and settle there. Whatever is in the boy's future, he will have this book she has made for him as a reference, a guide, an inheritance. *When you are old enough to wish to know something about your Father* . . . A person cannot go any distance, Beatrice believes, without that knowledge.

At the end. How shall she end her book? Gawen did become free in every way, as so many of the condolence notes said, soon after Beatrice wrote that letter to her darling boy. But it was not the freedom she had imagined for him.

Released and at peace—where nothing could disturb him anymore.

Increasingly, in addition to prayer, its constant comforts, Beatrice reads poetry. There is a poem of Shelley's she has found herself returning to often, a particular stanza that speaks to her. She includes selected lines from it at the end of her book. She has changed it slightly, though. An editor to the end. She has in mind what Claude Anderson wrote to her after seeing Gawen in his room that morning. Beatrice fixes Shelley's words, so they will say about her son what she wants them to say.

8th August, 1938

"Peace—peace—he is not dead he doth but sleep.
Tis we, who lost in stormy vision, keep
With phantoms an unprofitable strife.
He has outsoared the shadows of our life.
Envy and calumny and hate and pain
And that unrest which men miscall delight
Can touch him not and torture not again.
From the corrosion of the world's slow stain
He is secure, and now can never mourn
A heart grown cold, a head grown grey, in vain."

The Alvarado

+

NEW MEXICO.

Burnham could not get a feel for the state. It seemed raw, exposed. The light was starker here, the people unfamiliar. Very Spanish. Their hotel in Albuquerque, the Alvarado, was splendid, a grand, wide, Mission-style construction right by the railway station, so the transfer, when they arrived from the compact sleeper car to a cool, dark, high-ceilinged lobby, was seamless, even with a little boy, age five, who was tired and out of sorts from the long journey.

Los Angeles was Spanish, too, of course—look at the name—but he and his wife lived in Pasadena, confused with Los Angeles but quite separate from it, a lively enclave with calm sun and wide boulevards, where magnates settled and asthmatics came to get better. Pasadena was the Tournament of Roses, and proud of it. The city Burnham and his wife had both come from, and the city he had drawn her back to, where they now made a home together with her young, half-English son. The city from which they had, to Burnham's frustration, now been absent for several weeks, traveling on an itinerary of western states not of his own devising.

His wife was restless.

There were always further trips ahead, with more shops to discover and friends to look up in Chicago, where they had begun, city of her birth, and in a blur of other places on their progress west. Of course Lucia had a cousin in Colorado! How could she not? John

Burnham would like nothing better than to keep going through New Mexico, close his eyes in Arizona, and wake up back in California. But no, his wife knew someone in New Mexico who would host a dinner for them if they came to town, and someone else informed Lucia that Albuquerque was "a city on the rise," so she wanted to judge this for herself. The phrase came from a man she had met: his wife was always meeting men, or they were meeting her, and if John Burnham had thought that would cease to happen after they got married, he was wrong. At this distance from the man he had been two years earlier when the couple eloped to Nevada, John Burnham could easily enough see his own foolishness. Had he genuinely thought Lucia would change? Had he imagined himself capable of taming her— domesticating her?

"You're sure about this, John?" pressed his sister, Kaye, before the couple drove off to Nevada—without the child, Nicholas, whom they left with his grandparents in Pasadena. "I adore Lucia, as you know, but . . . is it really legal?"

"That's how they do it in Reno," he answered her breezily. "It's the divorce capital of the world. That's what they call it. Of course it's legal."

Her sisterly concern had scarcely penetrated John's excitement. He should not even have told Kaye of their plans: he and Lucia had sworn not to tell anyone other than her parents, but in his mind there was an obvious exception clause for his sister, as he told her everything; she was a second self. As such, she was voicing a hesitation that had coursed through him, too (making it all the more fiercely important to ignore her). They had been friendly with "the bold Von Borosini girl," as their mother called her, since they were teenagers, and though the fire off her was frankly irresistible, everyone knew what happened with fire. John Burnham felt that Kaye was right to wonder, and also that he was not going to worry about her wondering.

John Burnham Jr. was seen as an underformed man, including by John Burnham Sr., a successful investor, who once told his wife, not knowing their son could hear him: "It seems to me John is missing something—I don't know what it is. As though he doesn't have enough gas in him, is likely to stall out somewhere, along the highway." John Jr. planned to surprise his father and his mother, to prove he had spunk and daring. He had caught a prize, unexpectedly—he had opened the door of his rooms at the Huntington and in came a fierce and beautiful hawk. And faced with this wildness John Burnham found he did have the intelligence to seize the gift. She was older than he by a couple of years, but re-meeting now stirred them both, and when Lucia, warm in his arms, suggested a Reno divorce from her first husband and swift marriage with him, Burnham laughed, assuming she was kidding, then swallowed when he saw that she wasn't. And then he kissed her, as deeply as he knew how. He imagined he could see a future for them together. With her little boy, too, that funny fellow he intended to befriend. John Burnham Jr. would claim this lively, round-eyed, unpredictable young woman, lately returned, broken-winged, from her marriage to an English baronet-to-be who had not made her happy. She told chilling stories of her husband's distractions and his parents' attempt to take charge of young Nicholas, and of the strange, entangled world of London's writers and socialites, who played loosely in their affairs and were fast with their barbs and the worse for you if you couldn't keep up. Lucia had been wounded by the environment, and John Burnham wanted to soothe and to salve.

"You need an American, dear one," he said to her, "someone who understands you."

"I need a John," she murmured, unable not to tease him.

"You need an American John," John Burnham said, stomaching the joke and batting it back to her. And off they drove, not long after, to Nevada.

"MR. BURNHAM?"

A dapper man behind the main desk in the lobby extended a letter to him. Burnham had been there to inquire about dinner reservations for that evening.

"This came for your wife. Forwarded from Pasadena." Well-traveled, stamped with the profile of George VI. His wife collected stamps, one of her more innocent pastimes. Burnham thanked the clerk and carried the piece of mail up to their room, where on entry he found mother and son in a standoff, trading frowns that bore a comical resemblance to each other. (What powerful scowlers they both were!) Burnham found that his sympathies often went first to the boy. She could be short-tempered with him.

"Master Nicholas?" Burnham called him this with affection, a feigned formality, though Lucia's son did have an instinct for his future stature, doubtless encouraged by whispers in his ear from his mother. Lucia disparaged the world she and her son had fled, yet she showed off about it, too.

Burnham had insisted they take the boy with them on this extensive tour, rather than have him stay again with his grandparents, the nervous American mother and the rigid mustachioed Austrian baron, of whom Burnham continued to nurture a silent fear. Victor von Borosini's real passion was for scholarship, so they said, but Burnham felt that the soldier in the man was not far from the surface. He had been in a prisoner-of-war camp in England during the Great War, and the experience had stayed with him. Burnham's enthusiastic suggestion of a trip for three did reinforce his reputation as a genial stepfather, a quality valued by the grandparents at least, if less so by Lucia. She tended to prefer freedom from maternal duties, and would have had Nicky stay in Pasadena, but Burnham won this time, and the victory ensured that he would have a young person with them who seemed increasingly like an ally.

"Let's you and I go and wander the arcades, shall we?" Burnham suggested to the child. "Get some fresh air, see what we find. Your mother can stay and read her letter."

Nicky readily agreed to escape the irritation-aired room and go exploring with Burnham, a person he was fond of, whom his mother referred to as "your stepfather," as though the acquiring of John Burnham had been Nicky's idea. Burnham himself suggested that the boy call him, inaccurately, "Uncle John." They shared a tacit sense that *Father* was not the word to use, but *Uncle* had a warm, familial feeling, and so, when Lucia wasn't listening, that was the name the boy used. Burnham liked Lucia's son, moody though he could be, felt he was something of a lonely fellow and no wonder, having been hauled from California to England and back the first years of his life, and between London and Berkshire, as if he were yet another hatbox. The youngster could do with a few friends. He should stay in one place for a while, in Burnham's opinion, as he had told his wife, while the English father got up to whatever mischief he had going in Kenya. You heard things about the Brits over there. Not wholesome things, either.

Burnham took the five-year-old by the hand and strolled downstairs and then outside along the cool, shaded arcade. In the sun it would climb into the nineties later, Burnham had been told, the southwestern sun sterner than Pasadena's. It was the altitude, he supposed. But it drew artists to this landscape, and that interested Burnham. By day, he used to say wryly to Lucia, when they were still a couple capable of being playful, he might be in finance, but by night he had a secret appreciation for art. While they were here, he intended to take his wife to an Albuquerque gallerist he had read about: there were new southwestern artists Los Angeles and New York had not cottoned on to yet. Burnham was following those.

The architects had been clever about the Alvarado's design, the spaces moving people easily from staying to shopping. Burnham knew the place was famous for selling the wares of the local natives.

"Look!" the boy whispered suddenly, tugging on Burnham's hand. He had been strictly schooled not to point at people, but his blue-green eyes (again, uncannily his mother's) widened into an open stare at a suede-jacketed man sitting twenty yards away behind a table displaying blankets and baskets. The man wore his silver-black hair in two long black pigtails on either side of his long, walnut-colored face, and a leather hat like a softened version of what cowboys wore. He seemed absorbed in thought, not commerce, and worked with his hands on a small item that seemed to involve braiding. Burnham glimpsed a black feather glinting, almost hidden, in the man's hair, and was sure that the observant boy would have seen that, too.

Holding Nicky's hand, Burnham walked with deliberation to the table. He cleared his throat. "Good morning, sir," he said, removing his own hat. "Mind if my boy looks at your items here? His hands are clean."

The man looked up, his eyes dark and comment-less. He nodded.

"Are these pieces the works of your tribe? Are your people—"

"Tewa." He spoke the two syllables with equal emphasis, and as though the name were self-explanatory. It invoked a world, for himself anyway. He did not elaborate.

"The weavings are very fine," Burnham said into the uninviting silence. Still, the man must be here because he wanted to sell things. Burnham shrugged and focused on the work. It had not been an empty pleasantry: the weavings were striking in their colors and the geometry. There were aprons, a simple rectangular block of woven material attached to a couple of loose cotton ties; and thick, patterned blankets, rough to the touch but sturdy. Too much to pack and take home, though.

"Look at this pretty piece, Nicky—look at how the shapes fold over and repeat." He leaned over the boy to show him, tracing the diamonds and chevrons in deep rust reds and jet blacks, against a cloud-gray background. They made Burnham think of fire and of iron. The child was admiring a few woven neckties, too, which had bright splashes of beads near the narrower end. "What would your grandparents think if you wore that tie to your next Thanksgiving dinner, eh?" He chuckled, but his stepson was too fascinated to laugh, or perhaps even hear him.

"I like the slippers," he said shyly.

"Moccasins." The man behind the table corrected Nicky, but with a friendly tone. "Those are moccasins."

The word was new to them. The boy moved two plump fingers now across the ochre suede surface, marveling at its softness.

The man leaned toward him. "If you wear these, your steps are quiet. People can't hear you approach. People—or animals, either."

Nicky held his breath at the thought.

"Shall we bring something back for your mother?" Burnham suggested. "An apron? Not that she is famous for spending time in the kitchen . . ." Again he tried to coax his stepson into a conspiratorial laugh, with no luck. "But it is very decorative—I think she'd like the pattern, don't you? And it might inspire her, who knows?"

He discussed the price with the man. Nicky continued to look longingly at the moccasins, but Burnham imagined the row with Lucia over such a purchase and did not have the heart to defend buying her son such unusual shoes. The man went through the necessary motions of the sale transaction, and folded up the apron, as if this were part of some ancient, tedious ritual. Burnham saw that his real interest was in the little boy. When the exchange of money and item was complete, and Burnham was holding the rolled-up textile under his left arm, the man, now standing, reached into a pocket in his jacket. He looked at a small item for a moment, in the palm of his hand, while the child watched him keenly. He then held his hand out to Nicky.

"This is an arrowhead."

Nicky held out his palms, cupped together. The man held it suspended over Nicky's hands. You could feel the excitement pouring off the boy.

"Be careful with this. Someone used to hunt with it once. Don't lose it."

He placed, rather than dropped, the item in Nicky's palms, where the child stared at it.

"Thank you," Nicky said hastily. "Thank you, sir. Thank you very much."

Burnham had not even needed to nudge him.

The man nodded, satisfied that his gift would not be wasted. He had not smiled throughout this encounter, but his eyes had gentled. Burnham tipped his hat to the man before replacing it on his head. "Now, let's go back and find your mother. Show her our gift."

"Goodbye!" Nicky called out as they walked away, and from that point on he held the arrowhead tightly clasped in his left fist, until he was somewhere quiet and alone where he could examine it properly.

Burnham whistled a jaunty tune as they walked back in the warming air. At a time like this, with his stepson, he had brighter thoughts about what might lie ahead for himself and Lucia, for the three of them together. The road did not seem as short in that moment as it sometimes did in the dark hours of the night, when his wife made it clear to John Burnham that she found him, as a man, inadequate. Some marriages were short-lived. Her first had already taught her that.

Burnham and his stepson climbed the broad, gracious staircase to the second floor, then sauntered along the corridor to their room. Each had a different reason to feel not just pleased, but self-pleased, as though they had created their own luck.

"What's our room number?" he quizzed.

"Two-eighteen," Nicky promptly replied. He knew the importance of locating yourself at a hotel, while you were traveling. However temporary a home it was. The adults had impressed on him the value of swift attachments.

Burnham opened the door onto disaster. The sight of his stricken wife stilled his cheerful greeting after a half-strangled first syllable.

Lucia sat, stone white, on the edge of the bed. She looked up to them both, her cheeks streaked and blotched, icy eyes rounder than ever, rimmed in red. His wife looked harrowed, like someone in a painting of the damned.

"Nicky!" she cried. "Oh, Nicky—your father—"

She reached out for her son to run into her arms, a rare gesture, and for an instant Burnham felt the strong urge to hold his stepson back to protect him from whatever would follow. His last opportunity to offer himself as a shield; there would not be others. Burnham sensed that, even before hearing the news.

He would have released Nicky's hand, but he did not need to, the boy tore it away to fall into his mother's arms, and the hot urgency of an embrace he did not yet understand.

IT HAD BEEN true for so long already, and she had not known. Weeks. Weeks! That haunted his wife almost as much as the death itself. That she *hadn't known*.

"Why didn't they cable?" Lucia asked repeatedly, to which Burnham continued to reply that they had been traveling, and how could the Brownriggs have known where to cable? "There I was, having lunch with Nancy in Chicago and Gawen was already gone! And I didn't *know!*"

She was in shock, and Burnham was sympathetic, but eventually he blurted: "It wouldn't have changed things, honey."

This effort at comfort caused further eruption. "What a horrible thing to say. You don't understand—you can't. Not to have *known!*"

So he tried instead to hold or somehow console Nicky, but that road, too, was blocked. The child had retreated into a precocious silence and was unreachable, bewildered by the noise and drama but seeming to stand apart from its content. Nicky did not cry. Burnham had not known his stepson to talk about his English father, unless occasionally

Africa came up in a conversation, at which point he sat up and paid closer attention. The boy felt a connection to that far-off continent, Burnham had seen that.

In the room, after her initial outpouring of grief and protest, Lucia looked up to her husband with a practical question. "What am I to do? What should I do? Shall I send a telegram?"

Miraculously, he gave an answer that struck his wife as helpful. "Write his mother a letter. There's no reason to cable."

"To Lady B? Not—to both of them?"

"The letter you received came from his mother, didn't it?" He could not bring himself to use her cute nickname.

"Yes."

"Then reply to her. Write to Gawen's mother."

Not someone ordinarily to take direction, in this instance Lucia promptly obeyed. She sat down at the desk like a diligent student, or the finishing-school girl she once was, found a few sheets of hotel stationery, and composed a note directly. Tears pooled shallowly in her now blue eyes—they did change color, depending on her mood—but writing seemed to settle her, and she did not pause or cross out. The other two in the room fell out of her awareness altogether. Nicky, seated solemnly on the bed, examined his arrowhead: felt the sharpness with the tip of his index finger, then made light, experimental lines on his arm with the edge. Burnham thought of telling him not to, warning him he might cut himself, but the boy was concentrating so fiercely on this invisible writing on his body that his stepfather was loath to interrupt. The act seemed to calm him. Burnham resolved to let him be and instead gazed out the window at the fast new city around them, all beige and mud-colored and slathered in sun with, in the foreground, a silvered train on the nearby tracks. In a different moment Burnham would have pointed out the locomotive to Nicky, had him guess where he thought it might be headed.

"There."

His wife had finished. It had not taken her long; she was efficient in her communications, wrote almost every day to family or friends or admirers worldwide, in Burnham's impression, and this note now took its place with all the others, almost as though she had shed its meaning, on completing it. She went to the bathroom to freshen up—"I must look a fright"—and prepare for a broader outing.

She left the letter out on the desk, and Burnham scarcely hesitated before reading it. He glanced at Nicky, to see if he needed to fabricate an adult reason for such an intrusion, but the boy remained sealed off, in a private world.

THEY CONTINUED WITH one last day of their so-called holiday, exploring Albuquerque and meeting friends of Lucia's, or more precisely, people she was eager to know. Burnham insisted they make a short excursion to see the petroglyphs, though ancient sites tended to inspire indifference in his wife, and she was not fond of climbing. Burnham thought that Nicky's arrowhead might have sparked an imaginative interest in other, older peoples, and he was right—the boy found the indecipherable marks on the harsh and reddish rocks intriguing.

"What do they mean?" he asked.

"That is still being studied," his stepfather answered. "Perhaps one day we'll know."

Lucia changed toward John after that. Their life together in Pasadena was stained, and became unwearable. Burnham decided later that Lucia had already been on her way to changing in relation to him, the signs were certainly there (those ugly midnight words she had spoken, after an unsuccessful coupling, which he'd shudderingly tried to forget). Gawen's death hastened the distance. The loss, rather than drawing the couple closer, as a grief sometimes can, opened a wider chasm between them. He did not understand anything. He had no idea of the world she had lived in. She felt Burnham should simply *know* what it meant that Gawen had died, but he didn't, as Lucia made abundantly clear. If, in the nearly two years since their hasty elopement, John Burnham felt he had vanquished the unknown Englishman who was his rival—in America he was vanquished, anyway, though in England the couple remained legally married, which he had tried not to think about—the baronet's son was now wreaking a cold, posthumous revenge.

Lucia brought out stories she had never told before. How funny her first husband could be. "He was a terrible teaser. He did make me laugh." His humor had not been mentioned until now. And she had no need to make the analogy explicit: Burnham was well aware that she found him overly serious, slow to follow her jokes. The Englishman had been a novelist, of course, and Lucia mentioned that several well-respected people in London had predicted to her he would one day write something "very fine indeed." She spoke wistfully of how she and Gawen had both loved dogs—it was an early bond between them—and of the adorable Sealyham terrier puppy he gave her one Christmas that she named Opal. Burnham was not a man for dogs, one of the few items he had been firm on from the start, and to his relief Lucia's parents kindly took Opal off the couple's hands, renaming her Mitzi. Another in the growing loss column in his wife's ledger.

When he was not feeling bruised or belittled, Burnham could understand these changes in his wife's volatile heart, as he knew that losing someone raised them in value on the emotional market. It was unfightable. The more surprising difference was Lucia's sudden affection for her former in-laws. After two years of bitter commentary about their scheming and manipulations—particularly in relation to "Lady B," who according to Lucia had not disguised her skepticism about Lucia's capacities as a wife and a mother—there poured from Lucia now an authentic sympathy for the Englishwoman's loss of her son. "She adored him so much. You've no idea, John. He was the light of Lady B's eye." She had handled their wedding so graciously, Lucia now said, even if the Brownrigg parents had not fully approved of the couple's marrying so young. And how beautiful the wedding itself was, in "a sweet little Somerset church," like a picture from a storybook; it was all so charming, and in spite of the parents' doubts they had appeared genuinely happy for Gawen and Lucia. Hopeful even. Her second husband had not asked for these details and could have contentedly gone on without them, but that, of course, did not stop her.

Burnham's responses were the wrong ones. An appreciative chuckle at a long-ago witticism of Gawen's; brow-furrowed concern for Lady Brownrigg; speculation that Nicky's grandmother must want to see her grandson now more than ever—that last in particular lit a blaze of anger in his wife and closed the conversation down for days. Lucia found new ways to criticize Burnham. How could he pretend to know what life had been like for her and Gawen in London? (He didn't.) The people they met, the worlds they moved in? She diminished her husband in nearly every exchange they had, and it becomes wearying for a man to have to keep rebuilding his own stature. Burnham was more sensitive and worldly than his wife would ever give him credit for, but if the challenge was whether John Burnham Jr. had ever been presented at court, then—well, no, Lucia had him beat there.

A half year later, February 1939, news came that Sir Douglas Brownrigg, Gawen's father, had died, too. Suddenly, while traveling in France.

And that really was the end, for Burnham and his wife.

Now out came stories about "Jim," as this English aristocrat was mysteriously called, how amusing he was, how much he had always liked Lucia and had fun joking in mock German with her, how Lucia felt he was just about the only person she had ever known who could speak to her father, the alarming baron, on equal terms. It was clear, when Lucia said this, that she was perfectly aware of the degree to which Burnham was cowed by Victor von Borosini. (And why not? The man had the glare of an executioner.)

"To see Jim and Father together," Lucia said. "That was one of my favorite things."

She shed new tears over Jim's untimely death and wrote again to Lady B, though this time Burnham did not have the opportunity to read her condolences. Lucia was keeping things private, by that point. She had struck up a friendship with a man named Engel, and any letters from him, Burnham noticed, disappeared instantly.

It was John Burnham himself who ensured that the *Los Angeles Times* received the information he knew would interest them. Lucia waved her approval when he told her he would alert the paper. Local son makes good. The subject of the story, a little boy he used to refer to jokingly as Master Nicholas, was moving on from his former fondness for his stepfather, sensing the winds of change in his mother's sentiments, perhaps, or simply from his own developing awareness of his altered status.

PASADENA BOY, 7, TO RECEIVE TITLE OF ENGLISH BARONET
Nicholas lives with his mother and step-father, Mr. and Mrs. John
Burnham Jr., 3575 Yorkshire Road, Pasadena

WHEN THEY SPLIT, not long afterward, Burnham found himself
wondering whether in the future Lucia's views of her second dismissed
husband, would also mellow to something softer, as they had with
Gawen. Or would Burnham have to die, too, before she could bring
herself to be kind about him?

He had served a purpose for Lucia. She no longer needed him. Nicky
might have, but if so, no one would ever know. In his own second, happier marriage Burnham would become a loving stepfather to two older
girls. But even then, in his happy new family, he sometimes missed the
friendship he had had for a couple of years with a little round-faced
boy—who had already traveled great distances, for a child so young.

September 4th, Sunday 1938

From The Alvarado
Fred Harvey
Albuquerque, N.M.

Dearest Lady B,

You cannot imagine what a shock your letter was to me. As
we were traveling no mail was sent on regularly and therefore I
got your news days late. No words can possibly help you nor can
much but your own wisdom. Thinking only of what Gawen was
spared and that now he is really happy. They aren't very comforting while we who live feel the loss of him so keenly but what
else have we but that sort of consolation.

I am more grateful for our child now than ever before, and
although I couldn't love him more than I do already, I shall feel
somehow as though he were also Gawen. It is impossible for me
to express to you in a letter how this has affected me but I regret so terribly that our life had to run the course it did. Gawen
would have been so proud of Nicky and in time he would have
loved him I feel certain. He is all that Gawen wanted himself—

and by that I mean he has the qualities that Gawen thought lacking in himself and hoped Nicky would have. I am only glad that the shock of this will be over for him quickly and that as it had to be it was now while Nicky is still so very young and incapable of realizing what it means.

I hope that when you are able you will write to me more fully but I know that now you are unable to. If only I could be of some help to you Lady B. Please believe that I would gladly do anything in my power to help either you or Jim through these awful days.

Where is Gawen to be? And would you understand if I asked for something of his? The cigarette case I gave him, or some belonging of his—It is so very hard to believe, and all the years have melted away bringing back the past of seven years ago when we started out on our life together. I wish so very much that we could have seen each other again and somehow I had always thought we would. There was a bond between us even through all we went through and my letters from him in Kenya I saved with all his others.

Please do write to me again when you can. I wish that I could tell you how full my heart is and believe me

Lady B when I say

My love to you and to Jim,
Lucia

PART THREE

✦

A Life in Ukiah

I was something that lay under the sun and felt it, like the pumpkins, and I did not want to be anything more. I was entirely happy. Perhaps we feel like that when we die and become part of something entire, whether it is sun and air, or goodness and knowledge. At any rate, this is happiness; to be dissolved into something complete and great. When it comes to one, it comes as naturally as sleep.

—WILLA CATHER, *My Ántonia*

1.

SOMETHING COMPLETE
AND GREAT

✦

I DID FEEL THAT WAY, AT THE RANCH: PART OF SOME-thing entire.

There is a scattering of people I can still talk to who spent time at the Circle C. I have a particular connection with them, the way polar travelers feel with one another, or people who have climbed Kiliman-jaro. You've been washed by the same wilderness, and it's changed you.

If my dad, with the unlikely jostlings together of his personality—hippie and aristocrat, Beat writer and lumberjack—always seemed poised to become a fictional character, then the place he settled with my stepmother, those freeing unpeopled acres, offered from the start to be put into stories. Los Altos Hills, where I grew up, and Palo Alto, where I was schooled, gradually transformed into "Silicon Valley," a made-up geography where guys in garages had sparked a new industry and devel-opers began ripping up apricot orchards to build McMansions for the newly moneyed. After the turn into the new millennium, the phrase *tech billionaire* would become popular, a locally grown cliché.

Those changes desiccated my imagination and got me out of there quicker. When we were young, and not petting chickens, the Yu girls and I had played imaginative games outside across the open hillsides and by poison oak–choked creeks: we were usually orphans, as in all the best kids' yarns, escaping a blizzard or a mean aunt or sometimes, until Mrs. Yu scolded us that it was anti-German—she was consistent in her stance against prejudice—the Nazis. Soon enough, there would not have been anywhere for us to hide from the Nazis anyway, because fences were going up, property lines began to matter, and Los Altos Hills mutated into its mature identity as a real estate phenomenon. We put away childish things and took our tale-telling elsewhere.

"The future always looks good in the golden land," Joan Didion, our state's great essayist, wrote in *Slouching Towards Bethlehem*, about Californian amnesia, "because no one remembers the past." This seemed true of the self-erasing semi-agricultural countryside I grew up in, but up north at the Circle C—with the weathered, musty schoolhouse, the abandoned shack on the edge of the woods, the half-hidden abalone shells—you could get a feeling of an older time, an earlier California. The ranch had wild creatures, real or invented, and at night the crazy density of the Milky Way stretched overhead. You could find deep, true quiet there. And what *wasn't* around you proved at least as important as what was: no television, no traffic, no stores, no school. No others. People left you alone, and the woods were endless.

I loved it. If the chance to spend heat-baked days and starlight-scattered nights at the Circle C was all my dad had ever given me, that would have been enough.

2.

GROOVY KIDS

✦

MY DAD AND VALERIE MOVED TO THE CIRCLE C IN 1972, and lived off the grid there for nearly thirty years, with trucks and books, Valerie's piano, my dad's typewriter, and for road maintenance, an on-again off-again tractor he called Little Rhino. I used to think it was Nick's own playful nickname for the vehicle (he was an inveterate nicknamer), but I found out recently it is branded that way.

Friends and guests came for stretches of time, sometimes the younger of his Brosies, Peter, and occasionally his kids, but mostly the two had just each other for company. Plus the dogs. Plus the cats, though they were outside cats, so mostly standoffish, even the cute calico siblings Valerie named Fish and Ears, who featured in tales I penned when I was up there in the summer.

Around them: bears, redwoods, loggers, deer, mountain lions, old-timers, scorpions, rattlesnakes, quail. Bobcats and buzzards. Free spirits and weather. Downhill from them a mile or so, a river. The Circle C was no longer a working ranch in that they kept no livestock, but it did take a lot of work to live there. Nick and Valerie were without power—the fridge the single appliance that ran on propane, though eventually in the latest years they had a generator—and flow from the taps depended on the waterlines staying clear and the tanks in the forest supplied from deeper springs. There was no phone or nearby neighbor in case of an emergency. The iron potbelly stove was the central beating heart of the weathered nineteenth-century homestead, but if you wanted a shower, hot water relied on a good fire burning in the kitchen stove. Though we occasionally went to the ranch in the muddy, near impassable winter, mostly my brother and I visited the Circle C in summer: sweltering hundred-degree days, when my stepmother closed the shades to keep the sun out, chores had to be done by ten before it got too hot, and we played hearts to make the time pass during the long afternoons, snacking on radishes, cheese, and Triscuits, with scallion chasers for my dad. The heat reliably subsided into cold nights, whether starrily clear or damp with marine fog that had climbed over from the Pacific, and in the evenings we sat by the stove for warmth, reading by light of kerosene lamps. I got through all of *Anne of Green Gables* there. (Valerie got me started on that series, L. M. Montgomery's heroine the first of countless Annes in my life.) My dad generally went to bed early, after a quantity of wine, though if he had drunk enough, he occasionally sat at the upright piano, its top stacked high with my stepmother's Chopin and Mozart sheet music, and banged out some improvised boogie-woogie. My dad's blues moniker, he told me, was Fats Brownrigg. He once paid a fee at a small do-it-yourself recording studio and cut a record. Sadly, Fats Brownrigg's single is lost to history.

There was only one summer, early on, that my brother and I spent at the ranch with other kids. Three siblings with weird hippie names, their mom a friend of my stepmother's; and Adam, a boy my brother's age, son of Nick's buddy from Pasadena days. Nick and Bob had been fatherless boys together, and tennis pals in school; then Stanford undergraduates; then young men who got married and coveted, each in his way, the other's wife. The two marriages unraveled according to the mores of the time, Nick and Linda's with absolute abruptness, the other one later and more messily, after an extended Updikean love triangle on the East Coast. It was Bob, by then an English professor at Rutgers, who officiated at the 1971 wedding of my dad and Valerie on Mount Tamalpais, everyone wearing colorful clothes, as the occasion demanded. Grooviness prevailed. No children were in attendance, though surprisingly, Lucia was. Dress code was for bare feet, but I doubt my grandmother complied.

My dad wrote about the summer social experiment at the Circle C afterward to another close friend, the New Mexico writer and editor Gus Blaisdell (also a charismatic teacher, and described by the comedian Marc Maron as "the guy who changed my life on all levels"):

We had a month of children—or was it, simply, six different television stations blaring full volume simultaneously? A month of noise, chaos, SHIT EVERYWHERE, a year's supply of dishes every morning but, finally, for all my grumping, fun. Groovy kids, after all, Michael and Sylvia, Pam's three for a few weeks and, at end, Bob's son flown out from New Jersey.

I got along with Bob's son Adam, who wore a yellow T-shirt with HONDA on it and had a special affinity for Little Rhino, but not so much with the other kids, who used creepy slang and seemed San Francisco–mean. But there was only squabbling, no brawling. We slept outside, drank root beer, got dirty. We competed over who got to lie in the hammock that hung between two cherry trees, picked blackberries to put on morning bowls of Life cereal, ended each day with countless burs in our socks, and endured a case or two of poison oak, which grew along the borders between the grassy hillside and the woods. None of us got bitten by a rattlesnake or a scorpion or a black widow, though, or hacked a finger off while chopping wood for kindling, or crossed paths with a bear. We played games, including out-of-its-element croquet (a sport better suited to a manicured green, like the one at All Soul's College where we once played, with Philip), and endless fetch with their lovable black Lab, Buck, whose origins Nick described in the same letter:

> Our butcher, for instance, not only cuts us monster steaks, he also laid his son's Black Lab on us (didn't feel right keeping dog in house all day) and Mr. Buck-Buck is a super-duper dumb, loyal, beautiful, growly (towards strangers) pesty (with his fucking sticks always dropped on your bare tum or slobbered onto your lap) affectionate, eminently real dog-dog.

IN THE SURVIVING photograph of all of us from that August, grinning in our T-shirts and long hair and paisley pants, we look like a sunny, ragtag seventies group that could have hopped on an old school bus and toured around like the Partridge Family, if any of us could sing.

Fats Brownrigg could have been our band leader, though I probably would have preferred Shirley Jones.

3.

THE ANXIETY COMES

✦

THERE WERE NO OTHER SIMILAR SUMMERS, AND I DID not take any friends to the ranch until I was a senior in high school. What parent would have allowed it, even if they hadn't known that Nick let us take turns standing out on the truck's running board for short stretches of the drive on Low Gap Road, the lucky kid holding on to the sideview mirror to keep balance, too thrilled to mind swallowing mouthfuls of dust? That he taught us how to use a chainsaw, or ride Valerie's motorcycle? It would not have occurred to me to invite a friend to be hosted by a parent not like any other parents I knew. My dad drank and smoked, had no job, might talk about drugs or women, swore freely. The summer of all the kids visiting, maddened by the "noise, chaos, SHIT EVERYWHERE" described to Gus, Nick hauled a few of us in front of him one day to lecture us on not leaving used towels on the bathroom floor. "Not cool," he growled. "When you do that, it's like saying, *Fuck you!* to whoever comes into the bathroom next after you." The *Fuck you!* upset my child self, and I stayed sulkily mad at my dad all day. I did make sure to pick my towel up after that, though.

Our visits became even more irregular. We were in England a lot of the time, and then Mike was off to college. My brotherless stays at the ranch when I was back in high school in California were mostly difficult, until I got the idea of going up with company, people who could act as a buffer. My dad would find it harder to berate me about my suburban softness or naïveté if someone else was around. I went up once with my (unrequited) high school crush, a lean, soulful boy who played in a band, with whom I had always felt a kindredness about the wild. We camped out under the stars and had one of those perfect platonic moments you can write about later (though in the fiction, we probably would have slept together); afterward he was on his way to Idaho to build a cabin for himself and his new wife. He was the first of my friends to marry, and the first to divorce. After I graduated from college, I went to the Circle C with a writer friend who collected new words like keepsakes as Nick showed her around the ranch; I remember her jotting down in her notebook "smudge pot," the rusty funnel-shaped oil burner in one of the older vineyards, there to ward off frost. In my early twenties, I appeared at the ranch after a cross-country drive with a Florentine friend, who had taught me colorful Italian swear words on the road trip and was unfazed by Low Gap Road, used as she was to navigating dirt roads in Tuscany. Her appearance sparked a few memories in Nick of his time in Florence with my mother, though only good stories. He left all the bad ones untold. My mother filled in a few later, like her forever-stinging embarrassment that their disapproving Italian neighbors noticed the vast quantity of gin bottles stacked up in the couple's trash.

When I lived in London in the 1990s, I used to write author profiles for the American newspaper *Newsday*, and I had the luck to talk to writers I admired: Jane Gardam, Graham Swift, Penelope Fitzgerald. In East Anglia I met the great Rose Tremain, whose imagination has taken her all over—back to the English Restoration, into the sensibility of a transgender boy, and across the lives in London of recent immigrants from Eastern Europe. After our specific book-related interview, she and I spoke more generally about writing fiction, why we did it. She was interested to hear that my grandfather had been a novelist. Tremain's taut explanation of the alchemy we share has stayed with me: "The anxiety comes, and we answer it by making sense of our lives through telling stories." I'd never before heard it put so succinctly.

Getting at Nick, when I started writing about him for this book, required me to blur him into Frank, and myself to Sophie. Mike became Tom, Valerie Adele. (The most difficult to rename were the dogs.) The move simultaneously provided distance and proximity: I could see my child self at arm's length but the parent from closer to, like a perspective-altering telescope. It's why Gawen wrote best about callow young Val in sections narrated indirectly by Val's married lover, Camilla. He could see himself lucidly through Camilla's imagined eyes: "the two clear aspects of his character—his snobbishness and his misanthropy, his shyness and his insolence, his girlish recoil from fame and his theatrical flamboyance." It is a curious perk of the job that you learn things when you make yourself a character. Flaws are more easily made out, purplish white under fiction's black light of scrutiny. You find them on the page, and then know your own weaknesses a little better. Over two novels, Flannery Jansen taught me more than I ever knew before about why, and the many ways how, I am an imperfect protagonist.

My dad was not inherently frightening, but I was intimidated by him, and did not know what to expect; I was not inherently frightening, either, but he was wary of me, too. It is clear when I dip into his midlife letters—and for that matter, his life—that Nick's children did not take up a lot of space in his view of the world, so to draw him it is essential to picture him without us around. In his sixties and seventies, that prevailing self-reference began to change, especially after the death of his mother, who had so hobbled and obsessed him. With Lucia gone, Nick was liberated to pay a bit of attention to the descendants who had been piling up—he had seven grandchildren by the end, counting my stepson, whom he always welcomed. Before all that, when I was in my self-righteous twenties and Nick in his fifties, a point when the phrase *abandonment issues* had a vogue in the pop-psych lexicon, I had a festering anger about all the ways my dad *had never shown up* for events in my life. It would not have made an interesting story. Festering never does.

I used to wonder how this person who had come of age in Pasadena (not so different, in its wealthy and mostly white demographic, from Los Altos Hills) knew enough to make a go of this rugged life at the ranch, alongside my stepmother, who had grown up in Detroit. With Valerie, I think her strength, determination, and dexterity got her through: she could do almost anything she put her mind to, was a quick study, not someone ever to quit. And she loved Nick. They were in it together.

The dad I had known before the ranch had been a San Francisco guy—Giants fan, restaurant goer, apartment dweller on Telegraph Hill. On special occasions he took us to Ghirardelli Square. He had nothing of the country about him. But I learned, in the course of Nick's last years when his life finally opened to us, more about the high school he had gone to near Santa Barbara, the place where Lucia had sent him to get him out of her hair, or away from her busy New Mexico household with her third husband and younger sons. *Boarding school* sounded fancy to me, English even, so I had always pictured a place with uniforms and snobbish propriety—like the girls' school I had gone to in Oxford, maybe. It might have had Longriggs wandering the corridors, or like Mike's school been a place that made the boys wear ties. In fact, Midland, the school Nick attended, was the antithesis of what I had imagined. Started in the 1930s on the grounds of a former cattle ranch near Los Olivos, an area famous now for its vineyards (and as the setting for the movie *Sideways*), the school housed its boys in simple cabins heated by woodstoves, and in addition to scholastic learning they were taught to chop wood, build structures, and live close to the land. The school's mission emphasized self-reliance, participation in the community, and the safeguarding of natural resources. To us, Nick had nothing good to say about Stanford University, though he did root for their football team at the annual Big Game against Cal, but he remained loyal to Midland—and even reconnected, late, with people he had known there, one of whom claimed to remember Nick teaching him how to play the banjo.

The school's motto was *In robore virtus*, "Our strength lies in the oak." It is a cousin, if you want to see it that way, of the Brownrigg motto, *Virescit vulnere virtus*, "Valor strengthens from a wound."

The Brownrigg one is starker, though. You know. *Somber hues.*

The Winch

✦

SOPHIE DIDN'T LIKE GOING UP ALONE.

Tom was already at the ranch, though, so their dad was going to come collect Sophie in Ukiah, and then they would drive the last rugged stretch together to the ranch. Alone. Why had Tom gone already—couldn't he have waited for her? He must have been in a hurry to see their dad. That was never how Sophie felt.

It was always better to be with Tom on any of the crossings she and her brother had to make, county to county, parent to parent. They could play battleships or cards, or Tom could even tell Sophie to stop bugging him and punch her arm. It was hardly ever enough to hurt, and it was still company. When they were older their mother would get tired of the drive north and put Tom and Sophie on a Greyhound bus in San Francisco instead. She and her brother would learn the city sequence heading north on 101: San Rafael, Petaluma, Santa Rosa (where they switched buses, sometimes, allowing time to get a Coke or a pack of Wrigley's gum), Healdsburg, Cloverdale, and finally—Ukiah. Cloverdale sounded like a comic-book name, something you'd read about in the Archie stories, but Ukiah did not sound like anything. UKIAH—HOME OF MASONITE, read the sign as you entered town, and Sophie had imagined that to be a large concrete corporation, until her dad told her it had to do with cutting down trees.

The winter sky was gray and heavy as the road yielded before them. Sophie sat beside her mother in the passenger seat, head angled to look out the window. After the drama of the Golden Gate Bridge, when you felt you were sailing over the sea, there was a quick, dim tunnel. Now they passed a roadside strip with a liquor store, a pizza place, a motel. It was December. She and Tom were going to spend Christmas with their father for the first time. That was why Sophie had asked to come later; she had wanted to have her birthday party at home with her friends, other third graders, in a regular place with heat and electricity, before she went somewhere that had neither. The Circle C Ranch was like frontier times—like going back in time. Chopped wood for the fire. Light at night from kerosene lamps. No television. No phone.

"It will be an adventure," her mom said, trying to lift the pout off Sophie's face. "Your dad's place sounds kind of like *Little House on the Prairie.*"

"I never liked those books." There was something smug about Laura Ingalls Wilder's characters, as if they felt special for how hard their lives were. Sophie didn't buy it. She preferred books where girls dabbled in magic, altering reality. She had learned what it was to use telepathy, or have a familiar.

In Los Altos, Sophie befriended the gentle calico they had kept from the litter of the pure-white mother cat, five sealed kittens born on a blanket in Tom's closet. Lately, in the middle of the night, when Sophie heard a low growl outside her bedroom window—more moan than meow—she would wake just enough to sit up in bed and raise the screen, allowing the kitty to jump on the sill, then heavily onto Sophie, then down to the carpeted floor. There, in the dark, the creature would crunch, noisily, the bones of the mouse she had just caught, leaving in thanks for Sophie a heart or a kidney, which she had to clean up in the morning. It was a gross habit, but she had gotten used to it. You had to, with a familiar.

"I've put presents for all of you in a separate bag; you can give that to Adele when you get there. Your dad said you guys will be able to cut down a real Christmas tree together, from the forest! Doesn't that sound fun?"

Now, this was just weird: that her mother, who hated Sophie's dad with a deep, shuddering sincerity, was trying to sell Sophie on this holiday with him.

"I wish we were just having Christmas at home, like normal."

"Well"—her mother looked ahead, addressing the freeway—"your father and Adele asked if you and Tom could be with them this year, and it seemed a reasonable request."

Reasonable! When had reason ever come into it? There was no pattern to the back-and-forth, no rhyme or rhythm. They lived at their mom's, and now and then saw their dad. Before their father remarried, Sophie was not even allowed to spend the night with him, though Tom was. The difference went unexplained.

"What are you going to be doing?" Sophie turned away from the blurry landscape to look at her turtlenecked mother, whose smooth, ringless fingers were steady on the steering wheel. For the first time, it occurred to Sophie that if she were not with her mother at Christmas, then her mother wouldn't be with her, either.

"Oh, Leo and I are taking a trip down the coast, to Los Angeles," she said lightly, like a trip with her companion was so boring it was hardly worth telling her daughter about it. "We'll come to pick you up together, a few days after Christmas."

The four adults together in one place, at the same time? That did not bear thinking about, either, so Sophie didn't. She stared back at the silvered flats of the bay that had appeared beside the freeway as they neared Petaluma. The bay got around—there were fingers of it everywhere, and wherever it reached, birds came along, too, like ants that gathered around a smear of syrup across a tabletop. In the water's cloud-mirroring marshes stood a stately white egret, while overhead coasted a gray cluster of gulls.

"I bet this was Tom's idea." Sophie voiced her suspicion in a deliberate mumble, so her mom leaned sideways.

"What did you say? Tom . . . *what?*"

"Nothing. It doesn't matter. Never mind," Sophie answered, until they were both exasperated.

"Tom asked to go up right after school got out, to have more time with your father." Her mom, through telepathy, guessed Sophie's complaint. "You asked to stay here longer, so your friends could sleep over on your birthday. Remember?"

Maybe, but only Jeannie had slept over because Karen couldn't. The birthday party was okay, but Jeannie talked too much after the lights were out, not about anything interesting. It would have been funner with Karen.

"Believe me, I didn't *want* to do this drive twice in a week," her mother added, the tone sharpening. "I wanted to make it work for both of you."

As if Sophie were somehow at fault for how far away their dad had moved, after he and his new wife left the city to settle "out in the boonies," as Adele had said, laughing, when Sophie first visited the ranch last summer. Sophie waited till she got home to ask her mom what *the boonies* were. Adele had long blond hair like their mom but in her sturdiness, her practicality, her ready laughter—her ability to joke with but also stand tough against their dad, when necessary—was completely different. Sophie did not yet love Adele, but she didn't hate her, either. For now, her strongest feeling was curiosity: How would this story go? Having a stepmother placed Sophie in fairy-tale territory, like Cinderella. In Disney movies, the stepmothers were always wicked—the two words were practically glued together—and she felt a shimmer of glamour, telling kids at school she had a stepmother now. She was the only person she knew who did.

Sophie sank into silence. Her mom called it sulking and scolded her for it, but what was so bad about just not talking? She stared out the window, thinking about Tom. He pulled them more toward their dad, and Sophie had to follow. It was always her following him. He was a nice big brother mostly, but he thought she was weird, playing pretend games, whispering lines to herself as she wandered across the unfenced orchards near their home. He would never have understood about having a familiar. If she wanted her brother's company, she had to do what he wanted: play baseball or basketball, or balloon volleyball or else a wrestling match on a rainy day when they had to stay inside. Three years older, Tom was stronger than her, so usually the wrestling matches ended up with Tom sitting on top of her, pinning her arms to the ground. "Say 'I submit.' Say it!" he'd demand, until Sophie, defiant but helpless, eked out between clenched teeth, "I submit." Only then could she get back up.

The car was quiet for a long while, apart from the conversational hum of passing traffic. Her mom turned up the classical music station as they passed Santa Rosa and came into more open countryside. "Look at all the new vineyards, honey." It was a gentle, peacemaking effort. "There didn't used to be so many." The hillsides her mom gestured to looked like fields lined with crooked soldiers all yoked together into one large, gnarled army.

They were headed to the Denny's in Ukiah. Denny's was their usual place for what Sophie heard them call "a handoff," as if her mother and father were robbers trading loot. Long into their adult lives, and with their own established families, Tom and Sophie each nurtured a revulsion at the mention of Denny's. "No!" Sophie once barked at her sweet kindergartner son, who saw the bright yellow-and-red sign for the diner chain and asked if they could pull off the road and have lunch there. "Not Denny's. We're going to Arby's."

But at just-turned-eight, Sophie was years away from being in the driver's seat. She made no decisions. It was Denny's again, as always, and after Denny's Sophie would be with her dad, alone, going up to the Circle C.

FRANK GOT INTO town later than he'd intended. Before he left, he made oatmeal on the kitchen range for Tom so that Adele did not have to deal with that, and gave his son chores to do later. Refilling the kerosene lamps with fuel—"Be careful when you use the funnel not to spill; Adele can show you"—bringing more logs inside to stack up by the living room stove so they wouldn't get damp outside. There was a winter storm in the forecast; you could feel it hanging in the dense, expectant air.

After a few miles, Frank was stopped by a downed tree on Low Gap, the unpaved county road that wound its way through forested hills into Ukiah from their property's private access road. On a good day, the drive into town took an hour; it was not much more than thirty miles' distance, but there were curves and switchbacks over the ridges that separated their ranch from Ukiah's flat, populated valley. On a bad day something intervened, in this case a suicidal tan oak from a steep roadside bank that had given in to the night winds and now sprawled, melodramatically, in Frank's way.

"Shit," he complained to an uncaring universe. This was why they

kept a chainsaw in the back of the truck; it wasn't the first time Frank
(or Adele) had had to hack through some obstacle. He thought of
walking back on the road a hundred yards to the Yellow House to
see if the hippie Keith was around and wanted to give a hand. Keith
and his mellow wife, Debbie, their nearest neighbors, lived at that
roadside house with an uncountable number of kids, getting educated
who knew how. Keith wasn't one of those macho logger types who
would sneer at Frank for seeking help; still, Frank imagined having
to get into a conversation about picking up Sophie, which could raise
the specter of a suggestion that their two families could meet up over
the holiday, and Frank was not up for that god-awful possibility. (If
he had that kind of social capacity, he'd have stayed in San Francisco.)
Frank rarely talked to anyone about his son, and never his daughter, and he was not about to start. Instead he got out the chainsaw
and filled the forest with its whiny racket—these machines always
sounded like they were criticizing you. With thick work gloves on, he
sawed the dead oak into manageable segments, then lugged the logs
and brush to the road's shoulder, sending it all back to the land. Frank
was a good citizen, thoroughly clearing the way for the next guy. It
took time, and he was annoyed and hungry by the time he finally
arrived in Ukiah.

He had planned to get to the post office and do the grocery run,
but both would have to wait. If he went to Groff's now, he'd shop for
stupid stuff, prompted by appetite, and end up scarfing down chips or
jerky in the truck. Besides, Adele had suggested he and Sophie go to
Groff's together. Frank had learned the hard way that you had better get the cereal they knew, the goddamned right brand of cookies, or
there would be mutiny in the ranks. Nothing was more irritating than
kids who would not eat perfectly good food put in front of them, but . . .
Okay, Okay. It was Christmas, Mr. Grinch. "Let Sophie find some stuff
at the grocery store," Adele had advised Frank the night before. "That'll
help. Get her to pick dessert." Funny how she had better instincts than
he did sometimes, and she didn't even have kids.

Frank went to the Black Bart, the bar and grill that had opened the
previous summer inside the Palace Hotel. Ukiah had been a logging
hub—and Masonite was still the main game in town, jobs-wise, as the

sign at the outskirts let you know—but the town was trying to pretty itself now, to appeal to San Francisco exiles like them. Plaid was making way for polo shirts, beer for Zinfandel. Frank and Adele walked the fine line of city people who move to the country, swallowing their snobberies about food or culture but embracing the changes as they arrived. When the local players scraped together funds to rebuild its theater, Frank and Adele went to its opening show, *You Can't Take It with You*, and Frank threw his laughter up into the auditorium's new rafters; and when the whiskey-voiced gal who ran the bookstore said she planned to expand, Frank and Adele egged her on, stocking up on yet more paperback mysteries and hardback biographies, their company on long, TV-free evenings. On a downtown corner near city hall, the Black Bart beckoned urbanites with its broad wine list and novelty snacks like bruschetta, a fancy word for pizza toast. Frank was happy to take that bait.

As he entered the saloon doors from the foyer, Frank saw on the facing wall the familiar sketch of the bar's mustachioed namesake, a famed Gold Rush outlaw who ripped off stagecoaches but never killed anyone, and occasionally left behind a poem as a souvenir:

> I've labored long and hard for bread,
> For honor, and for riches,
> But on my corns too long you've tread,
> You fine-haired sons of bitches.

"Hey, Hank!" Standing behind the long bar, drying beer glasses, was one of the co-owners, a man with a blue chambray work shirt and a thick dark mustache that competed with Black Bart's. Jim had decided long ago that Frank was *Hank*, and Frank had decided not to correct him.

"How are you doing, Jim, man?" Frank had hoped honey-haired Naomi would be around today to flirt with, with her big hoop earrings and suggestive laugh, but no luck.

"Not too bad. Storm's coming, though. Not far off now. It will be quiet in here today." Frank hadn't yet figured out Jim's backstory—gay? There was some of that around here, too. Jim's business partner was a lean, solemn man with the self-containment of a Zen priest, a foil to Jim's boisterous front-of-house persona.

"Yeah, Low Gap's going to be hairy getting home. I already had to chop up an oak that was across the road, coming in." Frank took a seat at a round, dark wooden table. "But I've got to go pick up my daughter in a while. The ex is dropping her off."

"Good luck with that!" Jim's voice had a barked edge; maybe that was part of the backstory. "So what can I get you? A scotch? A double?"

Frank laughed and ordered a Cabernet and a cheeseburger, medium rare.

If he had gotten to the post office, he would have had something to read while he ate; though he would have found the seed catalogs irresistible, and that wouldn't have been a great look, city bumpkin thumbing through shiny pictures of peppers and lettuces while he sipped his cab. There would be a separate one just for roses—those were for Adele, with the outlandish names and post-impressionist colors. Frank lit a cigarette to give himself something to do, resigning himself to more weather talk, but mercifully a group of lawyers came in from the county courthouse and Jim had to see to his customers. When the burger came, Frank slathered it with ketchup and mustard and attacked it, and having made quick work of the first glass, he raised a hand to Jim for a second. After that he'd better quit. He might find Louise easier after a couple of glasses, but not Low Gap, and Jim was right: the rain would start soon. The sky was grouchy, glowering. Frank knew how it felt.

DARLING DENNY'S. "OH *goodie*, Daddy!" he said aloud in a falsetto once he was back in the Toyota. "It's *Denny's*! Can I have some *pancakes* shaped like *Mickey Mouse*?"

His daughter did not actually talk that way. He was just warming up.

He saw Louise's white Volvo wagon in the parking lot, and his stomach oozed acid. In its suburban smugness, the car itself seemed to judge him, find him wanting as a parent. *How will you fuck up next?* it asked. Frank pulled the truck in a few spaces away and checked his watch. Two thirty. They had agreed on two. Well, he was close. Frank lit another cigarette and smoked for one defiant minute, then crushed the lit end in the near-overflowing ashtray below the radio. What a waste of a Winston. He coughed, got out of the car, braced himself. If he had been wearing a holster, he'd have patted his gun.

Louise and Sophie sat in a curved booth close to the front, Louise facing the entrance, keeping a sharp eye out for Frank as she drank her coffee. The girl had her back to the door. There was a flicker of eye contact between his former wife and him. *You're late.* She did not have to say it. The girl had finished eating, it looked like; the plate was pushed away, her chin resting in her palm, elbow on the beige Formica table.

"He's here."

"Hello, Louise," Frank said, then put a hand on his daughter's rolled shoulder. The kid startled, as if Frank were the last person she was expecting. She turned, her eyes wide. Her little button nose twitched. He smelled of cigarettes, he realized. Well, tough shit. He smoked.

"Hi, Soph, old girl." Frank gave her shoulder a lighter pat, and her face relaxed. Somewhat.

"Hi."

Frank gestured for her to come out of the booth. She looked at her mother, who nodded, and having been given the green light, this girl, Frank's daughter, scooched off the red plastic seat and stood up. They hugged each other. It could have been awkward—Frank was tall, and big, so of course he loomed over her—but in spite of everything, once his arms were around this strange, often inaudible person, he felt better.

Until he saw her shoes. Tennis shoes.

"She has boots packed, right?" he said over her head to Louise. "There's a big winter storm coming."

"It was sunny when we left Palo Alto." Louise shrugged and folded her arms. Maybe she knew it was an idiotic answer. "We were going to get her new boots after Christmas, in the sales. She doesn't have any that fit her anymore. So—no. Just tennis shoes."

"I have to go to the bathroom," the child announced, scuttling off like a beetle darting for shelter in the woodpile.

Her absence freed Frank to tell Louise in his best, deliberate tone, that a *storm* meant that it would be *rainy*, which would in turn cause *mud* that was likely to get all over *nice white tennis shoes.*

"For God's sake, Frank, don't lecture me. I gave you Christmas. If those shoes aren't good enough for her, get her new ones! There are stores in this town, aren't there? Or do you have to order everything from the Sears catalog?"

Louise had been pretty once. She had been beautiful. Frank couldn't see it anymore, though she had the same long ash-blond hair—the Scandinavian in her—and the same forest-green eyes; but all her mouth did around him now was sourly frown, and it was hard to imagine that they had ever kissed, let alone that he had ever wanted to fuck her. He watched Louise's cool authority as she summoned the waitress for the check and paid it. It wasn't the right thing to be recalling in this context, but Frank found himself baffled, mystified even, at the unfathomable human contradiction, that a woman who had once been so intensely, distractingly attractive to Frank that he could not get her out of his head, thought about her night and day as the cliché had it, once went to the airport on a lovesick afternoon to watch her plane take off for her home in Los Angeles—that this same woman could have become so flatly ugly to Frank now. Repellent. She inhabited just a body, a sexless, nothing body. How could it be the same person? Frank looked away and muttered, "Fine." By the time Sophie emerged from the bathroom, after an improbably long time—as if she had been waiting for a break in the parental weather—the adults were quiet and stiff and ready to be rid of each other again. Each re-meeting, the two of them had gone through this kind of micro divorce, ending in the relief of separation.

Outside, by the Volvo, the rest of the transaction was straightforward, time and place arranged for the pickup in six days, and a reminder that Tom had to wear his retainer at night, to which Frank nodded as if he had already known this. Louise handed Frank a paper bag containing wrapped presents for under the tree, including, he could see, one for Adele. That was decent of her. Inevitably, he was empty-handed, as far as offerings for her and Leo went.

Louise turned to their daughter. Her face warmed and gentled, briefly lovely again, as she told Sophie to have a good time, and a Merry Christmas, and fun with Tom. She leaned in to murmur a few private words and give her back a soft, loving stroke followed by a kiss on top of her mousy head, but to her credit did not otherwise play the moment up for drama. Sophie fell gratefully into her mother's embrace and heaved one sob into her chest. Louise held her closer. Frank wondered how they would ever extract the girl, as he stood beside the two of them, waiting with the luggage like a stalwart bellhop.

THE TRUCK WAS quiet. Sophie knew better than to say anything, but she rolled down the window to get rid of some of the smoke smell. In blew a cool, busy air that had a thickness to it—a noise, almost. Like one of those whistles that only dogs can hear.

They drove up toward the center of town, where Frank told Sophie there were errands to run before they headed up to the ranch.

"Hey, old girl," he said suddenly as they approached a Baskin-Robbins. "Do you want to get some ice cream?"

She wasn't exactly hungry after the Denny's hamburger, but what was she going to say—no? Not to ice cream, she wasn't.

"Okay."

They each got a cone, and Frank let Sophie get sprinkles on hers. They sat in the pink plastic chairs inside that were stuck together at the base so you had to eat side by side, and they watched newspapers get blown up and down the sidewalk. Frank joked that it made him feel like an elephant, trying to sit in those tiny chairs, and Sophie smiled, in between licks of mint chocolate chip. Ice cream was one of her dad's best things; before he married Adele, when he still lived in San Francisco, their trips to Ghirardelli's for the occasional sundae were a mile better than all the other outings with her and Tom that had to do with sports: baseball games, bowling, three-person football on a stretch of grass by the bay. The only part of that Sophie liked was her dad saying to her *Hut, hut—hike!* Before she scooped the ball back to him through her legs.

From Baskin-Robbins they went to the post office, where he extracted mail from a glass-fronted box, like a safe, that he opened with a key. Sophie stood stiffly, arms held out like a robot's, with the job of holding "the keepers" as her dad sorted, throwing out junk, making a happy face at the catalogs and a cartoonish frown when he handed her bills. By the time they got back outside, drops flecked the air. "No more dawdling, Soph," he said, though she was sure she hadn't been. "We've got to get back on the road. Double quick now, through Groff's!" At the cramped, busy grocery store, he sent her off to the cereal aisle alone—Sophie knew he would let her get a sugary variety her mom would never have allowed in a million years—while he picked up meat, bread, jugs of wine. They met back at the register, where a top-heavy lady with a lined face reached, without his saying anything, for a carton of Winstons.

"My stars, you look just like your dad!" (This made Sophie uneasy. Did she?) "I didn't realize you had one so young, Frank." She started talking about her son's heart problems while she rang up and bagged the groceries.

Then Sophie saw a familiar impatience shadow her dad's eyes. "Well, Jean," he said when he found an opening, "we're going to try to get up Low Gap ahead of this bear, the worst of it anyway."

The rain was pelting down by then, hard diagonals from a fed-up sky. Her dad pretended to squeal in horror while he got wet stacking the grocery bags in the back, and he let Sophie stay dry in front. When he climbed back in, he pulled the door behind him with a holler of relief and shook off some of the rain like a dog. Sophie giggled.

It was new, getting her dad's attention. Tom wasn't around, or Adele, so he had to talk to *her*. Ordinarily, Sophie would have tagged along behind Tom, satisfied to be invisible. Maybe visibility had advantages she hadn't considered.

Low Gap Road started as a normal road. They drove past the cemetery and the high school, then a square building labeled WASTE WATER TREATMENT. "All the things nobody wants to think about," he joked. "Death, teenagers—and shit."

Sophie flinched: that wasn't a word said aloud at home, especially around kids. She tried not to mind. The swearing went along with the truck, the overflowing ashtray, the afternoon ice cream: just different. "It's not a choice, Soph," Tom had once told her before they went up to visit. They had been waiting with their luggage under the carport because their mother could not find her car keys and had gone back inside to look for them. She was agitated, so Sophie had been, too—head down, eyes salty. "You don't have to choose between them," her brother repeated, almost angrily, in response to her unhappy face. Sophie thought Tom was crazy. People had favorites with anything, like baseball teams. For Sophie it was no contest: their mother was the beautiful, gentle, familiar one. But now, as the rain slammed down and the wipers beat their drummed response, Sophie thought that might have been Tom's point. There was no contest. Maybe no one was keeping a scorecard. Maybe it was just different leagues, Mom and Leo, Dad and Adele.

The truck hit a surface edge and bounced, and the tires made a damp, sandy sound. "Well, that's it for the asphalt." Her dad hunched closer over the steering wheel. His voice was cheerful, though. He looked like one of the guys on the ads for that new brand of soup, called Chunky: bearded, rugged, wearing a denim jacket lined with fleece. "It's all dirt road from here to the ranch, Soph. Buckle up!"

They never wore seat belts in the truck, so she guessed he was kidding.

Up the initial gentle slopes, her dad told stories about Butch, the black Lab, and their new dog, a Siberian husky they got from a friend in the city who realized he couldn't keep her because she liked to run. She had been called Blue because of her amazing eyes, but Adele had changed her name to Sundance, as a partner for Butch. Her dad glanced at Sophie to see if she got the reference, which made the truck veer close to a scraggly outcrop of brush that scraped along Sophie's window, like a monster trying to get in.

"Jesus! Okay. Eyes on the road, old man." He maneuvered the long gear stick, and the truck growled back as he downshifted.

They jolted over big stones and through deep ruts, but Sophie felt secure, high up in the cab, even as some curves were enough to push her against the car door, or else pull her back toward her dad. If she thought of it as an amusement park ride, it was kind of fun. That was their other good adventure together, in Santa Cruz. Sophie was too short to do the scary rides Tom loved; he had to do those alone, or else with their dad, while Sophie waited for them at ride's end. But she was tall enough for Logger's Run, when her dad pretended on the slow climb up not to know a steep fall was coming. "Oh *noooooo!*" he shouted as Sophie's laughter burst out of her, along with the screams of other passengers, as down the car plunged for a few thrilling seconds, before braking at the bottom, then drifting into the mellow finish. A white teenage kid would help you out; you were soaked, but that was the idea. It was hot, so the wetter you were, the better.

Outside, the rain was heavy and loud, a stampede across the roof and windshield. The truck's atmosphere darkened. Behind a thousand clouds, the winter sun was getting tired. Night was not far off. Her dad concentrated. The drumming on the roof lessened as they entered the forest and trees intercepted some of the downpour.

"You can't see it very well now," he said, gesturing toward her side of the windshield, "but over there is an incredible old madrone. We call it the Michelangelo tree, because it looks like a sculpture—"

Sophie looked as they banked into a blind hairpin turn, before the truck juddered to a sudden stop.

"Shit!"

Another truck, bigger and more beat-up, was face-to-face with theirs.

"God bless it," her dad muttered, then reversed slowly into the wider outer bend of the road. He put the car in neutral, then faced the front, rolled down his window; the other driver did the same. A white-haired guy with a grizzled chin, Giants cap almost covering his eyes, a tarped mound in the back of his truck. He wasn't smiling, but he raised a denim arm, his hand up in thanks, or warning. Her dad answered with a similar half salute.

"Never seen him before." He tracked the guy's progress over his shoulder. "Bad day to be driving Low Gap, unless you live out here. Excuse me for a minute, Soph."

He cut the engine, got out, and walked to where the dim woods slid down the hill from the side of the road. His back was to Sophie, and she tried to understand what he was doing—could he really smoke a cigarette in this rain? Sometimes he got out to do that—before she saw that he was fiddling with his fly. He was going to the *bathroom*, right where she could see him! She closed her eyes and imagined she was somewhere else: back at her birthday party at the pizza place, when they brought out the cake that her mother had baked, SOPHIE 8! spelled out in chocolate icing across the vanilla surface.

"Nature called." Her dad climbed back in. "Okay, let's get going. No more fun and games. At least in the dark"—he switched the headlights on—"you get ample warning when someone is coming at you. That's the trade-off."

He tried the radio, but it was just static and he gave up. For a while all Sophie heard was the truck's noisy engine, whining and grumbling, and the slippery sound of it skidding, now and then, where the mud was slick.

"This is a hell of a rain." He slowed at one point, peering out the splattered window. "Can you see anything on your side, Soph? A tree stump, some branches and logs?"

She lied and said she could. Everything looked like branches and logs.

"That tree was down across the road when I drove into town this morning. I had to saw it into pieces so I could get in to meet you. That's why we keep a chainsaw in here."

The thought flitted across Sophie's mind that if he hadn't been able to make it into town, she could just have turned back around with her mom and gone home. This ride wasn't as much fun anymore, and now she had a new worry: that other trees might fall around them, or even on top of them, trapping them like a bug.

"How much longer?" she asked in a small voice. She knew her dad hated that question, but she couldn't help it. She missed Tom.

"This is the access road, right here!" His voice blended tiredness with relief as he maneuvered the vehicle up a sharp, steep left-hand turn. The road got, if possible, even rougher. "We're almost there, old girl. The access road is just a few miles long."

That sounded like a lot.

In the dark, Sophie slid around on her seat as the truck slid around on the road. "At least here," her dad grunted as a branch whipped against his window, "I know where the hairy parts are."

If this was meant to make Sophie feel better, it didn't.

Sometimes they slowed down, and she felt the wheels sinking into a puddled rut before escaping; sometimes he announced, "This one is better to take head-on," and they accelerated over some unseeable obstacle, and she bounced in her seat so hard her jaws clacked together. Then they were on a curving downhill, the truck slipping again, its back half seeming to want to go in a different direction from where her dad was steering. Sophie heard a dull thud and felt a tilt to the left. The wheel had gone somewhere it shouldn't. They stopped. Her dad's muddy boot pressed the gas, and he gunned the engine, yelling, "Come on, now!" the way he would if he was scolding one of them. "Goddamnit, come *on*!"

It didn't, though.

The truck would not come on.

You could feel something was wrong. Like the time Matt Wheeler fell off the monkey bars, and you just knew when you saw his arm bent in a weird way that that was not how an arm was supposed to look. Sophie had not forgotten Matt's pale, freckled face as he lay in the bark chips, whimpering.

Her dad pumped the gas, the engine whined, the tires spun. The truck pulled but went nowhere.

"Fuck!"

That was the worst one. The absolute worst. Sophie chewed on her lip.

Her dad tried once more, then shook his head, took his foot off the gas, and pulled the brake instead. He sat, staring ahead into the plastered darkness, headlights illuminating a muddy brown bank. His thoughts were moving, though the truck was not.

"It's too far to walk in this rain. Plus, we can't leave the truck here, with the groceries." He shook his head. "Goddamn it." But this was said conversationally, almost—not really to Sophie, but to some invisible witness, the one he had for his jokes and his outbursts, his life commentary. "Wouldn't you fucking know it. Tonight, of all nights."

Sophie's eyes stung, and she felt the crack in her windpipe that meant she was going to cry. She tried to be silent so that he might not know, but the tears came to her eyes and then jumped out, like parachuters from a helicopter, one after another, braving the fall.

"We're going to have to use the winch, Soph." He wasn't looking at her, but at least he remembered she was there. "It's for when you get stuck like this. I've never used it before, but this is why we have it. We'll use the winch."

Sophie nodded, as if she had been promoted to copilot and had to sign off on this maneuver. "Okay," she said in a scratchy voice.

She had heard of a *wrench* but not a *winch*; maybe they were similar.

"There's no Triple A out here, you know." Her dad's voice got louder with a familiar sarcasm. "It's up to us."

She got the gist of what he was saying. *You may never get home again.* Sophie swallowed and tried to get used to the idea: that this—the truck, the rain, the mud, the dark, her dad—could be the whole of her new life, from now on.

ABOUT HALF AN hour in, soaked, cold, half-blind, Frank did not see how they would get out of there. As he stood on the downslope behind the back of the truck, struggling in the rain with the equipment— heavy gloves on, he had already torn the grocery bags as he impatiently rearranged them while getting what he needed—Frank pictured the truck sliding back over him, crushing him in the mud, while his daughter sat unknowing up in the cab, ignorant contributor to his death.

The rain did not ease up just because Frank was out in it working his ass off. No pity from the weather gods, who didn't give a shit. Just him and the elements and a stuck vehicle, a mile or less from home, with a young kid who was no help at all. Sophie sat, hunched and miserable— and dry, by the way—and while Frank recognized that he could feel sorry for her, the weight of her sulky presence made him feel sorrier for himself. His jacket was drenched and heavy on him. Denim lined with sheep's wool was not your friend in a downpour. He had failed to put a rain slicker in the back of the truck before he left. Adele should have reminded him.

Frank had started smart, finding the manual for the winch, then returning to his seat, where by flashlight he tried to get through his sodden head a clear plan of what he had to do.

"You don't want to start the motor until you have the thing set up right," he told Sophie, whose eyes got rounder. *He has to read the instructions* was written in alarm across her smeary face. "We're going to use a tree to help us get out of the ditch, to help lift us out. See?" He shone the light on the book's line drawing, to calm her and himself. It depicted a sturdy man attaching a cable to a tree. The task looked doable. Frank resembled that man. Of course, the picture omitted the pitch blackness, the relentless rain, the scared kid. It wasn't a hundred percent realistic. "So I'll hook the back of the truck to a tree, get the winch going—and that should do it."

"Okay." The girl's voice was faint but had a hint of spunk in it— enough for Frank to catch. He appreciated that.

In the circumstance that met him, his truck's back wheel stuck in soggy clay down the side of a poorly maintained dirt road—the county never came out here to grade it, that was up to Frank and Adele—there was no perfectly placed tree waiting for Frank to attach the winch's hooked cable. Frank spent a good fifteen minutes, or it might have been an eternity, of *fucks* and *goddamnits* trying to loop the hook around something solid and strong enough to get them out. Close to the truck was a spiky manzanita bush that kept poking him, taunting him, as he unwound the canister. The cable was long and he felt like a cowboy, lassoing it around an oak tree first, fastening the hook to the looped cable, before he realized, visualizing what would happen, that he needed a tree higher up the slope.

What did you do if the perfect tree did not present itself? What the hell did you do then?

"Soph." He knocked on her window. A frightened face turned to him. He would have growled *I am the ghost of Christmas past* had he been in a better mood. Instead, Frank wiped rainwater out of his eyes, then gestured for her to come. "I'm going to need your help. Hop out."

She did, and the rain flung itself at a new target. He saw her startle at its intensity, but at least she had a real coat on, unlike Frank. He handed her the block flashlight and said, "Hold this, will you please, while I try to see if the madrone up there might work." He trudged up the bank to the madrone, spinning out cable as he went, but it would be the same problem with that trunk—it was not high enough above the level of the wheel. There was a thick branch that might work, ten or twelve feet up. He tried a few times to throw the hook around it, issuing *goddamnits* after each failure. How could he get more height?

"Do you want to try, Soph?" He assessed her as she held the flashlight steady. It wasn't completely far-fetched. "I'll help you up. All you need to do is throw the hook over the branch. You see? I can do the rest."

She didn't say *Okay*, but she didn't bolt, either.

"Good girl. You'll be fine." He planted the flashlight in the mud, to act like a spotlight. "Here," he said, lacing his gloved hands together and bending down to offer them. "I'll hoist you up, and then you'll try to get this end, the hook, over the branch." She was reluctant to put her muddy tennis shoes on his hands, but he told her it didn't matter. He lifted her up with a grunt, she tilted her face into the rain, and—blindly, had to be—threw the hook. Over it went.

"You got it!"

Frank gave her a damp hug when she squelched back down, and she stood up a bit straighter, with pride. Quickly he fastened the hook onto the round eye and pulled the cable taut around the thick branch. He told Sophie to stand far away, way up the road, and he gave her the flashlight for company. Then he jumped into the driver's seat, pulled the cable taut, turned on the motor, and eased the tires side to side, gently, as it said to do in the manual. *Please hold*, he said to the branch, the winch, the cable. *For God's sake, don't fucking break*. It wasn't exactly a prayer, though God got a mention. The madrone tree offered its strength to leverage the truck out of the ditch, and with an effortful heave on the reverse, the truck climbed back onto the surface of the road.

Sophie shouted something happy out in the rain, and Frank felt a huge surge of sweat, or adrenaline, pouring off him. He shouted, too.

The overwhelming wish was to immediately speed home the last mile, but first they had to get the cable back off the tree, rewind it, re-store the winch. He kept the truck running. The grocery bags had all spilled out, packs of ground beef over Gallo wine and gorpy cereal, but Frank didn't care. Sophie sat back inside, shivering, but shiny with relief. When Frank rejoined her he was slathered in mud and smelled worse than a wet dog.

"Jesus *Christ*," he said, in summary. "We did it, Soph! Okay. Onward."

They did not speak, and Frank looked nowhere but at the road till they were going down the home stretch, he heard Butch and Sundance barking, and finally saw the dogs out on the battered lawn in front of the Circle C, with two dim humans behind.

There was Tom on the porch, Adele next to him wrapped in rain gear. By this point she must have been pretty worried, and not good at hiding it; she had probably been on the edge of getting into their other truck to drive out to find them. From the house the kerosene lamps gave a friendly, subdued glow. It would be toasty in there, the stove hot. There was plenty of wood, especially if Tom had done his job.

The girl looked at Frank, her face dirty but with a pretty light in her eyes. She wiped her cheek with a wet sleeve. Frank would get the stuff out of the back in a minute, with Adele. Normally, he would have made Sophie do it herself—he wasn't her butler—but tonight he would give her a break so that she could get inside and warm up.

She made no immediate move to do that, though. Her brother ran out in the downpour, calling something. You could not hear anything over the rain. Tom lunged for the passenger door, but before he could get a purchase on the handle, the girl instinctively locked it. She turned to look at her brother through the spattered glass, with an expression Frank could not see, as her back was to him. It was as if his daughter were not planning to go anywhere else that night after all. She seemed to want to stay right here, as if the truck had, like a wild animal, become her friend.

Caught in Its Throat

✦

ONE OF THE GREAT THINGS ABOUT DOGS WAS THAT THEY didn't care if you drank. You could be a fuckup or a paragon—it was all the same to them. Frank reached for the brandy on the upper shelf, opened it, sniffed it reflexively, poured some into his coffee. Butch sat in the kitchen watching him without judgment. His tail gently thumped against the cracked linoleum floor.

It was morning, or night for others but morning for Frank, who got up in the deep dark of four o'clock to do the dishes from the night before, while listening to talk radio. There was a terrific Black guy in San Francisco who kept the night owls company. Frank loved Ray, talked back to the host while scraping onion crust off the iron skillet, or sponging clean the wineglasses and the aluminum cups he and Adele used for water, though Frank rarely touched the stuff. It had no flavor, and gave him a sinister feeling.

The beat-up red transistor sat on a grimy windowsill above the sink, perched beside a jar that held rattles from the snakes he and Adele had killed—Frank mostly, though his wife had bagged a few. Frank was tall, so he had to stoop over the old enamel farmhouse sink; they must have put it in eighty years back, when people were shorter. It meant he was face-to-face with the scratchy voices from the radio.

"Ray, come on, man, shut him down!" Frank didn't like it when Ray tolerated some crackpot or bigot mouthing off but chimed in—"That's right, Karen from Hayward. That's right! Absolute"—if he agreed with the caller. When the ads came on, Frank hummed to the jingles for car insurance or mattresses, or he might actually sing along, after he had downed his first cup. Butch did not mind that, either.

Ray's show ended at five. Afterward Frank built up the fire, went out to the porch to get more wood and bring it inside to stack neatly by the stove, and fed the dog and countless cats outside. The cats ate from one big metal bowl Frank placed up on the brick outdoor oven, under the walnut tree—it was a free-for-all up there beneath the thick green leaves—but Butch had the luxury of eating indoors. Next up was heading out to bury last night's compost in the garden. They kept having to fortify the metal fencing around the patchwork half acre of roses, lettuces, berries, potatoes, since the deer were greedy and would not quit. Don't be fooled by those pretty wide eyes: they were cunning animals, and they wanted your food. The sun was waking up now, turning the sky a pale rose behind the wooded ridge as Frank troweled down, packing their green leavings in the dry earth, then covered it over like it was evidence. He did a few other garden chores, weeding and watering now while it was still cool and could do some good. August: the heat would be punishing later. Water, as well as the ability to concentrate, would evaporate.

Frank came back into the living room to brew the second pot of coffee on the stove. He saw the unopened letter from his daughter where he had left it the night before, near the kerosene lamp by his armchair. She was living in another country. England. He would read it later. He'd get to it. Butch stood by the screen door, silently, and Frank let him out.

The nautical clock chimed a quarter before eight, which made it a safe time for Frank to bring a virgin coffee up the narrow flight to Adele, still in bed. He kept it quick, before she could smell his breath. He wasn't in the mood for nagging. "Heyo," he murmured, his all-purpose affectionate address. Adele's breathing was light, awake, but she chose to stay asleep-looking. He retreated.

Downstairs, Frank made his way to the john at the back of the house, past pine shelves groaning with cookbooks, almanacs, and volumes about country living—how to skin a bear or raise a windmill, guides to mushrooms, birds, plants that would heal you or kill you or get you high. Butch pattered along behind, as if going to the john were a group outing; on an impulse, Frank grabbed the bear book off the shelf, then closed the paint-chipped door in the dog's face. "Privacy, old boy," he said. "You understand."

When he was finished, Frank felt lighter, energized. He had had an idea. He reshelved the bear book, then opened the low adjacent door that led down to the cellar.

The naked yellow bulb came on with a pull of the string, illuminating casks of fermenting grapes, rusted unused traps, guns. Frank's underground den of vice. All he needed was a felt-covered table and a box of cigars, but they lived too far from any neighbors—a couple of miles as the buzzard flies—to pull a poker ring together. The only card game he and Adele used to play was hearts, on sweltering afternoons, but that was only when the kids visited, which wasn't often. You needed three or four for hearts.

Frank got his Smith & Wesson, checked that he had ammunition, and climbed back up the rickety wooden flight to find Butch waiting right there, golden light falling on him like an anointed beast in some renaissance painting. Saint Butch. Comforter of lost souls.

The dog knew what the gun meant; his black Labrador heart sped up, and he shuffled on his paws from side to side in excitement. They were going hunting! There was no better news for Butch, and in his small, purpose-built brain, the fact that it had been years since the last such outing did not register. Butch was ready. His master stumbled on the last step up and lurched forward, the rifle lurching, too, causing the dog to back up, lowering his head, as if this were part of a game.

"Ha!" Frank caught his balance without falling. "Had you fooled. You thought I was going to bayonet you."

Butch Lab-laughed at his joke, it seemed to Frank—mouth open, pink tongue out.

"Good boy." He patted the dog's head with a heavy hand, then stage-whispered, "What do you say, Butch Cassidy? Safari, eh? Shall we?"

Butch barked once, a yelp of anticipation, and Frank cuffed him, lightly. Adele hated barking.

"Discretion, old boy." He turned the cuff into an ear-scratch. "We don't want to rouse the natives."

Frank grabbed a flannel shirt from the back of a chair, took a last slug of spiked coffee. *Don't look, God.* Not that he believed in God. You could substitute *a higher power* if you wanted, they said. It was bullshit, in his opinion. A trick you tried to play on your own mind. Of course, an alkie's mind was weak and trickable—that's why those AA people did so well. They were like a cult, the way people followed them. That Jonestown psycho had gotten his start around here, not that many years ago. Look where that led.

Frank led the way out the screen door, holding it open for Butch, then closing it gently to avoid the slam. He leaned the rifle against the side of the house, put on his shirt, then grabbed his gun, and man and dog made their way into the yawning, pretty daylight, hoping to do a little killing. He had an appetite for it.

ACROSS THE OLD, uneven porch and a ceremonial rectangle of cropped, toast-brown grass was something like a driveway, inhabited by trucks. To the right, the road out, which wound past the vineyards Frank had planted along the blond hillside; to the left, a scattering of weathered outbuildings, projects past and ongoing, creatures, wood-piles, unfinished business.

That morning, Frank went left.

The road was their sole escape route if there was ever a fire—though they'd likeliest fry in place—and led to civilization. An hour's rugged drive to reach Ukiah, land of milk and honey, meat and ciggies—and booze. Social necessities, too: gossip, news, flirting with checkout girls or barmaids. Yawing about politics or the weather, which mattered here in a way it hardly ever had in the city. Others, those still living in San Francisco, sometimes called Frank and Adele back-to-the-landers, but Frank did not kid himself. What they got from the land was a partial existence, and town made up the rest of it.

No town today, though. Nor did he seek the upper meadow near the driveway's curve, the place he once started an outing with the kids, in promising open daylight. Frank turned left out of the house, aiming to reach the forest faster. He passed first the splinter-strewn wood-chopping area and called out, "Good morning, scorpions!" in a soft falsetto, like a louche call girl. He noticed an ax planted blade-down in the chopping block, left from yesterday morning's stint splitting kindling, and tsked. That was a poor show. "Put your bloody tools away, Officer." Frank's English colonel often found growling fault with his own habits, issuing praise when called for, but more often censure. That wasn't how they had built the empire, leaving axes lying around for others to pick up. Poor show.

He held his rifle loose in his left arm, the safety on (even with a morning buzz on, Frank made sure of that). He found himself entertaining. He contained multitudes; there was a cast of thousands in there.

He passed the scratchy dirt and sparse grass where the barn used to be, and a tumble of images fell through his mind. Last spring, Frank and Adele held the opposite of a barn-raising, inviting neighbors from surrounding ranches and friends from town for a liquored party of destruction. The weathered gray building was probably seventy years old—built by the homesteaders who first cleared this patch of land in the 1910s or '20s—and it leaned, ominously. Long ago, lightning had blackened part of the angled roof, and he and Adele agreed it was a firetrap and they should get rid of it. The old ranchers had kept feed in there, and probably livestock over icier winters, but Frank and Adele weren't shepherds and they weren't cowboys, so the barn had become an outsize junk haven. It would be safer to keep their tools and supplies in the small old schoolhouse, right across from the main house, instead.

The barn wasn't as easy to tear down as Frank had expected. Old things wanted to stay in place, Frank learned; they did not want to be hobbled or erased. Luckily, Dave Simpson from Goat Rock Ranch and old man Cliff from Kerr Springs, along with Cliff's son Matt, knew what the hell they were doing. They led the charge. Matt was one of those sober scolders—after he gave up booze (one DUI too many), the rugged forty-year-old didn't seem to want anyone else to have fun drinking, either, and thought it his place to make sure they didn't. So don't come to a party, tight ass! But Matt turned out to be indispensable: he knew about construction—he and Dave had built on some of the big ranches in the area—which meant he also knew about deconstruction and how to do it safely, which did not, as it happened, involve taking chainsaws to random support beams or doorjambs.

Frank had known it was more complicated than that. One clear-eyed morning he sat down with a legal pad and pen to try to diagram it at his cluttered desk upstairs, under the eaves, where he had pinned up photos of his and Adele's wedding day, on Mount Tam—long hair, bare feet, stoned smiles—along with an obituary of an English relative who had been admired by Winston Churchill. Frank's diagram was not worth much. He had no talent for art and scant instinct for geometry. It was all words with Frank, a cascade of language high and low, coinages and accents and even smatterings, here and there, of his mother's German. ("Jawohl!" he said under his breath if Adele was telling him what to do.) When Matt and Dave and Cliff came early, before the serious drinking started, Frank fluttered his paper diagram at them, then, feigning irony, folded it up and put it in his pocket. It was clear Matt, in his Marlboro Man getup, wanted to command the operation, and equally that Frank should let him. He swallowed his pride. So what if the guy had a rod up his ass? They did want the fucking barn down at the end of it, with limited casualties. That was the goal.

"Yes, Matthew. Very good, Matthew," Frank muttered now. Shards of grass were sticking up over the former floor, but bug-infested piles of ancient timber still lay at intervals, and they hadn't yet burned the remainder or hauled the rest of the non-burnable junk to the dump. An outside observer might wonder how much fire hazard had, finally, been removed. It had been a good party, though.

"Hello, dum-dums!" Frank hollered as the path continued down toward the chicken coops. He was far enough away now from the dozing Adele to make some noise. He clucked flamboyantly, and the birds clucked back.

If he hadn't been brandy-blurred, Frank would have thought to bring scraps from the bright pink plastic pail by the kitchen sink. The neon-green pail was for the garden, the pink one for the birds; kids' beach pails drafted into ranch duty, not that he had ever taken the kids to the beach, poor little neglected urchins. *Dial 1-800-OLIVERTWIST to make your donations now!* In the kitchen, the pink pail would be full of delicacies, wilted lettuce, tops and tails of green beans, melon rinds, eggshells—though there seemed something cannibalistic to Frank about hens devouring their own eggshells. His low opinion of the chickens was not just due to their intelligence; it was their iffy morality, too.

The birds crowded close to the wire fence looking for treats. Fat Rhode Island Reds, speckled Leghorns, bantam Japanese Silkies. Frank's daughter, Sophie, seeking objects of affection, treated the Silkies like kitty-cats when she came to stay. Once, worried the girl had gone missing, Adele had finally found Soph sitting cross-legged inside the dim light of the coop with a Silkie hen on her lap. Adele told Frank that the girl had been stroking its furlike feathers, the chicken's blue-black lids closed in a peaceful doze. God only knew what kind of mites she would get from the bird, though Frank did not worry about it. All part of the education his suburban kids got up here.

"I'm warning you, dum-dums," Frank said. "If I can't pull down a pigeon or some quail, I'll be back for one of you."

They continued to cluck and shuffle, lunging their heads either in deference to their master (ha!) or, more likely, keeping their beaks low to the ground to be first for a cucumber seed or an apple core. They seemed unworried by his threat.

"You think I'm kidding." Frank raised his left arm, loosely cradling the gun, and aimed it into the crowd. "Bang!" he called out. That didn't bother them, either. Butch had run ahead into the forest, across the concave dip that filled and became a pond in winter, so he had missed his master's show.

IT WAS IMMEDIATELY cooler under the canopy of redwoods, fir, and madrone, where solitude sheathed you like a second skin. The woods were full of creatures, Frank knew that, yet you felt more alone there than out on the hills, where anyone might see or swoop down on you from above. Here, enclosed by forest, the sky only glimpsable in patches, you fell into a philosophical feeling, as if you were the lone survivor of the apocalypse—a sense heightened by your dog having wandered off in his own pursuits. Frank heard his boots crushing leaves and needles, the forest's detritus. It made him think of the bills on his desk, the rinds in the pail, the box of empties out on the porch—all the other places where the sloughed-off and cast-aside gathered.

"Entropy."

He had meant to think it, not say it aloud.

Frank tried to return his focus to the task at hand. Snap into a heightened state of awareness, stay alert for wingbeats. Yet if he were seriously looking for birds, he had come to the wrong patch of land: he would have to climb toward the upper stretch of the road; they most often congregated near the edge of the woods, close to manzanita and pyracantha bushes, which needed sun to thrive. He thought of the time he had gone out with Tom and Sophie, years earlier when Frank had known less, traipsing up and down the forest along with the two dogs. They still had Sundance then, too, that gorgeous crazy husky mix. She was too independent to be part of the hunting team, really, but deigned to come along in case something interesting happened. It didn't, for an hour or two. They did not see any likely targets for so long that the kids had begun to get bored and restless.

Frank had gotten impatient, too. "Well, this is what real hunting is like. You don't always land something. We're not in Disneyland, you know. It's hard work."

The boy had gone quiet (the girl always was), whether mad or chastened it was hard to say, but soon after that, from yards ahead, his tow-headed son had whispered, "There, Dad! Look!"

Near an outcropping of pyracantha, a couple of fat pigeons sat on an overhanging branch. Frank gestured to both kids to get behind him; he wasn't going to undo the safety latch till they had. When he had the feel of them both at his back—their breaths, their tension—he planted his feet, raised the rifle, aimed, and fired.

A flutter, a drop, a papery thud. That sweet sound. Frank fired once more, but the second bird flew off into safer air. He lowered the gun.

"You got him!" Tom shouted, and ran alongside Butch to find the fallen body. Sophie was a few strides behind. When they got to the pigeon Tom hollered, "Butch, no! Drop it! *Dad*—Butch is trying to eat the bird!"

"It's fine! He's retrieving it. Let him do it." Not that Butch was the softest-mouthed dog, but it made him so happy to do it. "That's his job. It's why they call them Labrador *retrievers*." *You knucklehead*, Frank almost added, but he didn't want to lose the look of admiration in the boy's eyes. It was rare enough. Tom walked back toward Frank with pigeon-retrieving Butch: the dog looked proud, the boy almost jealous. "That's why they chase sticks and balls," Frank said. "You know that, right? It's bred into them."

Sophie hung back, picking berries and gathering them in her turned-up T-shirt, making up some game or story of her own. She was often in a private, imaginary world. Apparently distressed by the killing ("What did you think would happen, idiot?" said her brother. "*You're* an idiot," her timeless retort), she asked Frank if she could walk back on her own. Frank had said fine, pointed her toward the vineyard, and let her go. It wasn't far. He opened the leather game bag, eased the bird out of Butch's mouth, and fed the dog a treat from the bag, some bacon rind from that morning. Before placing the bird in the bag, Frank held it to show Tom, the crimson splatter on its soft gray chest, but Tom looked away, as if his father were showing him someone naked.

The berries in its throat that night.

Frank was getting hot now, tramping up an awkward diagonal toward somewhere with more light, more possibility of bird. He slid where the ground was still slick from the night's dampness.

"Shit!" He slipped. "Butch! Get the hell back here!" Like it was the dog's fault he had gone down on one knee. He held the rifle by the barrel, upright, as though it were a walking stick, or a scepter.

"Butch!"

Where the fuck . . . ?

"Goddamnit. Butch, come here!"

He could not hear his dog. Maybe a flicker? A rustle? But—no.

Frank should have eaten something before he left the house. That was dumb, coming out without eating breakfast. Hunting when hungry does not make you a better shot. It makes you sloppy, like the guy who left the ax out all night on the chopping block, where the dew might rust it.

The stillness was absolute. Frank did not have the urge to disturb it with the English colonel's voice, or one of his ad jingles. Everyone had gone home.

No. There was another rustle. Far away, intermittent, hard to tell what direction it was even coming from. Frank hauled himself back up, using the rifle. He cocked his head—like a dog, like the fucking dog he had who'd disappeared—and tried to listen.

Popping the berries out, at the sink.

Frank hawked from the back of his throat and spat. Nasty. Brandied, bilious, coffee-flavored wad of spit. Would it have killed him to bring an apple with him? A handful of nuts? When he went out with Tom and Sophie that day, eons ago, Adele had made sure they had chocolate chip cookies she had baked, wrapped in a paper towel, in the game bag. Adele was not a housewife, and Frank was the more inventive cook of the two, but she had more of a feel for what kids liked to eat than Frank did, despite the fact that the kids were his, not hers, and she had none of her own. (They had not tried again after that one time, and what happened. The bleeding, the loss.) Adele's cookies turned out to be game changers, during a low point after almost an hour or so, when the kids were flagging and sulky and on the cusp of rebellion.

He heard the rustle for a third time, a creature running through undergrowth with a labored, snorting breath. It was bigger than a dog. Frank's stomach growled, the sound of indignant emptiness. He was dizzy for a second; then the advancing noises grew louder, and the animal within Frank knew that coming toward him was some kind of danger.

HE PLANTED HIMSELF next to a redwood. Not a great-granddaddy—there was no old growth around here, too many loggers had tromped through over too many years—but a yards-wide giant, couple hundred years old maybe, fern and bracken in its shady shelter. The rough-ridged trunk, the color of dried blood, generously lent its solidity to him.

Frank looked through the sight's black cross and saw only trees, undergrowth, fallen branches: browns, reds, greens. The snorting had stopped. He wondered if he had heard it at all. What was real?

"Butch?" he murmured.

The creature came closer. Frank caught a blur of it fifty yards away, zigzagging, heavy, angry. Frank found a moving dark object in his sight line, moved the barrel ahead slightly in the direction of movement, and fired.

The kickback made him stumble.

The animal was neither hit nor put off. It kept coming at him. Faster now. Angrier.

Okay, Okay.

Frank leaned slightly against the redwood. He thought the animal might trample him, like a bull, as if he were in Pamplona again, where he'd once gone in his twenties. (Tough guy, right? Right.) Butch had abandoned his master, it seemed; it was every man for himself now, and every man's best friend, too. Probably made his way back to the ranch. Dogs had crazy compasses inside their boxy heads—Frank had seen it a hundred times, you could be miles down along the river and they knew how to get home. Clumsy human intelligence tried to think its way through landmarks—noting where the light was coming from, what side of the trees the moss was growing, Frank had read those tricks in books, whereas dogs just felt it, where home was.

Home sounded good to Frank right now.

The animal—or animals, there might be two—had stopped. They knew a gun meant a hunter, but they had an advantage over Frank: they knew where he was. They knew *what* he was. He could not tell which blur was theirs; which undergrowth hid them; where their sharp-toothed mouths were open, waiting; what they were planning. His hands leaked sweat, and he weighed the wisdom of taking another shot.

He could not say he saw one or both, but he did see a darkness within an area of wider darkness. Shapes shifted. He raised his rifle.

Don't go hunting when you're hungry.

If Tom came back to the ranch sometime—he was in college now, back east, with even less reason to see his dad, but he would come back sometime, probably—Frank would have new information for him. *There are more creatures here than we knew.*

He heard a blood-chilling squeal. A warning? A war cry, or a cry from wounding? Had Frank hit one of them after all?

Frank's heart thudded. He thought of English hunters riding with flasks of whiskey at the saddle, and it seemed an oversight that he had no such flask. The grunting continued, and Frank's ear could not discern whether it was approaching or gaining distance. He heard the crackle and pop of the leaves on the noisy forest floor.

He lowered the gun. His mouth was dry. He felt sick to his stomach, thought he might retch.

The one he missed most was Butch.

FRANK LET TOM hold the rifle after Sophie left, but not fire it. He got his son used to the weight of it in his arms, showed him (with the safety on) how you aimed through the sight, and explained the strength of the kickback and what caused it. "Watch it, next time I take a shot." And the boy did.

He downed two more pigeons that day, which would have to be enough. They had more meat on them than quail did, and anyway there was something about shooting those scurrying crested birds as they made a break out of the bushes that did not feel like sport. Sophie might not even eat any of what they brought home, Frank thought; she could be a fussy eater and might decide she did not like pigeon meat, opting for the macaroni dinner he and Adele had agreed on as the alternate for nitpicky kids.

The sun climbed back down the ridged horizon. Tom was flagging, Frank felt ready for a glass of wine, and even the dogs seemed done for the day. Blond-mopped Tom was weighed down by the bulging leather bag, but he wore it with an almost comic swagger, as though the haul belonged to him.

They emerged from the woods on a west-facing slope just below a clearing in which Frank had created a makeshift chopping block and a woodpile a few years back. It was a place to chainsaw felled trees into smaller logs, for easier stacking in the back of the pickup. Here, about halfway along their access road to Low Gap, Frank and Adele once caught a handlebar-mustached guy poaching wood one summer, claiming not to know he had strayed from his own land; though if you came upon a logging area you hadn't cleared yourself, wouldn't that tell you something? Then it turned out he was one of the drummers for the Grateful Dead, the conversation got friendlier, and it all ended with Bill giving them backstage passes to an upcoming show in San Francisco. Frank and Adele never got there, but it was a nice gesture.

"Hey, this is where we cut wood!" Tom shouted, his relief audible at returning to the light, and finding a familiar patch of land. "Where you let me use the chainsaw that time."

"You didn't tell your mother about that, I hope."

"No."

"Good lad."

Tom followed the trampled grass tire tracks to the dusty access road. Unpaved, rutted, rocky—but you knew where it went, at least. Back to the ranch.

The walk from that point took longer than either of them wanted, though, and Frank grew thirstier with every downward slope and dusty rise. He changed his mind as they went, settling on a whiskey soda—something that would hit harder and faster than wine. He'd earned it, after managing this ritual. Dad and son go hunting. Stuff of books, right? Fairy tales? Well, it started out as Dad and son and daughter go hunting, because Sophie hadn't wanted to get left out, and why should she be? She was a ruggeder kid than she sometimes seemed, and besides, Adele could do with the break. His wife liked space around her—a lot of space. She did her best with his kids, she did great as a matter of fact, but by the end of a two-week visit, the strain began to show.

"Are we going to have these tonight?" Tom continued his tilted walk, counterbalancing the bag's weight.

"Sure. But we have to pluck them first."

"Pluck them?"

Frank laughed. "What do you think—we cook them as is, feathers and all?"

Tom shrugged.

Whiskey soda: Frank could taste it. He picked up his pace.

"You and your sister can do it."

"She's not going to want to. She'll think it's gross."

"Too bad."

Suburban kids. They didn't know anything. Frank remembered the first bird he had to pluck, when he was sent to that boarding school in the southern California hills, the one that taught boys how to build their own beds and desks. How to live in the country and be self-sufficient. Straightened you out, it was meant to, though whether they had succeeded with Frank or not was anyone's guess. There was a working farm behind the two main classroom buildings, he remembered, and there in a high-ceilinged barn Frank had plucked his first chicken. He had not enjoyed it, not at all, but did not feel like telling his son that story.

"The feathers get all over the place," he said. An advantage of having the kids around—Frank was learning this, a minor revelation since they did not come often—was getting them to do some of the more unpleasant chores. "Up your nose, even, sometimes. It makes you sneeze."

Tom laughed.

"It's not that funny," Frank said sharply, "when it happens to you."

HE DID NOT get a hero's welcome that morning.

Every time one of them left, alone, on foot, into the wilderness, a scenario was always going to float in the mind of the other person back at the ranch: *What if they don't come back?* It happened with Sundance, that wild, beautiful blue-eyed dog, who lit out for undiscovered country one day and never returned. One of the kids had gotten the idea the husky was half-wolf and repeated it as fact to anyone who would listen, but Frank was relieved Tom and Sophie weren't around when the dog split for good. Hours he and Adele spent, over days, driving the roads, pulling over at intervals to get out and holler *SUN-DANCE!* into the echoing hills, like two people performing a ritual call to their indifferent gods. Frank could not one hundred percent pretend he had never wished Sundance would vanish; the animal was fidgety and demanding, the temperamental opposite of Butch with a direct, chilly gaze that cut right through you. She saw your flaws and failings. But Adele was hollowed out by Sundance's disappearance—she had loved that dog—and in a mostly unspoken way, she blamed Frank for her final run.

"I had a hankering for bacon this morning," Frank said to his wife as he came into the kitchen. He had been rehearsing the line as he surfaced at last, sweaty and withered, down near the chicken coop. He said nothing to the dum-dums at all as he passed. "But I guess the wild pigs weren't in the mood to be breakfast."

Adele had her back to Frank and did not turn. She was replacing the brandy bottle on the upper kitchen shelf. She was tall, too, and could reach, and did not have to say anything to make him aware of the act. Frank had not hidden his tracks.

He continued on with the story anyway; you had to do that on the stage, too, as he knew from the plays he had acted in at the community theater. Even when you felt the speech was bombing you could not just stop, mid-delivery—there was no shrugging and exiting, stage left. Adele was not going to ask him what pigs he meant, so Frank would just have to explain that he heard a terrible racket in the forest and could not identify the source, though it was enough to send Butch home out of fear. (Adele would have been alarmed to see the Labrador come back without Frank, he knew that, a masterless dog as eerie a sight as a riderless horse.) He had decided to go for comedy rather than thriller as the genre of the story he told, since his wife already knew by now that he had gotten home all right and underlining the risk, and his own fear, would somehow not impress her but rather add to her exasperation. Worry was like that, once it was over: the remaining adrenaline only left you irritated.

"So," he concluded, "I did not manage to bring home the bacon." He waited a beat, in case she laughed. She didn't. "And now I'm starving."

"Well, the hens laid plenty of eggs." Adele had clearly done chicken duty while Frank was gone, probably to keep herself busy. The scrap pail was now empty, he saw, and from the coop's wooden boxes she had gathered a collection of beige and brown eggs, with one pale green, some still smeared with chicken shit or stuck with straw, nestled in a shallow metal bowl. "I scrambled a few earlier."

Frank looked at Adele, brows raised, risking a wordless invitation. His wife acted like she had no idea what Frank meant, returning to the living room with her book and her coffee to read by the stove. Butch was already in there, crashed out.

Frank found some cold cuts in the cooler and made himself a giant sandwich, loaded with ham, cheese, lettuce, mayo, mustard, pickles, and onions. He threw in a few hot peppers. Defiantly, he got the jug of Gallo from the fridge and poured himself a glass. Well, she drank the stuff, too: Why else did they buy jugs? No need for his wife to be so prissy about it.

She was absorbed, anyway, in the other room and could not see him.

He sat at the Formica kitchen table with his sandwich, and he wolfed it down with a Gallo chaser. After he finished, his breath was fire.

FRANK AND TOM reached the upper gate at last, and there was just half a downhill mile after that. Frank and Adele never used to lock the aged metal-slatted gate—that did not go along with how they thought of their open-armed, backcountry living—until the time a truckful of drunk kids, yahoos, showed up right outside the house, the pack of them in the pickup's open back, like dogs. Scruffy white high schoolers feeling tough, they were more stupid than scary, and the dogs' barking kept any from climbing out, but Frank stood on the porch with his rifle just in case, though he felt cartoonish, a little like Elmer Fudd. It was probably clear he had no intention of firing the gun. Adele muttered to Frank that she ought to give the boys some food to sober them up before they went on their way, but Frank didn't want them on the property a minute longer and got the driver to turn the truck around. No biggie, ultimately, but it did make him and Adele realize that next time could be somebody worse, and they had better start locking the gate.

Frank fumbled with the lock. It was rusty, and the key fell to the ground.

"Fuck."

"Want me to try?"

"No!" Frank snapped, and the boy took a full step backward.

He got the lock open, finally, muttering "Hallefuckinglujah," then walked the gate forward and held it open for his son, like he was some goddamn servant. After Tom shuffled through, Frank closed and relocked it.

The dogs jogged ahead, giving advance notice of the hunting party's return. When they ambled down the dusty home stretch, Adele and Sophie were waiting out on the porch, standing framed by the leafy concord vines hanging overhead along the trellis. It was a nice vision, actually. Adele toasting them with her glass of wine.

"You made it!" she said, with a welcoming smile, and Sophie looked happy, too, her arms crossed.

"What did you get?"

"Three! Three pigeons!" Tom was like a junior herald, blowing his bugle. "We got two more after you left," he told his sister, trying to make her jealous.

"Yeah, right. *We.*" Frank might have underlined the sarcasm further, but he was interrupted by Adele.

"There's a drink waiting for you in the kitchen. And Sophie made up a plate of cheese and crackers for you guys in case you're hungry before dinner."

"Right on." God bless them both! Frank swung through the screen door like it was the way into the saloon: the whiskey was singing to him from the kitchen. On the porch, the brave hunter boy was giving his instructions.

"Dad says we have to pluck them. You and I do. You have to help me."

"Okay," the girl said, like this was no big deal.

Frank imagined the shrug. Well, good for her.

"I'll show you kids how to do it," Adele said, setting them up on that beat-up old love seat on the porch, with a paper bag to hold the feathers. Frank heard her showing and explaining as he downed his drink, knocked it back in a few gulps. Better. An immediate easing. He sighed with satisfaction. It had gone well, that outing. Considering. He topped up the whiskey and set to work peeling and slicing onions to put in with the birds when they were ready to roast. Tears were streaming down his face a few minutes later when he went back out to see how they were getting on.

Whatever squeamishness the girl had had earlier about killing the pigeon was gone now.

"I'm almost finished!" she crowed, like a little rooster.

Tom, on the other hand, was obviously finding the job distasteful though tried not to show it.

"Don't worry about the heads or the feet. We cut them off later."

"Is this one done?" Sophie held hers up proudly by a few tail feathers, as if she were a little David, and the pigeon Goliath's head.

"Looks like it. Good work, old girl."

She beamed.

A shadow on the bird's throat caught Frank's eye.

"Hey," he said to his daughter. "You want to see something?"

She nodded.

He turned back to the screen door, beckoning her in a theatrical way, like he was a magician. Drosselmeyer, maybe. "Bring it inside, to the sink."

Sophie followed, excited to be getting this attention.

Frank asked Tom, "You want to come, too?"

But his son shook his head, without raising his eyes from the bird. He was making a mess of it.

Frank stood beside the girl at the sink.

"Now, hold the bird in your hand, here, chest up, hands underneath."

She cradled the pigeon as if she were making an offering.

"You see these? Feel these?" Leaning over her, Frank took the girl's right hand in his own, and guided her fingers over the bird's throat. On touching it, the hidden beads, she instinctively pulled her hand back. Or tried to.

"What is that? What are they?"

"Here." Frank moved a step to his right and reached for a knife. His daughter flinched. What, did she think he was dangerous? "I'm going to show you."

He took the bird out of her hands for better purchase—he did not, actually, want to slip with the knife and hurt her—and cut a swift, short nick in its bulging throat.

Six or seven pyracantha berries, jammed in there, started to ooze out.

She squealed with disgust.

"Pyracantha berries," Frank said. "Pigeons love them. They get kind of drunk on them."

The girl's mouth was curled up in revulsion and also fascination, especially when Frank started pressuring from below to pop the berries out of the dead bird's throat.

"We're not going to eat the berries. At least the pigeon got to, though. She had a nice last meal."

Sophie stared a second longer, then asked, timidly, "Can I go wash my hands?"

Frank chuckled, indulgently. "Sure you can."

Tom appeared at the screen door, holding his not-so-well-plucked pigeon. "What is it?" he asked. "What?"

"It had berries in its throat. It had eaten berries, and they were still in its throat," the girl told her brother, then ran to the bathroom in the back to wash the evidence off her hands. When Tom came to the sink to take a look, he kept his expression neutral—bored, even.

Frank could see in the boy's eyes that he thought what they were doing was barbaric, but that it would be safer not to say so.

The Bear in the Night, and the
Bear in the Day

✦

IF A TRIP TO THE RANCH HAD DEPENDED ON SOPHIE, they would never have made it. She wanted to get there; she pictured showing that wild and past-haunted place to her husband and their young children, and the image had soft, sweet edges in her mind, as if it were melted candy. But the personality-wrangling required to visit the Circle C with Sophie's dad made it seem impossible. Too many wills crashing against the rocks, like the currents in the Pacific that met along the jagged coastline. There were other things Sophie would have liked, too: one serene night's sleep, or her friend Becca not to have died. She was not going to get those, either. The time in your early forties when your kids were small was not when wishes were mentionable, or grantable. You were feeding and loving people, and putting out fires. Wishes came later.

Max, though, was a rallier. Her husband had the circus ringleader's knack of getting people on board. He ran the show. It was a talent that Sophie admired. It was his literal job—he had a radio show—and many years of vanquishing unlikelihoods had taught him that people were persuadable. Even the unpersuadable ones. Sophie had been one of the animals, a lion or more likely a seal: directed to stand on the stool or scale the ladder, she stepped up, obedient, while Max called out patter and amusements. "Why don't we go see the ranch one day," Max suggested, picking up on an ambitious thought Sophie had once voiced, probably some morning after she had actually slept, "when we're up visiting your dad and Adele?" Sophie was at the sink, reliving the previous night's mac-and-cheese dinner with the aid of a green abrasive sponge, and it may have been the stubborn golden nuggets fixed to the stainless-steel pot like limpets that made her push past the easier deferral to a shrugged agreement. "Sure. I can ask Dad, at least."

She mentioned the idea to Frank later that day as they made arrangements for the family visit. For seven or eight years now Frank and his second wife had been living "back like normal people again" in a pleasant, windswept house off the remoter dunes north of Mendocino, a town they settled in after the risks and hardships of life on the ranch finally proved too much. There was only so much chopping and hauling wood and shooting of rattlesnakes and negotiating of deep-divoted dirt roads that two people in their late sixties could keep doing. Joints, even titanium ones, complained about the hard work. Frank and Adele had finally opted for having a home with warmth and light at the flick of a switch; cable television; a hot tub, for God's sake! And you could put to bed the worry that fire or animals or some maniac might get you, and no one would find your body for weeks. "It's so corrupting, Soph," Frank wrote to his daughter after they moved. "The luxury of an electric oven! I gotta say, we love it." They could happily have kept a telephone line at bay until they died, but it seemed a necessary evil of returning to a life in town.

"We'll just stay for a couple of days, Dad," Sophie told him, once he finally picked up the phone. "We're going to drive up Saturday. Does that sound okay?"

"So you'll head back Monday?"

"Right. Monday's a school holiday. But we'll leave in the morning, right after breakfast. It's a long drive." This was true, four hours on the freeway as well as car-sickness-inducing back roads, but also Sophie knew that reassuring Frank about how soon the family would be out of there was essential to making their stay palatable. The filling of the house with kid voices and energy would tax the patience of Frank and of Adele, who would use Suki, their aged Samoyed, as an excuse for a break or the need for children to settle down. "She doesn't like sudden movements, kids, okay?" Frank had anyway never had much tolerance for children in indoor spaces, preferring to keep them out of doors, like cats. "No *grabass!*" he used to command Sophie and her brother when they became rambunctious, on the rare occasions they were in a public place with their dad, burger joint or ice cream parlor. Until she finally saw it written in a letter of his, Sophie used to think Frank was using a foreign word the way he said it, gruh-*boss*. Maybe it was leftover Italian slang from the time before her existence when Frank and their mom had lived in Florence, the place their marriage disintegrated. *No greba-zio!* He might have been saying, but no: it turned out that he had been telling Sophie and Tom not to *grab ass*.

"Also," Sophie added, before she could chicken out, "Max had a nice idea, that on that Sunday we could maybe go take the kids to visit the ranch."

There was a beat.

"What ranch?"

Sophie gave a forced laugh. "The Circle C! I mean, if it's possible. Max would like to see it after all the stories I've told, and he thought it could be fun to show Luke and Elsa." Her hunch was that her dad was more likely to consider it as a Max plan than as one of hers.

"Huh."

Sophie heard the smothering of the phone receiver, then her dad's voice in a murky exchange with Adele for a long minute.

"Adele isn't sure."

Her stepmother's voluble, unclear commentary sounded like the teachers' voices in Charlie Brown cartoons. Tone audible, but not the words.

"We'd have to give the current owners a heads-up, you know, Soph—you can't just come toodling down the access road, unless you want to get shot."

He was saying that for effect, Sophie knew, and as part of an ancient argument between them about guns, but her maternal heart fluttered anyway. It wasn't worth doing this if it was going to be dangerous.

"Right. Well, it's just an idea. Max thought—"

"He's a decent guy, though, Steve, the guy who bought the place. Was an LP logger for years around there, so knows the territory. Logged some of those beautiful old redwoods, the ones in the Cathedral Grove up by the windmill, when he first bought it, to make some extra cash."

Frank was not exactly talking to Sophie, or even Adele. He was musing aloud. "Not surprising, we kind of knew he might. I mean he probably got ten to twelve thousand per. Still, you don't like to think about it. We heard he has horses, maybe even breeds horses there now."

"Okay. Well, we don't have to do it, we can just go miniature golfing or whatever—isn't there a place in town? The kids will be fine with that."

The line was still. Sophie could imagine the facial expressions Frank might be making to Adele: eye rolls, pursed lips, head shaking. He had a repertoire.

"Don't worry about it, Dad. Let's talk closer to that weekend, I'll let you know when we get on the road . . ."

"We'll chew it over here, Soph. I'll see if I can reach Steve. Let's play it by ear."

In her mind, the candy hardened. He was more open to it than she had expected, but still—likely a no. Sophie relaxed. *No* was always easier with kid outings, and her parental rule of thumb in those years—the opposite of Max's—was that easier things were better things. Sophie could focus on her main job for those two days, keeping the kids entertained and polite and not annoying to the older couple. Another long road trip would be a challenge; instead the family could just play a round or two of windswept miniature golf by the noisy side of Highway 1, and maybe Frank would come along, too, reprising his role in Sophie's childhood, taker of her and Tom to baseball games and bowling and miniature golf, in their allotted time together. Those were all before he and Adele married, and moved to the ranch.

Was nostalgia always ironic? Sophie wondered. These revisitings, did they ever come at you straight?

She doubted it.

* * *

The last time Sophie had been to the ranch had been with Becca. Seven or eight years back, as the crow flies, but really a lifetime ago. People used that phrase to convey the deep transformations in a period of life—a person's summits and her setbacks—but also it could be meant literally. Sophie's last visit to the ranch had been, to count precisely, three lifetimes ago: before Luke's and Elsa's lives began, and before Becca's ended.

A brain aneurysm had taken Sophie's friend. She had fluttered and died, like a frozen wren. Sophie had heard the news from a great distance, in an email from Becca's sister in London. She had gasped, alone at her laptop, on a morning she had managed to wake before anyone else. The kitchen filled soon after with its voices and its appetites, which kept the fact of Becca's death unreal for a while, hidden in an internet cabinet along with school bulletins and volunteer sign-ups. There was going to be a memorial, once Becca's youngest sister had returned from a summer in New Zealand. Sophie wondered if she would fly all the way to England to go. Becca, gone: it was difficult to fathom.

Sophie and Becca had been adventurers together once. They had driven across Germany for a group show in Frankfurt, Becca's wrapped paintings stacked carefully in the back of a borrowed Volvo; up into the cloudy ether of the Scottish Highlands, sketching and walking on a half-term break from Becca's school; and west from London alongside the motorway, then farmed and hedgerowed fields, to visit friends who lived at the edge of Exmoor. That heathered, windswept country always brought Sophie into an essential Brontëan self, one who walked through any storm, prayed to a complicated god, loved with defiance. (Becca never knew about the prayer. No one did.)

They both lived in London. For Becca, it was where her life was—studio, teaching job, siblings—whereas for Sophie the great city was just the place her postgrad freelance drift had taken her. She turned thirty there, in Dickens's city and Woolf's; Blur's and Blair's. England was shaking off the years of Tories and becoming *cool*. For a while the two women's friendship grounded them both, that way women's friendships can do. They talked about becoming flatmates but came up against an incompatibility: not the obvious and much-joked-about one, their English and American differences ("I couldn't *possibly* share a kitchen with someone who holds their knife and fork the way you do," Becca's mock propriety), but a practical creaturely difficulty. Becca had cats, Sophie cockatiels. They imagined a joint existence in Sophie's upper-floor flat, exotic birds flying around one slant-eaved, book-lined room while the two tabbies sat in the hallway, listening to wingbeats, planning their attack. The two women decided to leave that comedy as a story told, not lived. They traveled together instead.

Becca was an oldest sister and behaved like one, offering advice and direction to the rudderless, and Sophie loved her for that, and for much else. Becca had capable hands, a sturdiness of spirit, and a wide Slavic face so expressive that it required no makeup: her beauty was mobile and elemental. She wore elegant, often paint-spattered Italian shirts and drank coffee so dark it fueled the extended riffs of her dry and sometimes surreal humor. Faced with a turps disaster in her studio, Becca might assume the persona of an old bat who responded to crisis by invoking the spirit of Winston Churchill; other times she was an enthusiastic Edwardian lady confiding in the pages of her notebook: "Dear Diary, Marvelous day today, taking the students to an art museum in town. How lovely are Mr Constable's rivers!" Becca was neither soft nor maternal and too committed to her art to ever want children; her gift was to be a deeply loyal friend and have the unerring urge to help when you were in trouble. She avoided drama, and she never lied. She knew just the item of food that would comfort (an almond tartlet, a box of Turkish figs), and her simple, taut instructions—"Avoid her," "Bury it"—were always correct. When there was nothing further to say about a mess you had gotten yourself into, Becca did not fill the airwaves with empty chatter. But she might, soon after, suggest a new trip to take.

After one such skid, a bad breakup from a poor prospect, Sophie planned to go home to California for comfort; the timing coincided with a conference gig Becca had in Chicago, and Becca suggested they meet after for a few days in San Francisco. Sophie wanted to show her friend something more interesting than postcard places, the Golden Gate Bridge or the steep, cable-carred hills, so she had the idea of taking Becca to the ranch where her dad and stepmother lived, in Mendocino County.

It was a gamble. Sophie didn't know—she never did—what they would find up at the Circle C. The woods were unpredictable, and so were the people who lived in them. But Becca, as ever, was game.

Years later, after Sophie became a mother and discovered the need for outings with restless kids on yawning, empty weekends, she took them to the zoo, the little farm, the wildlife rescue center. Holding a small hand in hers, half leaning over, she would point out to her son or daughter the hyphen-eyed goat, or an elusive tiger at the back of an enclosure, or a mortified hawk behind glass, recovering from a broken wing. And she'd recall the card Becca had sent from England after Luke was born. "Congratulations! And give your sweet baby a kiss on the ear for me. PS Let him wander, when he's old enough, will you? And don't let him look at animals in cages. It teaches the wrong lesson." Sophie felt guilty, defying her friend's exhortation.

Sophie did not have to worry about bringing Becca to the Circle C. Her instinct had been correct. The farther off the highway the two women got, the rougher and more hairpin-turned the road as they climbed into timbered wilderness, the happier Sophie's English friend became. "Brilliant!" Becca said when they passed an old rusting truck resting on its back at the base of a drought-scorched hill, and the K E E P O U T signs along some of the fenced property borders delighted her, making her think of mustachioed Yosemite Sam in the cartoon, wielding his shotgun. "Do they all have pistols here? Are there saloons?" When Sophie tried, with late-breaking anxiety, to give Becca some explanatory background on her dad and stepmother, how they had come to move out here from San Francisco twenty years before, Becca placed a calm, broad hand on Sophie's arm. "Stop fussing," she said. "We'll be fine. You needn't give me the entire dossier." As they drove down the last dusty hundred yards to the house, a dog's high bark the starting soundtrack, Becca simply breathed. Sophie could hear the pleasure in her breathing.

It was Frank the host who greeted them, not Frank the curmudgeon or the faux redneck; Sophie could see it even as she cut the engine. Her father's eyes were clear, not bloodshot, and his wave, the lifting of his right hand, was salute-like, accompanied by a humorous nod. Next to him was planted a smiling, black-eyed dog whose intermittent bark seemed more of an announcement than a warning. Adele, shading her eyes, stood a few steps behind Frank, hands in her jeans pockets as she called out, "Hello and welcome! This is Suki—our new Samoyed. She's very friendly."

She did seem the sunniest dog Frank and Adele had ever had, a creature built for snow with thick white fur that made her look like a stuffed animal. Sophie would have thought the coat might be a liability in the heat, but Suki looked unbothered by it. Frank and Adele used to keep dogs in pairs or even threes, the way people often did in the country, so that you had backup in case of any trouble; but now, in their slowing-down years on the ranch, one must seem enough. Becca got out of the car and befriended the dog first, which immediately made her a great guest and allowed Sophie to re-meet her parent.

"Hey, Dad."

"How're you doing, Soph."

As they embraced, Frank clapped a heavy paw on Sophie's back, as he always had. When she was young, the thud of her dad's big hand had always startled her, the way a loud noise might, but now she found herself thudding him right back. In England people kissed in greeting, rather than hugging, and Sophie had missed the warmth and weight of American arms.

* * *

When it came to it, Adele did not want to go.

"There's not really enough room in your van," she told Sophie, then added frankly, "I don't think I could stand to see the place again." Adele had loved those trees and those acres more than almost anything in her life other than Frank. But one of the last times Adele had been at the ranch, in the days when she and Frank had already started to scout for easier houses, she had fallen badly, while up on a ladder picking grapes from the concord vines tangled round the roof's eaves. A helicopter had had to come to the ranch to get her out safely. Physically, Adele had recovered—her bones had healed—but the injury shadowed her, and made the leaving of the ranch, after all those dedicated years, like a bad breakup: the kind where you don't even want to hear any news of your ex, what they're up to, whether they're happy.

"Anyway, we couldn't take Suki, and it would be a long day for her to be locked in the pen. I'll stay here with her."

There had always been layers of excuses not to travel or visit: for Frank the excuse was Adele, and for Adele the excuse was their dog. "We can't stay for dinner. Adele wants to get back in time to spring

Suki from the kennel." It used to bother Sophie—*Why not just be honest about it, for God's sake? You're tired of us!*—until she found herself shamelessly using her own two adorable excuses anytime she could not face a social occasion or wanted to escape early. Luke and Elsa, now six and just-four, gave Sophie a pass to get out without guilt, and a new sympathy for her dad and stepmother's line.

Frank, standing by the van as Sophie did the requisite strapping in, almost quailed, too. "You don't really need me with you." Her father had made good on his offer, calling the former logger who had bought the property, setting up the time and day for the visit. "Steve will be happy to welcome you, whether I come or not. You're fine to go as you are."

Max stepped in to coax and jolly; Sophie imagined him with his top hat. "Soph has told me so many stories," he said charmingly, borrowing from Frank the nickname that he himself rarely used, "about you and Adele at the ranch. And I can't wait for Luke and Elsa to see where their grandfather used to make apple cider, and wine." It was a good move. Flattery worked with Frank, so long as it did not slide into the obsequious.

Sophie stayed neutral throughout the long, throat-clearing run-up to departure. She did not want to be disappointed if they didn't go. She was so deeply tired in her bones that she genuinely would not have minded if they had simply stayed and ambled the dunes with the kids. The sensation of fine sand pulling your own footsteps away from you as you moved uphill was so similar to what she felt all the time, these days—climbing and climbing yet somehow staying in place. The house was compact; keeping the children out of Adele's way was a challenge, as was getting Elsa to stop circling Suki's furry neck with her plump arms, something that bothered Adele more than it did the Samoyed. "Give her a little space, sweetie, okay?" Adele kept saying. "She likes a little space."

Luke took to correcting Elsa, too, showing his younger sister his idea of how Suki preferred to be petted. "Like this," he showed her. "Do it this way."

Sophie remembered how she and Tom used to fight over turns to play fetch with Frank and Adele's faithful Labrador, when they had run out of other things to do in the too-hot afternoons.

It had been so long since Sophie had been to the Circle C. She was not sure which memories would surface, whether from the tie-dyed seventies or sporadic adult stops or, more practically, how to navigate even a short visit with her two in tow. They were both younger than she had been the first time she went to the ranch, after Frank and Adele left San Francisco for good. Sophie's first short summer stay had been fun, like a kind of summer camp where you learned old-fashioned survivor skills, but the next muddy winter, getting stuck in a ditch on the stormy nighttime drive in, just her and Frank, had been no fun at all. That journey gave Sophie an awareness that never left her. The Circle C was not just far from everything familiar; it was also far from anyone who could come help. It did not make the place frightening, after you got used to the fact, but you just had to bear it in mind. Up there, they were on their own.

Sophie sat in the van's back with the kids, but the door stayed open as the bartering went on. Finally, Max clinched the deal. When she heard her father muttering in one of his English accents, Sophie knew Frank had conceded. After an affectionate farewell to Adele—and a rousing charge of "Once more unto the breach!"—Frank heaved himself up into the front passenger seat with a few theatrical groans. Max got behind the wheel, three generations successfully herded into the crumb-scattered van, and off they went.

The journey would take an hour or more, heading east and up through densely forested hills. Sophie began a Disney movie on the back-seat screen to make the drive bearable—*One Hundred and One Dalmatians*—but knew she could not get too lost in the landscape or her thoughts. She had to stay alert so that she could fast-forward through the scariest part, where Cruella De Vil seems ready to kill all the puppies.

* * *

Sophie had forgotten that her father could be courtly, a gentleman. He kept a set of old-world manners tucked in a drawer, along with a few clippings about his illustrious long-dead relatives, never mentioned. Becca's Englishness was of the funny, self-mocking kind that Frank responded to, and her attentive listening warmed and relaxed the sixty-five-year-old, who had devised an initial tour around what no one at the Circle C would ever call the grounds. A couple of coops, one now housing noisy guinea hens, a clearing to chop logs, the covered woodpile, Adele's compact shed-workshop. ("She makes stained-glass pieces in there," Frank told Becca. "Beautiful. She did the iris window in the front door. Make sure to look.") The highlight, Sophie realized, was going to be the grapes so that Frank could wax on about winemaking. On the way to the lower vineyard they walked through the old, overgrown apple orchard. Some of the gnarled, darkened trees had a few branches shorn off, and Becca asked whether there had recently been a windstorm.

"No, no." Frank tsked. "That's the goddamn bear."

Becca looked at Sophie, who shrugged.

"He comes around here at night; he's a greedy SOB. But all he wants are the apples, so we let him have 'em."

"I've seen elephants do similar damage to trees in Africa," Becca said.

Sophie thought the comment came via one of Becca's comic personae, perhaps an old colonial traveler, before she understood that Becca was speaking sincerely, as herself.

"I remember once in Tanzania . . . they occasionally trample the trees." She sounded subdued and remained politely quiet through Frank's proud and detailed lecture on wine production.

A couple of hours later Becca and Sophie were on the porch, Becca stretched out on the battered brown couch that lived out there, Sophie like an old lady in the rocking chair. Frank was inside prepping dinner, Adele practicing scales on the piano. Frank had poured them each a glass of a Circle C Cabernet—"It won't win any prizes," he said modestly, "but it's drinkable"— and Becca had presented him a bottle of an Haut-Médoc as a gift, adding to her favored-guest status.

Suki lay on the warped wooden floor between the women, dozing. They looked out toward the fenced half-acre garden, where Frank and Adele grew vegetables, herbs, berries, roses; and back behind it the orchard, with its bear-broken branches.

"This is the remotest place I have ever been," Becca told Sophie. "Apart from that trip to Tanzania. But even there, we were on a game reserve—it was different. The place was wild, but somehow managed. Humans were in charge, ultimately."

Sophie laughed. "Not here."

This was unexpected, that her bold, adventurous friend would seem the Londoner she was, at the ranch. The Africa analogy seemed fanciful to Sophie. But she perceived that, for Becca, urban streets were the natural order of things, and uncultivated land, while splendid, still set off a submerged city-dweller alarm.

"No one is really in charge at the Circle C," Sophie said, and she meant the surrounding woods, but as they had walked around with Frank she had noticed some of the outer buildings looking run-down. Frank and Adele could have used a day or ten of a younger person's help. "I hope that doesn't worry you," she added.

"It's fantastic," Becca answered without hesitation. "I love it." Her voice was as hushed and irony-free as Sophie had ever heard it. "I love it."

* * *

Pongo and Perdita were letting all the puppies watch television together, a black-and-white Western with a dog-hero character in it, while Sophie stared out the dusty window, trying again not to mind that Disney's scriptwriters had combined two of Dodie Smith's female characters, Perdita and Missus, into one mom-wife all-rounder. It was a less interesting setup than the original. Say what you liked about the English, but they were more tolerant of oddly shaped families than Americans were.

In front, Max drew Frank into telling stories of mishaps and misfits from the Circle C years: hermits and hippies, washed-out roads and clogged water lines, the artist neighbor whose angry teenage son lit a fire one hostile night that burned the cabin to the ground, though without them in it. The artist father retreated from the woods after that, back to the safer savagery of San Francisco.

Oaks and madrones gradually gave way to redwoods as Sophie listened half to Disney and half to her dad. Frank enjoyed the company of Sophie's husband, whom in letters he sometimes referred to as "the great panda," obscurely though with affection. It was an obvious daughterly courtesy to suggest Frank sit up front with Max, but it also returned Sophie, through the blurred dislocations of time, to the backseat role her kids were in now, when you passively went along to whatever the destination was, accepting an itinerary you had no hand in shaping.

After about an hour, Frank slowed Max down, though they were coming the opposite direction from the one Frank knew, and familiar landmarks were scarce. When a nearly invisible road, more of a fire trail, curved up to the right, Frank raised his left hand—conductor, traffic cop—and Max, slowing the Honda to an idle, asked, "Is this it?"

Frank leaned out of his window, as though that would give him a better vantage point. Maybe he just needed a second of air to himself. "They replaced the gate." He pulled his head back inside. "No surprise. Ours was crappy, and a mother to unlock." He stared straight ahead for a long instant, then collected himself. "But Steve left it open, like he said he would." He nodded to Max to carry on and Max, playing the role of chauffeur, nodded back, maneuvering the van up an awkward, narrow slope. They continued along the rough access road she remembered.

"Five-minute warning," Sophie said to the kids, who might as well have been on I-5 for all the difference their surroundings made. "We're going to be there soon, guys, and will have to turn this off." Luke uttered a faint syllable of protest, but Elsa was so engrossed she heard her mother's voice as white noise and had no response.

Sophie had never expected to come back to the Circle C, after that last time here with Becca. When she learned that her dad and stepmother had moved, she figured the ranch would survive for her in photographs and stories, and some of Becca's sketches from a scuffed green sketchbook Becca gave her when Sophie moved back to California. In it, the grassy hills were that milky oat color of high summer, the forest across the river valley a scratchy thickness of varied greens. The house itself, when it appeared, was a diminutive taupe rectangle, a dwarfed outpost of human effort. The gift now seemed a posthumous one, and it would be a while before Sophie could look at those sketches again.

They went down the long slow curve in the opener meadowed land, and then the van stopped. Sophie jumped out, sliding open the unwieldy door with its exhausted mechanical sigh, her strapped-in kids blinking at the sudden light and ceasing of the movie, while a middle-aged couple, clean-cut, T-shirted and jeaned, smiled their welcome from a patch of grass Sophie had known when she and it were younger. All was instantly different: they had removed the wrought-iron circled C from the wooden posts by the house, a couple of horse trailers and an ATV were parked where Frank used to cut wood, and the old school-house had been modernized with a tin roof and red-painted board and batten siding. There were other changes, too, but Sophie focused on the cheerful introductions, shaking the hands of Steve and his wife, Beth, before going back to the car to extract her children. Max chatted with the couple about the drive while Frank, Sophie could tell, was waiting for a wave of emotion to pass before getting out. On his own ground, Sophie's dad was blustery, jokey, assertive. He was not on his own ground here, though. Not anymore.

He inhaled, and steeled himself, and then down he came, the old gunslinger dismounting before tying up around the hitching post. Frank walked around the front of the Honda and reached out a hand to the younger man, who eyed him with a glint of wariness.

"Hey, Frank, good to see you."

"How're you doing, Steve, man."

Between them hung unspoken words about the Cathedral Grove, as Frank had christened it, those old redwoods Steve had had logged from there, majestic trees that must have stood for a couple of hundred years, Frank and Adele figured, in a circle that had always seemed sacred to them, unreligious though they were. A place of ancestors from this land. *Yes, but,* ran an unspoken defensive line from the guy who had moved here eight years earlier and was still trying to make his business viable, *we needed the money; not everyone has trust money backing them up, old man*—matched, silently, by the geezer's resigned reply, *You needed the dough. I know, I know.* With the handshake the two men shared an acknowledgment that they did not have to speak of this, and wouldn't.

"Welcome to the Sunshine Horse Ranch." Steve's smile was taut, slowly unwinding. Frank had, fortunately, warned Sophie of the name change before they got here, but Steve went immediately to an explanation. "We let our daughter name this place, when she was about ten, not much older than you, sir, I bet," he said, addressing Luke. Always good to flatter a kid about looking older than he was. "You guys want to see the horses, and the stables?"

It was a good place to start. The lower meadow, where Frank and Adele had never done much, not even get rid of a rusted-out '50s Dodge that had become a home for critters, was now developed, given over to a fenced-in practice ring and a huge modern barn complex. They went inside where it was cooler, a vast airplane hangar smelling of horses, the grays and chestnuts in their stalls. Steve knew kids, offered them each a carrot to feed one, and Max held Elsa up to reach. She squealed with pleasure to feel the velour lips against her small palm. None of Sophie's family was especially horsey, so they listened to details of what was, as Frank would later tell Adele, "not a Mickey Mouse operation at all— very impressive," without feeling that their past had been stepped on or eradicated. In this part of the Sunshine Ranch it was as if they had stopped by to visit a place none of them had ever been.

Sophie knew that would change when they went inside the house.

* * *

Dinner with Becca was raucous and delicious. Frank was a fine cook, and on the blackened wood-fired kitchen stove he made a perfectly tender ribeye and served it, as a cultural joke, with Yorkshire pudding, while Adele created a salad of peppers, tomatoes, and greens from the garden. Becca's Médoc was put to good use. She got on to stories of the trip she and Sophie took through Germany, embellishing a few near calamities for greater entertainment; then she and Frank improvised a humorous routine about German food, and some of the more extreme things done in that country to pork. Adele chipped in with a note on Polish dumplings she and Frank once sampled in Warsaw, where she had some cousins. Frank had baked an apple pie for dessert, "to keep America on the menu," using their own apples. When Becca tried to help with the dishes after, Frank and Adele both waved her off, telling her that Frank always did them in the small hours of morning.

As they moved toward the downstairs bedroom, Sophie spontaneously asked her stepmother if they could sleep outside.

"Like you used to when you were kids?"

"I was telling Becca about that. I think she's game."

Becca nodded.

"Well—sure. Why not? You're past mosquito hour. Let me find a couple of the old army sleeping bags and I'll set you up." Adele found what they needed, had them grab pillows and one of the giant flashlights, and out they all went onto the back deck that looked out and up toward the windmill. Sophie's stepmother unfolded two of the creaky weather-worn recliners that would lead the two friends into a fierce whispered debate later about whether the phrase was *chaise lounge* or *chaise longue*, an argument that dissolved finally into hysteria.

There were a thousand stars, and the soothe of cricketsong, and after Adele wished them good night Frank came padding out, Suki too, to make sure they were all right.

"All looks shipshape," he said. "You got everything you need?"

"We're good, Dad, thanks."

"The dog will sleep out on the deck with you. That okay?"

"Of course."

"Usually she stays inside, but I think it's better if she is out here." Frank looked up at the Milky Way, spent a moment contemplating eternity. He blinked. In the starlight, Sophie could see her dad's face clearly: his large museum-bust head with the tangled brows, silvered hair, booze-plumped nose. Part chieftain, part bon vivant. With an absent-minded hand, Frank stroked the lower part of his beard. "Anyway, if Sophie starts barking, which she might, don't worry about it. It just means she hears the bear. It's good actually. Sophie might scare him."

Sophie heard Becca begin to titter, as if Frank were joking, then pause. Sophie felt a stab of pity and cut in before her friend could tease him about his mistake.

"Thanks, Dad. Suki will be great company. We'll be fine." She touched his sweatshirted arm. He did not notice the correction. "Good night."

"Okay, old girl," he said. "Good night." He turned his face into the shadow. "And glad to have you here, Becca." Frank retreated back into the house, and for a while they heard the couple murmuring and moving around in their bedroom on the upper floor.

Later the women laughed about it, of course: Frank calling the dog by his daughter's name. On the drive back to the Bay Area, Sophie worked up her imitation of Suki's bark of alarm—which did wake them up, once, when for some nervous minutes they listened out for a giant beast crashing around in the fruit trees. Over the next couple of days Becca would paint sketches from the top of the hill beneath the windmill, and get poison oak, and not find funny Sophie's joshing about the risk of rattlesnakes. The Englishwoman actually blanched at the sight of Frank's famous jar of rattles he kept in the kitchen from snakes he had killed (shot mostly, though on occasion in the vegetable garden you had to think quick and bring a shovel down on its slithering neck). There was one dramatic afternoon when they went into town with Frank and on the way back were stopped on the road by a sheriff who warned there had been gunfire exchanged outside a nearby ranch, and a manhunt was underway in the forest. (That was the word he used, Sophie recalled: *manhunt*.) Their last starlit night the friends squabbled over something minor, and after sparring, for the first and only time they turned to kissing and an embrace they never spoke of, after. One of Becca's sketches developed, back in her London studio, into a textured, evocative oil painting, and she found a way via Sophie to give it to Frank and Adele as a thank-you present. It went up on the wall in their new house on the coast, above the watercolor portrait of their long-gone husky.

Becca flew home to England a few days later armed with great stories, gradually exaggerated in the telling, about her stay at the Circle C. And Sophie returned to her cramped flat with a joke she sometimes told about her apparent resemblance to a Samoyed—"My bark is worse than my bite"—and the start of a desire within her, related to childhood and woods and wildness, to find her way back to California and, once there, to motherhood.

* * *

"Do you like dolls, Elsa?"

Ponytailed Beth spoke to Sophie's daughter with the friendly ease of a kindergarten teacher. They had walked up to the house's wooden porch and stood outside the living room, where a stained-glass purple iris of Adele's still colored the door's window square. Steve, with permission, offered to give Luke a ride on the ATV (Luke was thrilled), while Max walked about with Frank, listening to his father-in-law flex his memory.

The four-year-old nodded to Beth. "She loves dolls, don't you, honey?" Sophie said, supplying the dialogue. "Her first word was *baby*." The two mothers traded a knowing smile, and Sophie added, "It's funny—I wasn't a doll kid at all, I was more of a tomboy, but Elsa has loved dolls since she was tiny."

"They make up their own minds about things." Beth smiled, ushering them in to a living room as cool and dim as it had always been, with what looked like the same iron stove at one end and the door to the stairway at the other. Beth offered her hand, and the trusting girl placed hers into it, checking to see that her mom was right behind her as they climbed the creaking steps to the upper floor. Behind these wooden walls, Sophie remembered, she and Tom once hid a plastic tarantula to surprise any future remodelers.

She heard her daughter's gasp, on arriving upstairs, and understood it an instant later. Around the broad room, angled into the eaves along one side, ran one long, wide, crowded shelf. Sophie had the immediate animal sensation that she was being watched—as she was, by dozens of blond and dark and redheaded dolls, too many to count. They were mostly old-fashioned in their pretty dresses and pinafores, some on rocking chairs, one on a bicycle, one at a miniature piano. To Sophie, the collection had a horror-movie eeriness, but she had never liked dolls. For her daughter it was pure enchantment.

Elsa was speechless. Sophie could see her gray-green eyes widen, taking in all the material here. *So many characters.*

Beth looked at Elsa and laughed. "It's a lot, right? This is my daughter Kayla's collection. She has mostly outgrown them now, so she says, but she still comes up here and checks in on them when she comes home." Beth squatted beside Elsa, looking up with her. "Would you like to choose one to take home, Elsa? Kayla said she'd be happy for you to do that. Is that all right with you, Mom?"

Elsa's eyes grew even wider.

"Of course!" said Sophie. "That is so nice of you. What do you say, Elsa?"

The girl dutifully produced her "Thank you" before turning to the impossible task of choosing. Beth started to tell her quietly about the different dolls, their names and other things, so Sophie allowed herself a moment to look around. To the left she glimpsed the wide bright bedroom that Frank and Adele had added on, overhanging the deck; and in the room where they stood, she restored in her mind Frank's desk, once wedged up against the eaves, on which he kept stacks of the canary-yellow typing paper used for writing letters. His typewriter had been there, too.

"Oh that's a good one." Elsa had pointed at one, and Beth affirmed the girl's selection. "She's called Lulu." Beth reached for a copper-ringleted blue-eyed doll wearing a floral nightgown. She brushed a little dust off the doll's front, and when she placed it in the girl's arms, Sophie's daughter's face softened and became rosy, with new love.

* * *

When they went downstairs again Sophie found Frank and Steve talking in the room behind the kitchen, where the four of them used to play cards on hundred-degree days, after chores were done, when it was too hot to do anything else. Through the window Sophie could see Max standing by the tall brick oven and the broad-leaved walnut tree that grew around and above it. Her husband was spotting Luke as the boy clambered on the lower branches.

Frank's back was to her as Sophie approached the two men from the kitchen, but she could tell from her father's rounded shoulders that he had become easier with the Sunshine Ranch's proprietor. Sophie paused, listening; back in the living room, Elsa had sat down in a chair by the window and started whispering to her new doll. She was introducing herself, and getting to know her.

The men were laughing. Well, that was good. Steve nodding, Frank saying, "Oh, man!" when Sophie noticed the dead body hanging on the wall between them.

She startled and froze. Her first thought was *Elsa had better not see this.* Sophie put a hand up to her nose, somehow expecting a stench to hit her, but there was no smell.

Maybe you would not call it a body, hanging on the wall where full shelves of cookbooks and stacks of *National Geographic*s used to be. Maybe you would call it a skin or a pelt. It did have a head, though. A furred, withered head, snout pointing upward, nearly touching the low ceiling so that there was room for the rest of it to sprawl. The bear occupied that entire space now. Her eyes moved back up to its head, and she was grateful that she could not see what they had done about the eyes.

"That's when I got the permit from Fish and Wildlife to take him out," Steve said. "I told them, 'Look guys, with kids here, and our horses—we can't be having this animal come around at night.'"

"Especially when the apples come on."

"Exactly! That's when I did it, when it got to be apple season. He was coming every night. And after Buster died—our Doberman—we didn't even have a hound to scare him off."

"God, do I remember!" Frank's mouth was open, laughing, like a dog's. "The apple trees mangled in the morning, and those big piles of chunky bear shit in the road." He was enjoying himself. "Gotta be the same one."

"They tell you exactly how they want you to do it. And they make you inform them when it's done. I told them I was keeping the skin, though."

"That's fair. You bagged him."

"Exactly." Steve looked up at the trophy, pride in his eyes.

"I remember him, all right," Frank said.

Sophie, still in the anteroom of the kitchen, thought better of entering. She turned around to rejoin Elsa in the living room, just as Frank was asking Steve what gun he used on the animal, and Steve went into a practiced narrative about the weapon and the killing.

Steve's wife had gone back outside. She was a good host, engaging Max in conversation. As a mother, she knew the importance of fairness and so found something for Luke to take home as a souvenir also from the Sunshine Ranch. Sophie planned to signal to Max that they should leave soon, using lunch, the kids' appetite, as an excuse. Frank would be wanting to get back to Adele and for his afternoon nap. Adele was making sandwiches for all of them.

On the drive home, the kids found out for the fiftieth time how Pongo and family got the better of Cruella De Vil. Frank was quiet; not even Max could draw him out. After they pulled up in the driveway of the duneside house again, Suki barking her heroes' welcome from the deck, Sophie asked her son to show what Beth had given him. He unclenched his fist and held out to her a small, slate-gray arrowhead Beth told him they had found down in the lower meadow when they were clearing it to build the barn. Boys, in Sophie's opinion, often got the cooler stuff, though Elsa was holding Lulu close to her like she was never going to let her go.

Jocasta

✦

WHEN HIS MOTHER DIED, FRANK CAME INTO A SIGNIFICANT
amount of money. She had dallied with the stock market over the years,
keeping her secrets close, and had built up a substantial portfolio. Her
broker had been her readiest friend.

One of his first purchases, after buying Adele a nice piece of jewelry,
was a comfortable new car. They had recently moved back into civilization from the wilderness, and no longer had to drive vehicles that could
eat mud for breakfast. He decided they could go ahead with a remodel,
add a guest room on the ground floor and install climate controls in the
basement, where he kept his wine, near the dust-gathering exercise bike
and some Kerouac first editions. The next time he flew—not that they
flew anywhere much, maybe to friends in Palm Springs or Colorado for
a fishing trip with his brothers—he thought he might fly first class. Just
for the hell of it. Because he could.

He was seventy-one.

Frank used to refer to his mother as Jocasta, jokingly, though he
never explained why. At dinner after the funeral, in Santa Fe, his
brother Carl told the story about a trip he had taken to Europe with
their mother ten years back or so, when she thought it made sense
to economize by staying in rooms with one bed. He and his mother
both found the confusion of the hotel staff amusing, as they dealt with
an eighty-year-old woman and her fifty-something male companion.
They had a good laugh about it. Carl, married thirty years, with grown

children and a couple of grandchildren—"the ankle-biters," he called them—enjoyed the titter of discomfort at the table caused by the story. Frank, the eldest, had listened to Carl and arched his brow in mute commentary; Frank had overgrown *Old Man and the Sea* eyebrows, and he knew they produced a dramatic effect. His brother ignored him, probably smart.

The new car gave him and Adele a lot of pleasure. It had broad, soft seats, a luxurious skin, and it went easy on the old bones, demanding little of joints that no longer moved as he wanted them to, that had had a tough run through the decades on the ranch. Basically, Frank had pain all over now, and the new car went some way to distracting him from it. You could tell it was solidly made. The doors, he liked to say to Adele, went *thunk* when you closed them. Not *tink*. That was how you could tell it was well-built.

He had not wanted to buy a Cadillac. His mother had driven Cadillacs, one big boat after another, in which she kept an umbrella that she could use to press the automatic locking and unlocking button on the passenger side from where she sat, behind the wheel. She kept driving into her nineties. It wasn't something you wanted to think about, this saber-toothed ninety-year-old matriarch—still sound of mind and clear of vision, though largely deaf and hectoring and impatient, and weak from arthritis—cruising along the broad, bright avenues of Albuquerque in her Cadillac, shouting unheard at all the incompetents on the road. She never got into an accident, improbably enough. The only thing that happened was the night someone set fire to her Cadillac, which was parked out in her driveway.

The car was a charred shell by morning, the umbrella a blackened skeleton. The police never discovered who had done it. Frank guessed the insurance must have covered the cost of the replacement.

THE LAST TIME he had seen her was three or four years before. He had flown out, finally, to visit her, mostly because Adele wouldn't stop bugging him about it. *You'll regret it if you don't,* she would say to him, though he doubted that was true. *She's survived bladder cancer and breast cancer, but she isn't going to live forever.* He doubted that, too. His brothers and he had a line in morbid banter about knocking Mama off so they could finally get their hands on her estate—before it was too late, for Christ's sake, to enjoy it.

"Pity, Franco," Carl said, his own private nickname for his big brother. "They'll be cutting the check for you out in the old folks' home, hermano, by the time it happens." Eight years between the two of them. Different fathers. Carl had the foxed, sharp-toothed face that came from the other side.

"Don't you worry about me," Frank had answered. "I'll endorse that check with my dying hand, if I have to." Had gentler Walter, the youngest, been part of this jokey vulture round? Frank couldn't recall. "But the three of us know that she's going to bury us all."

Nonetheless, to placate his wife, Frank went.

Pulling up outside her home in the rental car—*tink* went the doors, *gong gong gong* to remind you to take the keys out of the ignition, like you were an imbecile—he saw the baby-blue Cadillac in the driveway of the sanded yellow house he and his brothers called El Dorado. A high shadow in the kitchen window must be her moving around in preparation for his arrival. His bowels clenched. Really, he did not want to see his mother. Why had he come?

"Mama," he said when she opened the door. She still stood six feet, or just under, and was dressed in a long emerald silk housecoat. Her white hair, cut in an elegant bob, looked regally beautiful against the jeweled green. *Aging geisha* was the phrase that sprang to his mind. She wore a vital red lipstick, and held her yappy dog, Cindy, close to her, for warmth or possibly protection. But his mother's blue, ice-shelf eyes, fiery and alive, were surprisingly welcome.

"Frank. Come in." She reached a stiffened hand out to his shoulder and drew him in for a cheek brush, a tall embrace.

He hoped she would not actually leave a mark on his face or collar with her lipstick; it had just been applied, he could tell, and might come right off. Cindy growled, a comical, diminutive rumble, and his mother pulled diamonded fingers through the dog's scruffy neck fur.

"Don't be silly, Cindy. We can let him in. He's not going to hurt us."

He inhaled, and entered.

But he found that once inside, surrounded by the familiar clutter of pills and collectibles, dog toys and hardbacks, *Forbes* magazines and doctors' bills, he stopped minding being there. The place was a known quantity: the smells of perfume and Purina, the dust and dander, the ticking clocks; the lapping waves of wealth and chaos. He decided to try to enjoy himself. What else was there to do?

His mother led him back to the room where he'd be sleeping, Lloyd's old study, and he did not mind that, either. The walls were still covered with photographs of Lloyd, a few of his encounters with the great and the good: in one, he shook hands with LBJ; in another, he was laughing with John Glenn. Frank decided it was poignant rather than sinister, that his mother kept these photographs up fully thirty years after Lloyd had died. He was the favorite of her husbands, not merely the last. She did not tell tales on Lloyd as she did on all the others. (Stinginess, impotence, poor manners; she went into detail you would as soon she left out.) Lloyd's being a member of the Philadelphia establishment gave him a social standing that elevated him, decades on, above his mother's countless pettinesses, and for that Lloyd was the husband Frank liked best, too. Frank's own father, the first, was a dissolute Englishman he knew only by the blighted reputation his mother insisted on; the next one, a marriage sealed in Reno on a western journey of pine trees and casinos, was short-lived, finished practically before it started; and Frank had difficulty, as a rebellious teen, with her third, Lawrence, the man who fathered his two brothers. This stepfather had a rude bark for a laugh and an asphyxiating handshake, and would not let Frank drive the family car, even when he came back from his spell in the air force. That divorce had not been pretty. Lloyd, on the other hand, older, sedate, a financier, had offered a late promise of contentment to the hard-to-contain Jocasta. Poor guy: the effort must have killed him. They were married two years; then he died of a massive coronary. Nothing they could do.

Frank had worried about dinner. He had quickly put away a burrito at the airport in case there would be nothing when he arrived at El Dorado. He could get by on olives or cashews if he had to—Mama usually had plenty of those around—but if she offered to cook, unlikely though it was, Frank would demur. He remembered an evening some years before when his mother had served him corned beef from a can, half reheated on the stove, which would have been hard to swallow even if he hadn't seen the can already opened on the kitchen counter when he first came in, leaving him to wonder if it might just be left over from lunch, or from dinner the night before. It was a miracle that botulism had never visited the place, given what went on before Mary arrived to pull everything into shape. God bless Mary, her patience and unflappability, and even if Frank didn't believe in God, Mary certainly did, so He was doubtless on her side.

The difference the resolute Irishwoman had made was striking. Frank saw clean surfaces and tidied pantry shelves, plates and glasses where you might expect them, no half-filled dog dishes out on the counter, attracting flies. Mary had prepared a meal for them, too, left it in the fridge for Mrs. D to warm up later in the oven. Lamb chops and potatoes and string beans cooked to the point of disintegration, like she liked them.

They ate together in the small breakfast nook off the kitchen—he wondered when she had last cleared off the mahogany dining table and eaten at it—chattered over by a pair of zebra finches called Standard and Poor. Cindy sat at their feet, waiting for scraps.

"This poor dog," his mother said, handing down pieces of lamb and gristle, "is so poorly treated. Really, it's a shame. Don't you feel sorry for her?"

The dog gazed at its mistress, eyes wetly pooled with adoration and greed.

"Yes," he said to play along. "I'll have to report you to the SPCA, Mama. Clear case of abuse and neglect."

And the wine flowed. If there was one thing you could count on his mother for, it was a healthy appetite for wine, and resources to get the good stuff. He appreciated this and was grateful that no well-meaning killjoy (including Mary) had tried to persuade her to change her ways. At ninety, what would have been the point? She opened two bottles of a gorgeous Margaux and he was touched, because she did have plenty of cases of plonk around the place, too, and if she was in a bitter mood, or not planning to have any fun, that's what she would pour.

After they had eaten, she started telling him stories. Her food was mostly untouched apart from what she had fed to the dog. Travel stories, this cruise ship or that one, Antarctica or the Galapagos, the Baltic Sea or the Mediterranean—though the Mediterranean bored her, the dullness of smug socialites and azure seas. She preferred places where she could see turtles or penguins, or a gray whale lurching up to the surface to exhale a spray of spume. It wasn't the millionaires his mama traveled for. She was tired of millionaires by now. It was the wildlife, when she was still able to get up and see it, and the idea of the wildlife when she wasn't. She was happiest nestled in the soothing rhythms of ship life, enjoying the meals and company on board. She ate at the captain's table, generally, which pleased her. The Scandinavian captain of one cruise line was, by now, a friend. She had bought a painting made by his wife. (Parallel acrylic bands of mauve and ochre—a Nordic Rothko, was how Frank thought of it.) Every Christmas the couple sent her a box of beautiful Swedish jams. The captain had been particularly solicitous of her since the time—was it Baja, or Costa Rica? she couldn't recall—when she had fallen out of one of the Zodiac boats on a short excursion to the shore. She had a lifejacket on, of course, and the water wasn't positively polar, but nonetheless she was eighty-five, and floundering around in wet, cold clothes and a lifejacket was, as Mama put it, "not part of her health and exercise regimen." A helpful crew member, "a handsome, butch young thing, she had the pretty purser eating out of her hand," deftly brought Mama back onto the Zodiac, and she was taken back on board in a state of mild shock, though good humor. Shortly afterward she caught a chest cold that stayed in her lungs, and she had to spend the rest of the journey in bed taking antibiotics. "I won't sue you, Olaf," she told her friend, the captain. "But I wouldn't say no to a free ticket for my next cruise." Which, to his credit, he gave her.

The story made Frank laugh. His mother had always, in spite of everything, been able to make him laugh. "You've got balls, Mama," he told her, and seeing her thinning lips pulled back over broad yellowed teeth in amusement, he knew that he was watching his own mouth laughing. They looked too much alike. It was one of the problems. "I'll give you that," he repeated. "You've got balls."

As far as he knew, she took the remark as a compliment. Certainly, that was how he meant it.

FRANK COULD NOT remember precisely why they stopped talking to each other a year or two ago. He could not remember if he had offended her, or she him. A gift sent with no thanks received, might have been; or the obnoxious comment Mama made to Adele about their Samoyed, Sirius, who had been reduced to hopping about on three legs now, post cancer surgery. Not everyone held with rescuing a dog in those circs, Frank got that, but you would think, given Mama's passion for that yappy little Cindy, that she'd know better than to question the decision. Adele was better at letting things go than Frank was. It might have been something else, another time his mother's whip tongue had finally lashed him too harshly, over the telephone, and he decided he was terminally sick of it. Mocking his appearance—"that lovely underbrush on your chest you insist on showing the world, with your open shirts"—or how they lived now—"I must say, Frank, I never imagined you as a beach bum in your sunset years." Whoever thought you should forgive everything in a person who was ninety-two years old did not know how badly behaved a ninety-two-year-old could continue to be. Did not, in short, know his mother. Toward the end, even Adele had stopped making a case for reconciliation.

He had not arrived in Albuquerque in time for her death. The final illness was a pneumonia, and he arrived the day after, in time for the viewing. This seemed about right to Frank. His brother Walter, the beloved youngest who even as a grown man Mama used to call her "little puppy," was at her bedside when she passed, though he was too decent to press that emotional advantage over Frank or Carl. According to the nurse and to Mary, "Mrs. D didn't know anyone by then, except for God," and it was under his breath, so no one but himself could hear it, that Frank added, "And her broker." The three brothers met together at the funeral home, out on some depressing outskirt of town near a public storage unit and packaging plant. The reedy, stooped manager was kind enough to stay open later than usual so they could all make it (Carl's flight had been delayed, due to winter storms). Frank wiped sweaty palms on his jeans before he went inside, as if he were a teenager about to sit for an exam, but once he saw her, his nerves steadied. It was dim and arid-aired inside, almost like a movie theater, with tinkling music fluting unwantedly through discreet speakers. There she was, at the end of the room, on a platform, laid out like a queen.

He had wondered, on the plane ride out, whether he would choke up when he saw his mother's body. He did not, then or later. There she lay, recognizably Mama but powerless now, her face thinner than when he'd last seen it, her hair papery and styled. The expression looked angry to him. Couldn't they have fixed that—made her unnaturally benign-looking? They had put coloring on her lips, but her skin was lightlessly pale. He saw Carl press his fingers to his eyes and hunch his shoulders. Frank turned away not only to give his brother privacy but also because he himself was finished. He nodded, sighed, left. Waited for the other two outside.

IT TOOK SOME months before everyone got their money. Lawyers first, meetings, phone calls, Federal Express envelopes—items Frank had little use for in his normal life. He was not required to weigh in, significantly: Carl was the executor; Mama would never have entrusted the Englishman's son with the job, even though Frank was the oldest. (As if making mistakes with wills were a genetically inherited trait.) It did not matter now, and Frank did not begrudge his younger brother the role. Carol handled the business competently and fairly, and all three got what was coming to them after these many years. First the money. Then the objects: china, silver, jewels.

Frank's wife now wore one of Mama's eye-catching rings on her finger. A band of white gold studded with several yellow diamonds. Mrs. D had singled out this piece for Adele, which was curious since Mama had directed a fair share of snidery at Frank's wife over the years—as she had at all of the wives. None of them were good enough for her sons, even if the sons themselves had countless flaws, too many to list. The gift reminded Frank of an evening on that last visit. She had been wearing the ring, and he admired it, not because it was new, but because he knew there was a story behind it that his mother liked to tell. The stones were urine-colored, to Frank's eye, but that perception might explain why he didn't do better picking out gifts of jewelry.

"Have I ever told you about this ring?" his mother asked.

"Tell me." He took a slug of the Margaux. Goddamn, that was a beautiful wine. Velvet. Violet. Blackcurrant. "Go ahead."

"When I was in my twenties—after you were born, but before the others—I finally discovered my favorite jewel. Every girl has to have a favorite jewel. I saw mine in a shop window in New York—a yellow diamond, in a divine setting, just gleaming like bright liquid gold against the black panel. I had never seen anything like it, so I went right in and asked them what it was. 'Yellow diamonds,' a suave gentleman there told me. 'They are very rare.' Ordinary diamonds are wonderful, of course, but there is nothing as magical as a yellow diamond. Do you know how they sort the quality of the stones? Fancy, Fancy Intense, Fancy Deep . . ." She laughed. "So ever after that, if I had an admirer, I made sure to let him know I was especially partial to yellow diamonds." It was an almost flirtatious look she gave Frank. It must have worked on them, he supposed. "That way I could tell how serious a man was about me, and I could also judge something about his means, if I didn't already know. This one, you see"—she looked down at the ring and pointed to a small piece of faceted sunlight—"came from Mr. Gibbs. Do you remember him? The man who owned the stables? And this one came from Lawrence; he gave it to me out of guilt about the affair with Barbara." Her lips compressed, briefly. "And this one . . . Well, I don't want to tell you about that one—a lady has to keep *some* secrets. But this one, this big, beautiful stone—this was from darling Lloyd." She fingered the ring for a moment, turning it around, caught in a strobe of memory, her face leached of irony or anger. "I had them all put together on one ring, you see. So they could all be with me, at once."

Frank nodded, as if this made perfect sense. "Have a drink, Mama," he said, refilling her glass.

She smiled at him, almost wistfully, like a girl.

"Does one of them," he asked her, though as he asked the wine turned bitter in his mouth, and he knew that framing this question was a mistake, "come from my father?"

"Oh, no!" She found the thought almost laughable. "He had long since left us, by the time I was walking in New York that day and saw the display in the window." She admired the ring on her finger again. "Besides, he could never have afforded a yellow diamond."

She drank, then stood. Teetered, slightly. The music stopped. She had no feeling for music, his mother. It was something Frank had wondered at, often—why, then, did he?—but it was as though she were a pianist who had lifted her hands from the keys. She turned her back on Frank and retreated to her bedroom.

He emptied the second bottle into his own glass. Well, that might be it for the night. Cindy trotted off behind her mistress, on that assumption. Frank had no feeling about it, either way.

She returned, though, holding something in her right hand.

"This."

She cupped her palm, and he saw that something lay in her pale, wrinkled hand. For a moment, though, the object itself was blurry to him, as all Frank could see was how old that hand was, the leathered wrinkles and folds, the lifelines that had gone everywhere, to places Frank never wanted to have to think about. He blinked, and saw a ring there.

"His signet ring," she said. "This was all he left us. This was what we got when your father died." It was a simple gold signet ring with an etched black stone, on which the symbol looked like some Chinese character.

We?

In the sorting out with his brothers after—an irreverent venture through El Dorado, not unlike soldiers looting a town after riotous victory—Frank claimed a painting or two he liked, and some pleasant trinkets. There was no sign of the signet ring. In the will, Mama had specified that the yellow diamond ring was to go to Adele. Frank did not worry for his brothers, though: their spurned wives got other treasures, a heavy gold charm bracelet, a smooth jade necklace.

When he gave the ring to his wife, he decided not to tell her the story behind it. She knew enough about his mother already. Why add new details, now that it was over? Adele could find her own new meaning for the ring. She really loved it, wore it all the time; it suited her better, as it turned out, than the pearl necklace he had gotten for her in the first flush of his inheritance. The irregular cluster gave off a yellow-white light from Adele's hands when she drove the new car. The two were paired, in Frank's tiring mind, ring and car: passports, both, to other countries.

Vanity Plates

✦

MOST DAYS THERE IS SOMEBODY, BUT SOME DAYS THERE is nobody, and they are on their own.

The dog barks and jumps up, barks and jumps up.

"Star, goddamnit!" Frank, mussed hair, eyes ablaze, barks back from his seat at the kitchen table. "Awful dog." He says this often, not to anyone in particular. Star's a border collie. She ought to have hours a day roaming across miles of open land, stalking a flock of sheep as she guides them to safety. She could learn a hundred words, as other collies have, identifying balls, toys, friends. Instead, kept from going upstairs to Frank's room by a flimsy wooden toddler gate, Star moves tautly around the ground floor of this beachside house with two old people—herding her humans away from their remaining memories, or toward them.

Neither direction is safe.

But Adele loves Star, and Star is devoted to her mistress. The black-and-white animal quivers with her adoration as if with a fever. Adele needs somebody to love, now that Frank doesn't really count; though, even in the old days, back on the ranch, there were days when Adele's affections for the dogs and for Frank seemed about even.

She misses him.

Adele talks to Frank like he's still in there, but there are three of them living together now with Star: Adele; Frank who seems like himself; and a third party, the ghost of Frank, who sits at the kitchen table and speaks gibberish or aggravates Adele by contradicting a basic fact, adamantly denying an incident from the day before. She might repeat the story—"Sophie was here yesterday, remember? She brought those blueberry muffins and took Star out to the beach?"—as if on hearing it a second or third time, Frank might admit his daughter had visited.

"You're driving me crazy, you know." Adele stands by the round oak table, which is scattered with uneven stacks of catalogs, like molehills in the garden. She holds a steaming cup of chamomile tea and leans slightly on the walking stick with her other hand. Her knee still hurts from the fall. She is half facing Frank, half facing the view of the dunes and the sea beyond. Light from the morning Pacific pours over them both through the wide, salt-sprayed windows. "If you drive me all the way crazy, Frank, there will be two of us, and then what'll happen?" Star sits at Adele's splayed feet, head tilted up, listening with every fiber of her furred being. "Star, honey, I don't see you taking care of us."

"Where's the little girl?"

"Lizzie comes back on Monday." Adele blows on the top of her tea. "That's tomorrow. Today's Sunday."

"Oh."

"She needs a break from us, Frank. I mean, I can understand that. Can't you?"

Lizzie is in fact an adult but a petite one: compact, blue-jeaned, androgynous. She is the caregiver with the most hours and the one Frank likes best, though the older tattooed rocker Steve is a close second. (Cross-wearing Grace is alarmed by Frank's language, and young Eric is just flaky, sometimes shows, sometimes doesn't.) When Lizzie first came to the house for an interview, Adele opened the screen door and laughed out loud. This five-foot-tall elfin person was going to try to handle Frank, who stood over six feet and had always been hefty? The idea that Lizzie could commandeer this half-mad hulk of a man seemed comical to Adele. Santa Claus, one of Sophie's kids used to call their grandfather, with his white head of hair, his bushy beard, his jolly round belly.

His mental frailty is worse than the physical. Frank is in better shape than some eighty-four-year-olds, upright and mostly mobile, though his shuffle is heavy and his internal parts have got to be in advanced decay. No one wants to imagine the state Frank's liver must be in now, a year into the return of the cancer; and imagination is all anyone has to go on since Frank decided, when he was still able to, not to submit to any more scans. Pills either. Fuck it, he thought and may have said—Adele can't remember—but the attitude was clear. What's the point now? Frank had tossed out all his meds. She could not stop him—there was no one stubborner than Frank when he had made up his mind, even a broken mind—and she couldn't say anything when he started drinking again, either. *Fuck it. Why not?* Adele wonders if Frank's body will just give out one day, the way an old car might eventually stall right on the freeway. It's probably how he'd want to go.

She felt bad about bursting into laughter at the sight of Lizzie, a reaction that may have had something to do with the diminutive carer having been found by Frank's kids: they were bugging her about getting more help, though she told them there just weren't many options in this remote town, so of course they had to prove her wrong and find Lizzie. Adele, who is tall, too—she had to be to stand her ground opposite Frank—felt like a different species, looming over the younger woman. (Fortyish? It was hard to tell, and Adele didn't ask.) Adele almost sent her straight home. Like someone who showed up to audition and couldn't carry a tune. Next!

But, partly to compensate for her own rudeness, Adele invited Lizzie in, and by interview's end she was convinced that there was a lot of sense and competence compressed into Lizzie's small person. And she was from Michigan, like Adele. Lizzie was unfazed by Frank—by his bulk, his confusion, his cursing. She seemed to like him right away, and he liked her, too, treated her like his niece, if he had had a relationship with his niece (she lived in Virginia and sent Christmas cards with pictures of her kids). Almost immediately he gave her a nickname, Lassie, a good sign. It stuck until the stranger nicknames that came later. Lizzie reminded Adele of a tugboat taking a great container ship out of the bay: I may be a tenth your size, but I'll get you there, whatever your cargo. Once we make it to the open waters, though, you're on your own.

SUNDAYS ARE BLANK days. A short preview of death, of nothingness; of there being no one in charge. Occasionally, Adele thinks of church, almost wistfully, though she has not been since she left Michigan, after college, decades ago.

She gets through by holding on to Star and throwing remarks at Frank: some, like darts, sticking near the target, others bouncing off uselessly. And by having the TV on. If they sit side by side watching together, Adele in her tan recliner grayed by dog hair, Frank in his walnut brown, she can pretend for a spell that life is normal again, and their troubles limited to the ache of joints that need to be replaced or just have been, the stiffness that comes with arthritis, the rises and falls of diabetes, an irregular heartbeat here or there. Kids' stuff, Adele thinks now. The Golden Era, she jokes to herself or to Star. Who knew how special it was to be able to tell your husband that the heart doctor had pissed you off by changing your medicine again, and have him know what the hell you were talking about? Who knew how much you'd miss the grunt, the noncommittal shrug, even, when they were gone?

If there's a game on, that's best. When it was summer and baseball, it was usually the Giants and they were usually throwing the game away, one more thing that's gone to hell lately. Now it's fall and football, and since there's no team they care much about anymore it's easy to watch whoever it is, college or NFL, one color against another is what it comes down to. Adele has a few people she hates—Tom Brady especially, a Republican, a Trump guy. Adele yells at the TV when Brady is playing, though that gets Frank flustered and makes Star start barking.

Politics is upsetting. The awful 2016 election and every awful thing that followed from it. In retrospect, that was the beginning of the wreckage.

When the news shows air from midafternoon on—exhaustively chronicling corruption, evil, idiocy, chaos—the air in the room gets frizzier and more charged, Adele feels her hair standing on end and can't make herself shut up. "It's unbelievable." She has lost count of how many times she has said this. Finally, she gets up to pour herself a glass of wine. Four o'clock is not that different from five o'clock, when you think about it.

"Is that Thump?"

"Yup," she says, from the kitchen.

She doesn't correct Frank on the man's name. It's what he always calls him, and though it's possible it started as a joke, the syllable seems apt to Adele since the president does seem like a blunt instrument, a cudgel or a shovel. It bothers her, though, that *thump* has also become one of Frank's all-purpose words, meaning something like love, pain, heart, loss. He will pound his fist against his chest sometimes, a geriatric Tarzan, saying, "And when you think about it, and when you see it, it's like thump, right here, you know?" "Thump, thump, thump: that's how it is, man. That's just how it is. The rest is all BS."

She knows Frank still feels love: for his son, Tom, who makes him proud in a general way (Frank wasn't very attentive to specifics even before, and Tom's finance job is complicated); for his daughter, Sophie, though when he sees her he usually calls her by the dog's name; even for Lizzie, the "little girl" who cooks for him, helps him dress, cleans up his messes, takes him out for a drive if he wants a change of scene or a lunch out, giving Adele some breathing room and needed quiet. Frank jokes around with Lizzie, and she can better tolerate his incomprehensible commentary, the dead-end stories, the sudden exclamations studded with *fuck*s and *shit*s that Lizzie finds funny, not offensive. "You're a card, Frank," Lizzie says, and he gets from her voice that that must be a good thing.

Frank loves Adele, too. She knows that. They yell at each other freely on the days when there's nobody, no one to witness the things Adele occasionally allows herself say to him, partly in the hope that he'll understand and partly with the certainty that he won't. Those days Frank, too, lets go, sounding more the way he used to when he was drunk. That mean streak he always had, the withering sarcasm.

"Wait till I tell you about my wife," Frank said to Adele one Sunday a few weeks earlier, rolling his eyes. She was trying to get him to help her bring in bottles of sparkling water from the garage. He sounded as though he was joking with one of the guys at the gas station or the lumber yard.

"Frank." Adele had looked him right in his ice-blue eye. "I am your wife."

The red veins pulsed across her husband's cheeks, and he furrowed his tangled snowy eyebrows and grimaced—a comical, sheepish look. But when Adele started laughing, he did, too, with relief. "Oh," he said simply. "Oops."

She switches the channel from news to a movie. War: perfect. Guns, action, heroism, handsome guys, pretty girls. That will keep them going.

They settle down, Star squirming for the first hour on Adele's lap, shivering with nervous energy, until she finally gives up on finding any sheep, and goes to sleep.

SUNDAY IS LIZZIE'S free day. No bedpans or Depends, no cleaning of intimate places, none of the brisk matter-of-factness required to manage somebody else's personal hygiene. The way someone looks at you, half grateful and half ashamed, realizing they have become something like your baby or your pet. Whole chunks of memory can be gone in a patient, but the submission in that relation is still understood.

On Lizzie's day off, the only cleanliness that matters is her own.

There is no going up to dress Frank, where he waits in his lair like an ogre in a fairy tale, in a room whose walls are lined with colorful pictures, paintings and photographs, of landscapes he has seen or maybe still dreams of visiting. Sitting on the edge of the bed, hands on his knees, his large head down as if he is thinking about the great questions, he is sometimes cheerful, sometimes fierce and prone to snap. Goddamnit! Shit! Not that way—if an arm gets stuck in a sleeve when she is helping him and accidentally jostles his bad shoulder. The swearing is worse, or there's more of it, if he has had a glass of wine, found a bottle and started swigging already. That happens. Lizzie has shown up at eight in the morning and found Frank crooning along to the Rolling Stones, plastered, Adele asleep in her downstairs room or pretending to be, leaving Lizzie to sober Frank up with breakfast and strong coffee. Adele still drinks wine, and Frank, with a hound's instinct, finds the bottles no matter where she stashes them. Early on, Lizzie tried talking to Adele about whether she might stop drinking, or at least lock the bottles away out of Frank's reach, but the conversation hit an immediate roadblock and Lizzie has never tried going back that way again.

You pick your battles. Like people say about their kids. You can't stop a patient doing every single thing that's bad for them, or their loved ones letting them. They'll get upset, their heart rate will go up, and you'll lose their trust, which is what makes the work possible; or worse, they'll submit and become resigned, lose any urge to enjoy their lives, and that does not actually make things easier either; it is like handling a mannequin, a deadweight. Lizzie makes sure Frank walks, and eats well, and stays as much off the sugar as he can. (If she isn't careful, he'll pour a thick stream of it into his coffee, calling it sand.) She talks to him to keep his mind active and doesn't worry when she can't understand his replies. Lizzie knows about the liver cancer recurrence, that some years back he had a third of the organ removed. She hasn't talked to a doctor about the issue—Adele waves off Lizzie's questions about the doctor, so she is in the dark about the details—but given Frank's history, Lizzie guesses that alcohol in any quantity ought to kill him.

But Frank's an odds-defying guy. Lizzie's been doing this long enough to have seen longevity pop up in the strangest places, ambushing bewildered family members braced for loss. Her stint before this was providing hospice care for a ninety-year-old retired pilot with advanced pulmonary and heart disease. He was given a month to live, which stretched to two, then six, then twelve. Everyone around Vince was tired and broke, but he had been clear that he wanted every possible intervention to prolong his life, and so on he went. Lizzie finally left that job for this one, after making sure they found a replacement caregiver. You can't keep preparing someone for death if they won't die. You feel like you're not doing the job right.

It is why, when she got the email from Sophie via the website, Lizzie answered it. She was ready for a change. And she likes working for Frank and Adele, generally. Adele can be short; she won't hide her sighs of annoyance if Lizzie doesn't fold the laundry just so, or puts plates away in the wrong order, or cooks Frank beef stew because it keeps him strong, though Adele has a thing about red meat. But Frank, confused though he often is, has a good heart, or at least is funny and warm, dealing with his impairment as well as anyone could. It's harder when they fight it—when they struggle against the loss of memory, the evaporation of words, the falling away of self. There is a grace in giving in.

Lizzie and Frank have their moments together. After she has dressed him in his khaki coat and corduroys, Frank looks distinguished, with his white hair combed back and his beard trimmed, and he carries himself with that old-school dignity, especially when they go out. Lizzie takes him to the seafood place near the harbor, where he'll shuffle stiffly in, nod to the barman, engage in garbled banter with a pretty waitress, and then settle down to enjoy, really savor, his food. He can't make sense of the menu, but Lizzie orders for him, and when it is time for dessert, Frank marvels at a sundae with chocolate sauce as if it is the rarest oyster.

"For me?" he says with a girlish flutter of his eyelashes. At the first mouthful, his face lights up like a kid's. "Oh, man! That's good. Jesus! That dark stuff."

"It's chocolate," Lizzie tells him.

"Fuck, yeah." Frank clenches his fist and stabs the air with it, a charge of victory. "Das Chocolat. *Sehr gut, mein Commandant.* Das Chocolat!"

Frank goes into characters like this—a jolly Nazi, a quavery old lady, a fancy Englishman. Lizzie doesn't know where they come from; when Adele hears Frank do it, she shakes her head, rolls her eyes, and on a good day gives a snort of amusement. Some spouses are eager— desperate, even—for you to understand who this person was before they crumbled. Vince's wife used to try to tell Lizzie some of Vince's pi-lot stories, though she stumbled over the technical details, which made her feel worse. Lizzie understands the urge, though. It's like someone trying to fill you in on the plot of the movie when you're only going to see the last ten minutes. They want you to have a grasp of the story.

Adele has not made a lot of effort in that direction. Lizzie is not even sure what Frank used to do for a living. Early on, when she asked, Adele talked about a lot of land they used to live on, up in the forested hills inland, where they had Labs. It took Lizzie a minute to get that Adele meant dogs. Sundance and Dutch, they were called, and one of them was a good hunting dog, and Frank grew grapes, and Adele learned to cut wood and kept a huge vegetable garden. "We were hippies, basi-cally," Adele told her, "hard though it is to picture it now."

There was a divorce, a long time back—hence Tom and Sophie. Liz-zie gradually realized Frank's kids must be closer to their mom, since they don't come to visit Frank all that often, just once every couple of months. They are middle-aged and live down in the city with their fam-ilies. Nice but neglectful: it's a more common combination than peo-ple might think in families. Sometimes it's the mean ones who hold on tight, interfere with everything, and that is harder. Lizzie has seen plenty of permutations of grief and jealousy, siblings embattled with each other or with their parents (or stepparents—those can turn nasty). When Tom or Sophie comes up, Lizzie often has questions stored up to ask them. They'll usually tell her.

Like Frank's German voice, his English voice—who these characters are. They make Lizzie laugh. Frank is a ham, when you come down to it, which makes working for him all right, even when Adele is grouchy or the dog is frantic (though Lizzie has developed a fondness for that dog), or Frank growls at her. A week ago, Frank called Lizzie an asshole for emptying out the dregs of his wine before he had finished it. Frequently, when he and Adele bicker, he tells Adele to shut up, though judging by Adele's reactions—she gives as good as she gets—Lizzie guesses that these outbursts are not so much dementia-related as snapshots of exchanges the two have had over the length of their marriage. "Forty-five years," Adele told Lizzie when she came for the interview. "I don't know how it happened." She sounded genuinely surprised. "I don't know how we managed to hang in there, but here we are."

They did not have kids together, and that probably helped. In calmer moments, when Frank is asleep, Lizzie and Adele sometimes talk a little. It's awkward. They don't have a lot of common ground, though they can talk about Michigan, and both like to garden, or Lizzie used to when she lived somewhere she could. The two women can trade stories of their failures and successes with plants, the shade lovers and the sun lovers and the temperamental ones that don't do well in either. They never mention their other similarity—the fact that neither of them is a mother.

Lizzie used to spend most of her days off in the garden. It was a great counter to a week spent mostly in a stifling indoors, breathing air that was often a mixture of body excretions and the antiseptics used to disguise them. Lizzie used to live in a converted garage behind a friendly couple's main house, several miles east of here, on a gentle slope a stone's throw from the redwoods. Lizzie loved being so near the hush of the forest, and best of all her landlord let her work a patch of the garden, where she grew peppers, lettuce, flowers. He even put a wire fence up so the deer wouldn't destroy all Lizzie's hard work.

Then the guy's wife's sister showed up in some kind of trouble, and they needed the garage back. Lizzie tried to fend off the details (a violent husband featured), though the landlord really wanted to explain it to her because he felt bad about kicking her out. Lizzie left pretty fast, though, moved into the first place she found, the upper floor of a duplex in town. There's only room for potted plants on a narrow back deck, which is a big disappointment, but Lizzie tries to make herself feel that being close enough to hear the ocean makes up for it.

Now she often spends her Sundays walking in the pretty tourist town a half hour south, the one with sweeping views of the jagged coastline and dramatic rock formations below that look like sea monsters. Lizzie mingles with out-of-towners who have brought along their sweatered terriers and their romantic dreams. The place is a popular spot for weddings; it is not unusual to bump into a flock of giggling young women wearing matching dresses. Lizzie isn't interested in trinkets or five-dollar coffees, though, so after a while she makes her way down to the beach. She wishes she had Star with her for company. To deal with her own restlessness, under cover of dealing with the collie's, Lizzie often offers to take Star for a walk when Frank is napping. She has to keep her leashed along the old coast road, the dog pulling the nylon taut while weaving back and forth low to the ground, as if sniffing for murder clues in the ice plant. "Star light, Star bright," Lizzie calls her, thinking of the rhyme she learned as a kid, though that makes her miss her garage apartment by the woods, where you could better see the stars at night. Here, all too often, the coastal fog swallows them whole.

ON MONDAY LIZZIE gets groceries. The other caregivers do a run later in the week, but by Monday Frank and Adele have run out of basics like eggs, bananas, and Chardonnay.

Adele urges Lizzie to take the Mercedes; it needs to be driven so that the battery doesn't die. Adele has a Subaru. It isn't clear to Lizzie why they have kept the luxury car since it's so low that Frank can't even get into it anymore.

"It was Tom's idea, a couple of years ago." Adele talks about the car like it was a gym membership or a spa gift certificate—one of those things a younger person imagines an older person might want. "He drove up here and then took Frank all the way down to the city to go car shopping. When they found this model in royal blue, Frank went nuts." Adele shook her head. "Six months later the doc took Frank's license away. Frank couldn't feel his feet anymore! It wasn't safe. Was Frank furious, though. He made me find him a different doctor, not that that changed anything. It's a small town; we used to run into Dr. Ron in the street, and Frank would completely ice the guy. He'd probably still do it if you ran into Ron. He doesn't remember why anymore, just knows he hates him."

Driving: it's one of the worst losses for people, especially up here, where they are a couple of miles from any stores. Adele can't drive, either, right now; she threw out her knee a month or so back. She heard a giant thud coming from Frank's room upstairs and ran to see if he had fallen. He had. She couldn't get him up, so she rushed downstairs to dial 911 but went too fast and tripped on her way to the phone. Only later, after the paramedics left—Frank fine, tucked back in bed, oblivious—did Adele realize that her knee was the size of a football. She upped Lizzie's hours after that, but still doesn't want someone at the house 24/7. If Frank falls again, he will be stuck. It's like a game of chicken. Who is going to give in first: fate or Adele?

One of Lizzie's older patients, a retired coast guard officer named Stan, used to steal the car keys from his wife when she was asleep. He would get up early morning when it was dark, take a little drive, and then come back and park the car exactly how he found it. He wouldn't tell either of them for days. Lizzie learned how to recognize when Stan had had one of his adventures, by his barely suppressed smile of satisfaction. She liked Stan for trying, but she knew that her task was to come up with a better hiding place for the car keys, though not so good that his wife couldn't find them.

Lizzie is nervous about driving Frank's car. She has considered telling Adele she would prefer not to. Lizzie does not flinch at the more repulsive tasks, cleaning stains and messes out of bedsheets, clothes, rugs, bathrooms. Lizzie learned soon after she started doing this work that it was best to be direct about bodily functions. Patients prefer it. You've got to match the words to the person, though: in Lizzie's experience women often prefer to speak of *bowel movements* and *urine*, but Frank is very much of the *shit*, *piss*, and *puke* school. The last one hardly comes up, though; Frank's not much of a vomiter. His stomach seems to be made of steel, able to withstand hot sauce, onions, alcohol, and any amount of coffee.

Driving the Mercedes fills Lizzie with dread. It's too big. She feels like a child sitting behind the wheel of a tractor pretending to be a grown-up. She's afraid that one day she is going to mistime her turn across two lanes of oncoming traffic into the Safeway parking lot, or knock against another car while trying to maneuver the giant vehicle into one of the diagonal spaces. She doesn't like to think about how expensive it would be to repair a car like this.

When she makes it to Safeway and back without incident, Lizzie is so relieved she does not even mind the sticky mechanism of the outside gate, which opens with an expressive judder, or Star's ear-splitting barking from the pen as Lizzie as pulls up the graveled driveway. Star jumps against the fence as she barks, jumps and barks in a repetitive loop, like a cartoon, but in Lizzie's hearing the sound is a congratulations for her making one more trip without a calamity. She parks by the weather-beaten garage, cuts the engine, and exhales. Safe! Except that the parking brake is just a button you press, not a lever you crank—another feature Lizzie doesn't trust. She pops the trunk open and gets out.

"The brake is on, all right? So you can't run me over, even if you want to," Lizzie mutters to the Mercedes. It's a habit left over from her job with Vince, who virtually never spoke to Lizzie in the year she was caring for him. She had one-way conversations with her patient when the family wasn't around, and eventually with the machines, too—the catheter, the heart monitor, the ventilator. She began to go a little crazy, maybe. Vince's family didn't have a dog or cat or even a bird, and Lizzie had to talk to somebody.

"Did they have everything?"

Lizzie startles. Adele is on the wooden steps of the deck, watching Lizzie. She had not noticed Adele up there, standing still with her cane.

"Well, the bananas were green." Lizzie blushes about getting caught talking to the Mercedes. "But I got them anyway. Everything else was easy."

"That's okay. They'll ripen eventually. We all do."

Lizzie laughs at Adele's small joke, but she's still embarrassed. She takes the bag of groceries from the trunk, and then as a diversion, but also because she has often wondered but forgets to ask, she says, "What does the license plate mean?"

It reads 5TH BT.

"Fifth BT." Adele smiles. Maybe ironically, it's hard to tell. "Fifth baronet."

"Oh." Is Lizzie supposed to know what that means?

"Ask Frank about it." Adele turns to open the screen door.

Lizzie comes up the stairs behind her, while Star barks furiously at being left out of this exchange.

"Hold on, sweetie! I'll throw the ball for you in a minute," Adele hollers back over her shoulder, more or less right into Lizzie's face. "Ask Frank," she repeats, in less of a shout. "See if he remembers."

"Ask me what?" Frank is sitting at the kitchen table going through catalogs, bathed in ocean light. He loves one of the shoe catalogs especially. He has told Lizzie over and over how pretty the black-haired girl with the blue clogs is ("Cute, but not Barbie doll. You know?"), and tells some sarcastic story Lizzie can't make sense of about the suave, gray-haired man in loafers. These are the two models Frank returns to, every time. "What?"

"About your license plates," Adele says loudly, as though Frank's deaf. Adele's hearing is worse than Frank's. "Fifth BT. Fifth baronet. You want to tell Lizzie what it means?"

Frank looks wary, as though this might be a trap. He stares at Adele. His face is not blank—Lizzie sees a flicker of comprehension in it—but he does not speak.

Lizzie has seen spouses do this, when they're fed up or bored or want to show off their loneliness. They quiz the demented patient on some detail or history almost certainly irretrievable. They are willing their spouse to fail, as if that failure will finally prove to God, or to the caregiver, how put-upon they are, with this empty shell of a person to call their own.

No caregiver likes to play along with this game.

"We were just talking about your license plate, Frank. On the Mercedes." Lizzie puts the paper bag on the kitchen counter and starts taking out groceries. "Look, I got some of the pastrami you like. They had just sliced it in the deli. We can have sandwiches for lunch, later."

"What license plate?" Frank directs the question to Adele.

"On the Mercedes. Lizzie just told you. Fifth BT. Do you remember what it means?" Adele gazes steadily at Frank, her brown eyes unblinking behind her glasses. Frank's eyes are a cool northern-European blue, one of his most striking features. Almost a greenish blue, though frequently bloodshot. He hardly ever wears his glasses anymore, since he no longer tries to read. "Who's the fifth baronet?" Adele presses him. She is unforgiving. She did not sign up for this, she has told Lizzie: watching TV with a guy who insists five minutes after they've finished dinner that he's starving, who doesn't know the name of the country's god-awful president. Who gets up at four in the morning and starts puttering in the kitchen, just like he used to, only where before he would be doing last night's dishes and brewing a pot of coffee, now he is putting the coffee beans in a pan with onions and frying them till they burn, creating a foul-smelling mess, or he is nosing out Adele's wine and glugging it down, till he staggers.

Adele did sign up for this, of course. She and Frank are married. Have been, for forty-five years. It's in the contract. You make a promise.

Lizzie is about to ask Frank what kind of eggs he wants this morning—scrambled, or fried over easy, sometimes it makes him laugh when she says sunny-side up—but she sees that Frank is focused on Adele.

"*I am.*" Frank's voice is subdued but clear. He is addressing his wife with a *So there* expression on his face. "That's me. Fifth BT."

Lizzie has no idea what they're talking about. It sounds like a spy code, Agent 007. Lizzie will have to ask Sophie about it next time she comes up for a visit. She just came last week, though, so it will be a while before she can clear up the mystery.

Still, Lizzie sees that Frank has won this particular showdown with Adele.

"Sir Frank," Frank booms in his fancy English voice, and there is intention in his eyes. You could even say they are twinkling. "Very good, chaps! Very good. Carry on!"

Adele laughs. She is gracious in defeat, unexpectedly. "That's right, Frank. That's you, all right." His wife thumps him on the back, like he's a good boy, and he laughs with an open mouth. "Okay, Sir Frank. You have your breakfast, and I'm going to throw the ball for Star. I've got to get that poor animal out of her pen."

Frank is still seated, hands on his knees, staring out the window at the breaking waves. He doesn't say any more, and Lizzie gets the idea that the English character has gone back into the costume closet in Frank's mind.

"I'll explain it to you sometime," Adele throws over her shoulder to Lizzie, right before the screen door slams shut, but Lizzie knows how those kinds of promises go. She won't hold her breath.

Outside, you can hear Star yip-barking with excitement, the frenzy of anticipation, and Adele talking steadily to her as she unlatches the gate and lets the collie out.

The two have a joyful reunion. It's one for the ages.

Harbor House

+

IT WAS A PLACE FOR HONEYMOONS, FOR ROMANCE. TEN miles south of the tourist town and its crowds of day-trippers, the cliff-side inn had been written up in magazines as a destination for weddings and fine dining. The restaurant's talented chef served adventurous dishes in a gracious, open dining room whose expansive windows offered a panoramic tableau of the emotional Pacific. This was the early 1990s, when the French-leaning word *gourmet* had not yet ceded to the childish *foodie* to describe people with enough excess cash and leisure time to throw at improbable restaurant concoctions and ten-course tasting menus. But there had always been people who liked to eat well, and Frank and Adele were among them.

Harbor was in the name, but there was no harbor there, so you could interpret that as you liked. A functional harbor, Noyo, had been developed in the 1800s in a narrow natural bay half an hour farther north. Here at the inn, the view from high above the surf was rarely serene; generally casting you back to some earlier, prehuman landscape where giant, creaturely rocks crouched in a roiling ocean, as if biding their time for return or reincarnation. The painterly sunsets were life-changing, but if you wanted warm shallows or breezy palm trees, try Hawaii. Here, along this rebellious part of the Northern California coast, the land met the water not gently but severely, and from the pretty, windswept garden behind the inn a narrow path wound down to a rough-cut strip of beach. Walking there, you felt dramatic saltwater on your face and heard the waves shouting as they struck the shore, and it was often too loud to talk to anyone. For some couples, that forced end to conversation was just right.

There were four in this party of guests. Celebrating a parent, not a marriage: it was the father's sixtieth. Frank and Adele had booked two of the outer cottages for a couple of nights, one for themselves, the other for Frank's adult son and daughter. In this lull between Christmas and New Year's you sometimes got such odd groupings. The staff were told to be especially welcoming to the graying, jovial Frank, as he had loaned them, some years before, a grand, gilt-framed painting, nineteenth-century-ish, of an elegant seated lady and her small white dog. The picture hung beneath the railing at the top of the stairway in the main building, so guests saw it whenever they descended. She was apparently a distant relative of Frank's, a man who lived up in the redwoods someplace where "she is not as comfortable as she would be here," he chuckled to the then owners when coming to the loan agreement. They must have laughed and agreed, feeling that the graceful lady, hair pulled up with a hint of flowers, lent class to the place. Subsequently, the inn had been sold on to new owners, who did not share this affinity for the painting but knew their business enough to tell Mara, likely the one who would check the couple in, to be nice to them. Frank and Adele. The Harbor House meant something to them; you found that a lot at a place like this—there were new guests and magazine reviewers, but, too, there were scores of repeat visitors who came with their memories and their stories, and it was your job, as greeter, chef, or owner—to act as though these mattered to you, and were interesting.

FRANK WAS NERVOUS as he and Adele set out for the inn, dog-less. Frank had taken Suki to the kennel the day before, and Adele was slightly off-balance without Suki around, like someone who's quit smoking and can't remember anymore what to do with their hands. It was not as if anyone ever asked you to choose between your dog and the kids—if they had, Frank doubted Adele would have hesitated, but then they weren't her kids, though she had known them since they were pups—but when you had to watch that ever-sunny Samoyed face stop smiling when she realized you were going to abandon her, it did make you pause. For a moment, Frank had a wild thought of canceling the two-day trip to the coast with Tom and Sophie. He could find excuses. Was it too much to do? The kids had their own busy lives, they probably wouldn't mind. Maybe they'd even be relieved—?

He shook off the temptation. *Come on, old man. It is a far, far better thing . . .* He handed over Suki's leash and special toy to the unattractive, lank-haired woman of no known age who ran the place. Her bright grin made her briefly younger. "Don't worry, Frank!" she cajoled, in a voice with a lifetime of cigarettes in it. Almost made him miss smoking. "We'll take good care of her." Like any person good with dogs or horses, Lonnie had an animal feel for others, and sensed Frank's anxiety. "You two go and have a nice time. Suki'll be fine."

Adele drove them to the coast the next morning. There had been a rain dump two days before, and though the drive into town had not been too hairy, they didn't know what they'd find heading the other way. Frank was ready to jump out if needed, clear the road of branches or other debris. Who knew? Maybe they'd come across a landslide that had washed the road out and they would have to turn back, after all.

Ten years ago, this worm in his gut, Frank would have known just what to do—knock back a slug or two of brandy before they left. Steady the nerves with a light bit of numbing. Not full-on anesthetic, just a shot of local. He had not felt the urge for a while, but that morning it surged strong. Weird how the instinct waited in you, a hibernating bear.

He had shed alcohol, though, along with some of the weight that went with it. Frank had a paunch now, no longer a whole bowling ball. It was physical weight he had lost, yes, but also the heavy role of the Grinch. Frank told himself he was not going to complain to Adele; he could have that much self-control. Enjoy a Grinch-free Christmas with your kids and your wife, you old sourpuss. Feel that heart pumping in you, the way Dr. Seuss showed it. The cartoon's little dog had made Frank laugh, with those fake reindeer antlers tied onto his tired head. Seuss drew a good villain, and stories were better with villains, even or maybe especially when they reformed at the end. Frank worried sometimes these days that he had become a pale cliché, with his demons at a distance.

It was one reason he enjoyed playing Drosselmeyer in their town's annual production of *The Nutcracker*. Frank kept the clever toymaker just this side of sinister, but with his eye patch and his mysterious magic, you had to wonder what he was up to. When Frank bulged his blue-green eye wide open, you could believe him capable of evil. He could feel it in himself on the stage: his powers of destruction were at the ready, and you never knew when he might use them.

THE SIBLINGS DROVE up together, with a craft project for their dad's birthday in a bag on the back seat. Like old times, except traveling by car rather than on the Greyhound they often took when they were a bit older and their mother wanted to skip the drive.

It had been Tom's idea to create a hand-drawn calendar with pictures he had dug up, and Sophie, too, from across the years. A classic seventies ranch shot, Sophie with scraggly hair and a Snoopy T-shirt, Tom in a magenta button-down, posing near the old red Toyota truck; Tom and Frank fishing together, slightly blurred over some jade-green river; Frank and Adele laughing in their finery at Tom's recent wedding. Tom had married someone who expressed to him a strong preference that Sophie not bring her girlfriend along to the great event—"She just wants a normal wedding," he explained to his sister. Sophie, after feeling a dread-clench deep in her stomach, refused the request, telling him she would attend only if her girlfriend could come, too; but she also promised Tom that the two women would not make any "political statement," which seemed to be part of the bride-to-be's concern. She hoped her brother heard the sarcasm, but she wasn't sure. In any case, he secured his fiancée's agreement to that deal and they all got through without incident. Sophie was even included in the bridal party, an ivory-clad set of young women with sprays of flowers in their hair who had fun chatting about their makeup. The wedding was a cheerful and photogenic affair, and Tom and Sophie never discussed the matter afterward. Tom did his best to forget about it, a useful skill he had. The negotiation was one of Tom's first acts of spousal diplomacy, and good practice for his future work.

They met in a shuffling awkwardness in the Harbor House lobby. At first, the four were faintly nervous around one other. Before they sat down for dinner, Frank led Tom and Sophie upstairs and showed them the painting of the lady with the dog, which they duly admired. Frank provided no backstory for the woman in the picture, so there was not much to do but nod "She's pretty," and agree that the painting looked good there. "I wonder if she ever imagined she'd end up in Mendocino," Sophie breathed to Tom as they descended again. "It wasn't really on the map of empire."

No one could remember what they liked to talk about together. Frank, drinkless and also beardless, looked strange to Tom and Sophie, less the grizzled lumberjack and more of a sobered-up seventies rocker. The wordy menu gave them an opening, and Frank dived in there right away, bantering with the waiter about different dishes and then prompted, after they ordered, to launch stories about the recent stint he had, for reasons mysterious to his children, who had never known him to have a paying job, working as a sous-chef a few nights a week at an upscale restaurant an hour away from the ranch. Had it been part of his drying-out regime, proving he could work around alcohol? Frank did not bartend, but prepped plates and veggies and baskets of bread. He loved regaling them with the near disasters, the tetchy customers, and the kitchen camaraderie, which gave him a good buzz.

"The old biddies are the ones who *really* can't wait for the food to arrive." He shook his head. "Man, are they fierce when their roast lamb with polenta is not in front of them when they want it! The fat cats from the city don't care; once they get their Zin and a plate of focaccia they're good to wait. Scott sent me out to do a soft-shoe for old Mrs. Anderson one evening." Adele started chuckling. "She's no spring chicken, and still dresses like she's going to the opera. You could *see* the steam coming out of her head." He puckered his lips in campy imitation of the lady's sour expression. "*The waitress should have warned her* the lamb takes a while. Like Sierra had put her in physical danger, by making her wait."

"Sierra's the owner's daughter," Adele added. "Cute, but an awful waitress."

"No one can say anything, though. *Don't tell Daddy!*" Frank said, in his falsetto. He bugged his eyes out for extra effect.

After that icebreaker, they could move on to dogs. At twenty-eight, Sophie still enjoyed that subject most, the animals at the ranch. It united them. The Circle C dog count was down to one, a new Samoyed, and Adele relaxed and warmed when describing Suki. "She's only a little past being a puppy, but she's just a sweetie, no trouble at all. Wants what's best for everyone." Adele's Midwestern practicality had always lived alongside sympathy for animals and a deep, ranging creativity that could surprise people. Visitors to the ranch discovered Adele in the tiny, compact stained-glass studio she had built for herself out past the woodpile, where she shaped flowers, suns, a windowed bird; in her artful photographs of their land, in poetic lights; in her knowledge of astronomy, furthered by a serious telescope Frank gave her one Christmas, through which she traced the movements of a hundred stars. Above all, when she played piano. From their dusty upright Adele's strong, deft hands drew sounds that took you far beyond the ranch, back to some older, different country, when you furtively listened while rocking on the deck and petting one of the half-feral cats, or playing a hot game of croquet on the dead, weathered grass behind the house. The music poured into you on those days, and it never left. It would be Adele who presented Tom and Sophie with prettily wrapped Christmas gifts at the end of this visit. It was Adele who sustained Frank, in every way. They scraped against each other at times, and Adele was never afraid to be tough or sharp with Frank when he got out of hand, which he did, but her face warmed when she talked about him, too.

From there they went naturally into older stories about their late, plodding black Lab, much loved by the kids, and the legendary, glamorous husky who had fled after a feisty couple of years, though not before giving birth to a litter of cute, mottled Lab-husky mixes, one of whom Frank named Black Bart after the famous outlaw. In the Circle C's living room, on the wooden wall behind the stove, Adele kept a pretty watercolor someone had done of that blue-eyed runaway; it hung in the place a portrait of ancestors might have gone, or a sketch of the homestead.

Against the vivid color of these ranch memories, current realities paled. The wider world seemed tamer, even though they all had adventures ahead. In the summer Tom was moving with his wife to his next foreign posting, likely Hong Kong; before that, Frank and Adele were traveling to Tanzania for a safari trip ("Africa without alcohol!" Frank said, mock-shuddering). And Sophie had decided to settle in London for a while. She was not sure why, but she felt it was the place for her to write. Not that she risked saying that aloud, in case it made their dad laugh at her, a lasting fear; she buried her real intentions under some blandery about wanting to live in England again, as she and Tom had when they were young, and having a few leads in journalism. Her omission did not matter, though. No one was following the others' details closely. They were each of them wrapped up in their own story.

"SO," TOM SAID, shyly, "I've got some news."

It was brunch the next morning at one of Frank's favorite places in Mendocino, a historic town that had long ago abandoned woodcutting and laid itself down for tourists instead. Restaurants, galleries, bed-and-breakfasts. Shoes, tchotchkes, crystals. An annual music festival. Mendocino lacked the bejeweled geriatric wealth of Carmel, not least because it was harder to get to and a greater distance from high-end health care, but as a beacon for cultured coast-loving explorers it worked on a similar principle. Trapezoidal water towers, shaded the gray of racoons, stood on stilts at intervals along the salted-and-sanded streets, like scattered monuments to some lapsed religion. Frank was on friendly terms with some of the gallery owners, and bought the restaurants' cookbooks so that he could re-create their delicacies in the Circle C kitchen.

"Oink, oink," Frank said as they tucked in. For him it was already lunchtime; he had as usual been up since dark. Sophie, still on East Coast time, had also wakened early and heard her dad stirring and talking to himself through the thin walls of the next room. She recalled the sounds of his groaning and muttering from ranch mornings in the past. It was strange, too, to be sleeping so near her brother for the first time in years, made Sophie feel they ought to get into a game of Stratego or battleships together, start tossing insults around, though more of their sibling fights when they were young had been physical. Wrestling, tripping each other up, wrist burns, rather than verbal cruelties. Punching the other one on the arm. Never the face.

Sophie saw Tom waiting until forks paused over cinnamon French toast slathered in berries, or a goat cheese omelet with sundried tomatoes, beside a glistening pile of bacon. He allowed a dramatic beat, then said: "You're going to be a grandfather, Dad!" (swiftly amended to "You're going to be grandparents!" to take in Adele). "And you'll be an auntie, Soph."

There was a buttery silence. Unsurprising information can still strike a momentary shock, like the shudder from thunder after lightning has streaked across the sky. You're waiting, but the percussion startles you, anyway.

"That's so great, Tom!" Sophie got there first. She held her coffee cup up. "Cheers! Congratulations!"

Frank and Adele, blinking, joined in to give a caffeinated toast to the thirty-one-year-old, whose proud smile had a flicker of doubt in it.

"We're excited," he said. "Molly's feeling good."

"When is she due?"

"Summer."

"Before you go?"

"Before Hong Kong. Right. So"—the young husband lifted his fair eyebrows, as though this were a fun adventure they had added on to a vacation—"there will be three of us moving to Asia! Not just two."

"Boy or girl?" Sophie asked.

"We're going to keep it a surprise." Behind his smile, Tom's face shuttered. It was unclear whether the surprise stretched to the married couple, or just everyone else.

What did you say in this circumstance, after that? None of them had any experience, or could guess. They returned to their cooling eggs, bacon, French toast. Frank speculated about the nature of breakfast in Hong Kong. Adele listed all the shots they had to get before they went to Tanzania. Sophie had a muddle of words in her head, *baby, Hong Kong, American embassy*, but she could not sort them into a legible order. A walk would help, she felt, and she suggested one after brunch, along the headlands.

To get there, you simply ambled until the town gave out. At a point, the shops stopped and the land took over and walkers carried on to a broad shelf of earth that broke off, along ragged edges, into a steep downward drop to the agitated ocean. The place brought eternity to mind, as horizons often do, and for a melancholic like Sophie, the unvoiced curiosity about suicide was inescapable. The paths did not take people quite to the edges—the state park did not want to encourage plungers to seek out this spot—but they were not far from the line where solid ground ended and salt-sprayed air took over. Did people jump from here? They must—those rocks, thirty yards down, mixed in with the waves, would kill you right away. A relative of Tom's and Sophie's had died that way, Frank's father. By pills, not jumping, but the fact haunted Sophie, though she had never heard the story behind it. Frank did not speak of him.

"It's so exciting," Sophie made herself say again to Tom as the wind whipped their hair and chafed their skin. Sophie's dark blonde was cut then in a short bob, a look of hers that did not last long when she discovered it did not correspond to her personality. But at least it meant the strands of her hair did not blow into her mouth, as they always used to at the beach.

"I know," Tom said. "It really is."

"A baby!" Sophie had never had much feeling for babies, not being one of those girls attached to dolls. It was always animals that had sparked her imagination.

Adele was not a big cooer over babies, either, it seemed. Tom and Sophie had been kids when she met them, and she had suffered a late miscarriage in the early days with Frank, after which a door apparently closed.

"You'll have to learn how to change a diaper, Tom," she teased. "Molly's not going to want to do them all by herself."

"Oh, I know! She's already made that clear."

A baby.

"So you're really not going to find out the sex ahead of time?"

"We want to keep it a surprise," Tom repeated, sticking with the ambiguity.

"But do you secretly have a preference?" Sophie nudged her brother, who smoothed things over so effectively she was sometimes provoked into trying to ruffle him. A successful diplomat erased his own decisions or preferences in order to facilitate the negotiation. Neutrality was an art. "Like, are you hoping for a boy?"

"Boys are great. Girls are great, too!"

"Ah, come on, Tom—everyone wants boys," Adele stated. "People say they're easier. You know girls—so fussy." She was laughing, though whether at memories of Sophie, age eight or nine and a sometime sulker, or with general female self-deprecation, was hard to tell.

"Well," Tom said, heaving his not-robust voice into the wind—he had not inherited their dad's deeper timbre—"I'll be going to the kid's Little League games, either way."

"In Hong Kong?"

"By the time they're old enough to play sports, I'll be out there cheering 'em on." Tom practiced his proud sports-dad face, a look he wore happily. Not from having seen it modeled by Frank, who had never attended one of his son's myriad matches or games—a thought Sophie kept to herself. "Wherever we are. No matter what sport it is!"

"How about dance?" Frank asked.

It was their dad's first comment about Tom's forthcoming, still imaginary child. The *Nutcracker* run had just finished, and Frank was perhaps thinking of the dozens of tutued and leotarded urchins skipping and pirouetting around his all-powerful Drosselmeyer. As he had written in letters to Sophie, he loved watching those dancers, and kept an eye out for the ones with special grace. "Will you cheer them on if they dance?"

"Of course!" Tom buried his hands deeper in his jacket pockets. He had made a classic error of someone who left California a while ago, forgetting how cold it was, and wore only a wind-cheater, which was not cheating much of the strong wind. "If we have a little girl, and she gets into ballet, even though I don't know much about it—"

"Or a boy. It could be a boy," Frank noted, passing the idea forward, as if they were playing one of their old games of three-man football. "Boys get into ballet, too."

"*No.*"

The syllable was loud, easily audible.

"No. That's not gonna happen."

Frank started chuckling. He could tell, they all could, that he had hit a soft spot in his son. It was like Frank to keep prodding. "You don't know that for sure, Tommer, until it happens. You might find—"

"Nope."

He did too know. He was suddenly certain.

"If we have a son, he's not going to be a dancer."

Any of the three of them might have kept bugging Tom—there was clearly sport to be had in it—but Sophie felt a spasm of sympathy for her bristling brother and cut off Frank's further sarcasm.

"Where are you guys on names?" She created a diversion, the way you give a dog a bone, to make him drop the steak in his mouth. "That's the fun part. Like naming characters—one of my favorite things about writing a story." Sophie was aware as she said this that there were names she held aside from the huge pool of fictional options: a secret elite group she was keeping back in case she wanted to use them one day for her own children. If she ever had any. *Luke* was one. *Sam, Isabel, Elsa.* "If it's a girl," she asked, "what would you name her?"

Her brother's shoulders relaxed again, fielding a question from the press corps that he had been well briefed on that required no bluffing or evasion. He issued a list of approved possibilities, and did not even mind when some drew the inevitable reactions. "Ugh, no, not Alice! I had a terrible boss called Alice once." "Madison? Sounds like a president or a lawyer, not really a little girl." Tom weathered all these amiably, his good mood restored.

After a while, the air was getting cold. They got through some good options—Frances, Chloe, Rose—before Frank made noises about needing to take a nap. He was like a young child that way.

They returned to their safe harbor for some downtime, Frank humming the tune from the "Dance of the Sugar Plum Fairy" as he waved goodbye at the cottage door, a joke probably caught only by Adele.

THE CALENDAR WASN'T quite finished. "I still have some pictures to put in," Tom said, leaning over an open nylon sports bag in which Sophie could see a set of tape and scissors and glue sticks, like the luggage of a traveling kindergarten teacher. Sophie watched him from her narrow twin bed. While the inn itself was coherent and romantic, these outer cottages were character-free additions, with little light and no view of the sea. They could have been in a nice freeway-side hotel almost anywhere.

She liked the sports bag touch. This might change—and it did, to a degree—but her brother had not yet resolved to present himself to the world as a suave, suited, world-traveling diplomat with a leather brief-case of European origin and a status watch glittering from his wrist. In a cream cable-knit sweater and blue jeans he could be a graduate student on a research jaunt, or a guy getting ready for a fishing trip, as he probably wished he was, or a young man walking from an urban train station, as he did once when visiting Sophie at college, carrying two gift speakers for her in boxes all the way to her off-campus apart-ment. (She had been relieved and surprised he had not gotten mugged en route.) Such sibling visits had been rare and were now over. Sophie did not know what was ahead, but the *baby*, in word and image, hovered between them, like the ghost of Christmas future. It would open the gap between them wider than the mere miles. Sophie reminded herself that her brother and his wife *were just doing the normal thing.* Happened all the time.

"I want to make sure it's pretty even, you know?" He was paging through the months, seeing where there were still places to be filled.

"Yeah, just because I've been a total slacker and you've done most of the work, don't erase me."

He laughed. Sophie scooched off the bed to look at the work in progress. Tom, tall, just beginning to stoop, looked over her shoulder as she held it.

"Oh, that's a great one!"

March had a rare snap from their mother's house; she must have taken the picture, unthinkably, of a droopy-mustached Frank looking on as Sophie, her hair pulled back with two small pigtails by her face, read the words in some picture book. Her eyes were cast down to the page in concentration, Frank looking on beside her, Tom beside him. Perhaps Frank had just dropped them off after a visit, or was picking them up to drive them off to a baseball game. Maybe it was a special occasion; Sophie was in a yellow plaid dress, and dresses happened rarely.

"Dad looks like a total Deadhead in that one."

"I know. Then there's this one from England, seventies sometime. It's hard to find any with Adele in them, too; she was always behind the camera." Frank stood, a serious expression, beside his two teenage children. He was in a corduroy jacket, bearded, and smoking a pipe.

"I don't remember the pipe," Sophie said. "Was that a pose, for England's sake?"

"I wish there were more pictures of us fishing. Like at the ranch, down on the Navarro."

"We never had a camera with us. I could only find one from the Circle C, and it was just me with one of their hundred cats."

"Should this go in for August? It's between this and one other."

It was a Polaroid; Sophie had forgotten about those. Adele had a phase of taking plenty, expensive though they were—the instant gratification was irresistible, especially if you lived an hour away from the photo lab in town. In it Tom was standing tall and grinning, shoulder-length blond hair, next to his silver Fiat, parked incongruously on the dried grass at the ranch.

"Fix It All the Time!" Sophie said. "Oh my God, that car. I was so happy when you loaned it to me until I realized I had to bump start it almost every time I parked."

"Yeah, but it was super fun to drive. Basically a tin can, but who cared?"

"Put that one in. The Fiat should live on. Doesn't matter that I'm not in it."

"Okay, we've got one left. May." He shuffled through a pile of candidates, handed her one. "This is a nice shot . . ." It was of Tom and Frank in a Scandinavian landscape. Fjords, mountains, greenery. Tom, ten years old, had gone on a post-wedding trip with Frank and his new wife, a time when Sophie traveled instead with their mother and some friends of hers, including the English academic who proved to be significant, eventually becoming their other stepparent. "Then again," Tom said, always fair, "this one has all four of us together. Maybe we should go with this."

Another wedding photograph, Sophie barely recognizable to herself as a bridesmaid. The men looked good in their tuxes, Tom a smart and handsome groom. It was nice to see Adele, too, hair lightly permed, wearing a light blue dress with padded shoulders. She and Sophie looked similarly out of character, as though they were in drag. Both were people who belonged in jeans.

"Up to you," Sophie said. "But I like the fishing one—the countryside is beautiful."

"That was a great trip." Tom looked at it again, other memories flickering across his face. It struck Sophie that he did not probably recall that she had been absent from it. She wondered whose decision it had been to separate the siblings, though she imagined her going along would have made it less fun for Tom and for Frank. The allocation of each child to a different parent made some sense. "It was one of the first times," Tom continued, "Dad and I did real fishing—you know, not the trout-in-a-barrel kind."

"That was the kind I could do!" Sophie laughed. As she grew up, Sophie did get a little adept at fishing, enough to catch one or two on a line sometimes, down at the Navarro, feel the elemental thrill of pulling the flopping creature in. Once she had it out of the water, she had no idea what to do with it. Her dad had to come along and grab the wriggling silver creature, stun it to death against a rock.

"I'm going to put the wedding shot in there," Tom said. "It's nice that we are all in it. Plus—it's my wedding!"

"Perfect!" There was no trace of the controversy in the photograph, or for that matter of Sophie's girlfriend, who was probably in a corner somewhere wishing she could just read a book. "Good choice."

Sophie thought of the photographs you saw in the news of state visits, presidents shaking hands with emirs, chancellors with prime ministers. That was the world her brother was entering. His wife would be beside him.

And where was Sophie going? As usual, she did not know. Maybe when she turned thirty everything would miraculously become clear.

"I might have to learn to smoke a pipe when I move to London," she joked to Tom, who did not react as he focused, brow furrowed, on carefully pasting the wedding photo into May. Sophie did not mind. Like their dad, Sophie indulged in in-jokes sometimes, for the smallest audience. "And corduroy. I'd better not forget to pack my corduroy."

Tom half laughed, nodding. It was a great imitation of someone who had heard what she said.

PART FOUR

✦

The Whole
Staggering Mystery

A devilish grin. "I might be old, but I'm not dead."

"You've had a good life," I tell him.

"Well, I don't remember it," he says, then concludes happily, "so I don't forget it either."

—KEGGIE CAREW, *Dadland*

1.

A NANOSECOND ON THIS EARTH

✦

I SPENT MORE HOURS WITH MY DAD IN THE LAST THREE years of his life than at any other time. What I know best about him, finally, is how he faced his end.

It's a decision every person makes for herself or himself—whether you are of sound mind and body or not, whether given a heads-up by doctors that it's coming or just consulting the actuarial tables and making your own bet. The ones taken by a heart attack midsentence or deep in their sleep are robbed of the moment, which is otherwise the ultimate character reveal, as dramatists know. "Had I but time—" Hamlet says to Horatio, wondering if he can fit in a few last great lines before he is out of breath, "as this fell sergeant, Death, / Is strict in his arrest—O, I could tell you— / But let it be."

The prince lets it be. That is the heart of the task, whenever it comes.

Along the way to my dad's end, I started to learn about his beginnings. The structure was novelistic in that way, allowing us at the last to follow the whole of Nick's arc.

Discovering Gawen got me to explore some of the boxes I had inherited from Lucia, and among them I found her "Baby Book about Nicholas," along with a great tide of congratulatory notes that washed into their home in Pasadena from American, English, and Austrian friends and family from December 1932 into 1933. Names I did not know, like sketches of the couple's English life:

Dec 29th

My dear Lucia

We have only just heard through Mrs Rundell of the arrival
of the new member of the family, and send you, Gawen and him
our very best wishes for the future.

I hope the post fairie will bring him all the nicest gifts, and
that he will be strong & nothing but a pleasure to you.

We shall look forward to having you back though it must be
lovely in your sunshiney country. I hope Gawen is really strong
again.

We saw his father and mother in London—

We have had the vilest colds for weeks, and they linger affectionately with us—I want to get away somewhere.

With love & many congratulations

Yours affectionately
Aceituna Griffin
Wargrave, Berkshire

Strikingly, from Lucia's father-in-law, "Jim," as I learned Sir Douglas was known by those close to him. To Nick, Lucia gave an account of
his cold English father who abandoned and wanted nothing to do with
him, and of an English family manipulative and foreign. In this way
she secured the boy on her side and prevented him from meeting again
his surviving English relatives. My dad returned to England only after
he turned twenty-one and was untouchable by British courts. By that
time, his English grandmother had died.

Yet Lucia kept notes and letters that provided contradictory details
about the Brownriggs. She was not the editor that Beatrice was, and she
left documents from which you can tell a different story. From which I
have told these stories.

Friday 23rd December 1932
9 Victoria Street
Westminster, London
(The Fairfield Shipbuilding & Engineering Company Ltd)
Lucia, My Dear!! You have given your dear self a most mag-

nificent x mas present & to me also! Fancy me a grand Papa!!!! To say nothing of your von Grand Papa!!!! HE must be as proud as a Dog with two tails! The best thing you can do now is to give him cause to be as proud as a Dog with 3 (or more) tails!!!!! By the time this reaches you—when it brings you my warmest congratulations and love—You will I hope be up & about—only returning upstairs for "Old Nick's" meals . . . what I call the Jersey Cow business! & very nice too for him!!!! Mind you make Gawen B push the Pram about!!!!!! & send me a snap shot of him so employed! And don't let him introduce Bed side episodes with his forthcoming novel!!!! Look out!

My Mr J. L Wilson is all over himself this morning at your news!!! One would think he was the happy father—good soul that he is. I am rather excited too as I am off to Portsmouth for a 5 day change of air for Christmas. I shall try to assume a particularly dignified air—as becomes a grandfather—even though his HAIR is getting somewhat scanty! But then the times make business rather hair reducing! You are lucky to be where you are—out of the turmoil of politics and poor business.

Well my Dear, be good & wise and don't get doing too much—whether it is Ping Pong or Badminton or swimming!

God bless you my Dear: please give my sweetest messages to the local grand mamma & to the local Grand P von Papa (or should I say POP!?)

Your very loving F I L
Jim

In this alternate history, Lucia is warmly connected to her husband's parents—"Dear Lady B," she continues to address Beatrice, even years after the divorce—and is a more sentimental parent than I knew her to be. People change over a lifetime, of course, and new motherhood is its own state; but the best I ever heard from my grandmother about her sons was affectionate skepticism. She was critical of them—the more so, their wives or girlfriends—though with her youngest, Peter, she kept up sweet nicknames and a certain playfulness. She relied on Victor, named for her father, as the sensible one. Certainly she had the most uneven relationship with Nick, her eldest. They quarreled over the years, and did not speak for long stretches of time. He shed no tear at her death. I won't forget the stolid neutrality on Nick's face in the Albuquerque funeral home when I visited with him and his brothers after Lucia died. In a good spell, mother and son delighted in out-outlandishing one another, Nick's banter spiced with sexual innuendo and florid swear words, Lucia parrying with tart retorts. Nick and his Mama could make each other laugh, and when that happened it was the same smile, the same laugh. Their physical resemblance never lessened; in fact, in my dad's frailest last months, clean-shaven, his voice weakened, he resembled his mother more than ever.

To imagine this spiky, unconventional woman as a twenty-year-old doting on her newborn took extra imagination. It was hard to forget my uncles, the Brosies, laughing at a picture I had of Lucia seated at her kitchen table, smiling up at my infant son I am holding in my arms, in a photograph from 2001. Their jokey claim was that it had to be the only photograph ever taken of their mother smiling at a baby.

2.

SOMETHING TO MARVEL AT

+

YET LUCIA, THE NEW MOTHER, WAS THE WRITTEN PORTRAIT I found on my first visit up to Fort Bragg after my brother and stepmother had finally opened Beatrice's scrapbook. Early revelations from Beatrice's "Memoir of Gawen" had tumbled out swiftly: Beatrice's love for her grandson, Nicholas, her deep belief that her son had not died by suicide, and the lengths to which Lucia had gone to keep Nick unaware of Gawen's fatherly feelings. My stepmother recognized that the essential message of Beatrice's letter to Nicholas in 1939 was "to let him know how much his English family (and his father) loved him, how they were a family of love for each other, how they might not survive the war." Additional details would come more slowly, as we read through the many pages of the thick black book, but one of Mike's and Valerie's main takeaways was that Lucia's actions, claiming benefits from Gawen's complex and ambiguous estate, helped force the sale of the Brownriggs' home, which in turn led to Nick's enduring separation from his English family.

The living room in my dad and stepmother's Fort Bragg house was set up with two recliners, side by side, facing the TV. At the far end of the room, broad windows gave out over the dunes and the ocean. At the Circle C, the snug living room was also set up with two armchairs side by side, though as there was no television they were set up for reading, not far from the warmth of the potbelly stove. Nick used to sit in his corduroy-upholstered chair after dinner, a few glasses of wine in, sometimes patting the head of his loyal Lab, Buck, who lapped up Nick's muttered faux-English praise of some other-named character. "Very good, Woodley; as you were, Woodley; well *done*, Woodley . . ." Buck, often chided by day if he was being annoyingly persistent about fetch, was in heaven then, wagging his heavy tail with a thump. It was a tail we had to watch around the kerosene lamps, in case it knocked one over and set the place ablaze.

In Fort Bragg, I sat near my dad on a comfortable ottoman, Beatrice's scrapbook in my lap, trying to understand all that was in it. The book was so much fuller than I had imagined. He sat in his chair, attentive, making whatever sense he could of what I said to him. Paging through, I narrated Beatrice's titles on the various envelopes—"Letters after Gawen's death," "1928 Letters to Gawen from his Father on his becoming Captain of his school," "Letters on Voyage to Kenya 1937." Then there was one that seemed of special interest: "Letters 1931–1932–1934–1937 Marriage of Gawen and Lucia—Birth of Nicholas."

"'Birth of Nicholas.' Oh! Let's look at what's in here, Dad."

He neither encouraged nor discouraged this selection. He simply waited.

"I wonder what it says." I pulled the letter out of the envelope it had been sent in, addressed to White Waltham, in Maidenhead.

He had such small, neat handwriting, my grandfather. Lightly slanted, pretty, with trim, elegant loops for *y*'s, and *l*'s, and in perfect parallels whether or not on lined paper. Gawen's letter might have been sent the month before I was reading it that day. The paper was not yellowed; the ink looked fresh.

Nick was past reading by then, so I read the letter aloud.

Bienvenido
26 Circle Drive
Pasadena, California

24th December, 1932

Darling Mums and Daddy,

I haven't had a minute to write to you before, as you will readily understand. Nicholas was born on Thursday morning at 9:36 a.m. and weighed 7lb 10 oz. It all went off quite well, and it didn't last very long, although it seemed like ages to me, naturally. Lucia began feeling slight pains Wednesday evening, so we kept in touch with Dr Smith. She went to bed and got a little sleep and I took her to the hospital at 4 a.m. I stayed with her in the delivery room until they gave her gas which was about 8:15. They gave her ¼ gr. Morphine hypodermic about 7 am. and they didn't give her gas until the contractions became too painful. They had to use forceps at the end because the head was rather large, but as the worst part came after the gas had been administered I don't think she suffered unduly. Anyway she was very brave about it—much more than I was. I've never spent such a ghastly 6 hours in my life. However I held her hand for her, which was all I could do, and I was glad to be able to do something to help at all. She came round from the gas about 10:45 and I saw her for a moment and then went home & came back in the afternoon about 4. She had recovered amazingly well and was cheerful and happy, but still, of course, very weak from loss of blood. Yesterday she had rather a reaction—nervous— but was well on the whole. I'm told that will be all right as soon as she can nurse the baby satisfactorily, which is expected today or tomorrow. She has a delightful room, looking out over the mountains, and the nurses are excellent—sensitive as well as being very human, and she likes them which is the main thing.

Nicholas is a funny looking little man, still rather red and wizened, with a mop of mouse coloured hair, and a very lusty voice and strong little hands. His eyes, as far as can be ascertained are blue, and still rather swollen, because they put in silver nitrate and salt. It is a state law here apparently. But I am assured that he promises to be a big and healthy boy. He still has some forceps marks on the sides of his face, though I am assured that they will disappear in a few more days. Lucia simply adores him, and thinks he's the most beautiful thing that ever happened. I'm as pleased about this as I am surprised. I didn't expect such a violent and perfectly genuine display of mother-love from the very beginning. I think I'm going to like this little son of mine, too, when I get more accustomed to the idea. My strongest emotion at the moment is one of intense relief that it's all over and that all is well, and that the child is normal in every respect. Apparently the bony structure of the head is something to marvel at, according to Dr Smith. Lucia saw him last Monday, and he said to expect the baby next Monday the 26th. I'm very glad that it arrived a few days early, because the suspense and waiting wasn't so bad for Lucia. The nurse who is coming here afterwards is awfully nice and efficient. A woman of about 34 or 5, I'd say.

Lucia was awfully pleased with your card and appreciated it very much. Everyone has been very kind to her, and sent Christmas trees and flowers ad infini. She is getting lots of attention from everyone. Only her mother and I are allowed to see her at the moment, but she says that's all she wants to see, so she's quite happy and comfortable. She will come home about the 7th or 8th Jan. I expect, all being well.

I am quite pleased that it's a boy. It's no good being anything else, is it! But it is a great gratification to me to know that the future 6th Baronet has arrived. I hope and trust that you and Daddy feel the same way about it—I will go to the British Consulate and notify them, as soon as I have time to go over to Los Angeles. But what with Christmas as well as the baby and dashing to and from the hospital my time is just about full up. I haven't got the birth certificate yet and I shall collect it today. Did you put it in the papers?

Everyone has been very kind to me, and I have been asked out to dances etc, which I have refused, because I'm still rather tired and I want to recuperate my nerves. You will laugh when I tell you that I lost no less than 8 lb in those 6 hours between 4 and 10 am Thursday. But I have got back one of these already, and I feel rested and happy again today. My mother-in-law is still very tired and exhausted, and insists on rushing around the place without stopping. Just like all mothers. The Baron was delighted that it was a boy, and kissed me on both cheeks and shed a tear on my shoulder when I came back with the news. I was very touched. I haven't time to write any more now, but I'll write again soon after Christmas. I wanted you to know all about it as soon as possible. Lucia sends her love, and all my love to you both.

Like the baron, I shed a tear at the description of Nicholas's birth.

This letter, dated December 24, 1932, and mailed special delivery to England, had been waiting to be reread by its subject for about sixty years. Or eighty, depending on how you counted.

"That's you, you know?" I touched his blue-jeaned knee. "That's you as a baby, Dad, that he's talking about."

He nodded. His eyes were alert, his expression was inscrutable. I could not tell if this moving moment of discovery was one I was having alone, or if we were having it together.

Still, something of what I read had made its way through to him. Valerie said that Nick told her later, after they had started looking through this scrapbook and he understood some of what it contained, that something had changed for him. He said he finally felt like a Brownrigg.

3.

HITCHHIKER'S GUIDE

✦

IF YOU'RE DRIVING TO FORT BRAGG FROM BERKELEY, THERE are two ways to cut over to the coast from northbound 101. One route goes up past Ukiah, and familiar exit names, State Street, Perkins, that trigger memories for me of our childhood drop-offs. At Willits, the town where you turn off for State Route 20, you pass a Lumberjacks restaurant whose sign has a red-flanneled, suspendered man with a smile and an ax. SR 20 is the road the loggers use, hewing close to the route of the Skunk Train, a local line built in the 1880s to transport timber but now just for tourists. You often get caught behind a long truck, stacked high with long-dead bodies of redwood trees. This route might be the slightly shorter way to Fort Bragg but it winds steeply through expansive acres of a demonstration state forest, and the curves aren't great on an uneasy stomach. I associate that ride with a visit my husband and I made when I was pregnant with our son. We had to pull over so that I could throw my breakfast back up at the side of the road, while he and my stepson waited in the car, and I have tended to avoid the road since.

The other turnoff for the coast comes sooner. State Route 128 intersects the highway at Cloverdale, a pleasant valley town that used to be a stagecoach stop, and later a gas-and-diner stop, where you could get a sandwich or a burrito on Citrus Fair Drive. SR 128 starts out in rolling chaparral, scattered ranches hidden in the hills, then reaches the hamlet of Boonville and the pretty vineyards of Anderson Valley. We once went wine-tasting there when my English friend and I visited the ranch, a rare tourist outing, as usually the Circle C itself was the feature. It was fun until, after the boozy lunch, Nick insisted on taking the wheel for our return. Midafternoon was his naptime, and alarmed by his yawning I peppered him with questions about the previous day's Giants game to keep him awake.

One day in 2017, driving up alone as usual, though with our family dog in the way back, I passed a woman hitchhiker standing near the turnoff, wearing a hefty backpack. I went on for a bit, wavering. Buffered in my Volvo SUV, listening to a podcast, I felt like the clichéd suburbanite my dad used to snap at me for being, continuing some old argument with my mother (if not his own). Picking up a hitchhiker was not a Linda thing to do. It would be a Nick-inflected act, as that countryside was, too, the redwoods, the pot farms, the vineyards. Loggers, hippies, Subarus: those were my dad.

I turned around.

I saw her standing there (the Beatles were also Nick; he took Mike and me to see *Help!* and the *Yellow Submarine* in a double feature, though musically he was more of a Stones man), did another U-turn by the oak trees, and pulled over. I rolled down the window. The hitchhiker and I had a brief exchange, each trying to check that the other wasn't a serial killer, and then I invited her to hop in. The dog reassured us both: I figured he could protect me if anything went wrong, though he was a mellow creature, and she probably guessed that anyone with a friendly hound like him could not be too sinister. She put her backpack on a seat crowded with my various bags and then got comfortable beside me.

In her twenties, bundled in layers, she had white-girl dreads and an air of pot and patchouli. She was at ease making conversation, said she hitchhiked this route often. She had come early that morning from San Francisco and was trying to get to "Mendo." As we headed oceanward, my passenger chatted about her friends in the city, her younger siblings, their trials and talents, and how expensive and impossible life was getting everywhere. She talked about sleeping rough in Mendocino—fine, mostly, though a local mountain lion came into town from the woods sometimes, and you had to keep a lookout.

The first miles of that road have bends and switchbacks through the open country. When I asked if car sickness might be an issue, she answered cheerfully, "Nah. I smoked a bowl this morning so the drive wouldn't bother me. I'm good."

She mentioned that she did seasonal work for cannabis growers, mostly the laborious task of separating buds from stalks. When I asked how legalization had changed the industry, she said she did not think it had much improved conditions for workers like her. I told a pot story from Circle C days, probably to establish my wilderness cred and counter the image of the Volvo, the labradoodle, my blond highlights. (Before you know me, I can seem like I might be from Marin.) The back-to-the-landers around the Circle C mostly grew grass for their own or their friends' use; if there were larger-scale farmers in the surrounding hills in those days, Nick and Valerie were unaware of them. Then, when the former California governor Ronald Reagan became president, his lasting animosity toward hippies and pot smokers led him to create the federal Campaign Against Marijuana Production, an aggressive, military-style operation. Targeting the "Emerald Triangle" of northern counties, which included Ukiah and environs, CAMP deployed armed troops that removed families at gunpoint from their houses and searched vehicles without warrants. In the eighties, CAMP helicopters flew low over the forested hills, giving local Vietnam vets disturbing flashbacks, and with these high stakes—people, growers or not, could be shot and killed in raids—it's the more surprising to recall Valerie's pranking of CAMP officials. Sometimes, hearing a helicopter overhead, she went through a pantomime of running indoors with small planters of roses or other flowers, to taunt the pilots into thinking she and my dad were growing weed. They never were.

I told my passenger a version of this story and she laughed, but I decided against adding the bookend tale from soon before Nick and Valerie left the ranch. By the 1990s, when CAMP and its excesses were over, serious growers had returned to the area. Now the violence began to go the other way: hikers straying unknowingly onto land owned by new drug cartels (as some considered them) had been shot, the wilderness becoming less safe in a way that had to do with humans, not animals. On one of my last visits to the Circle C, with my English friend, Nick's truck was stopped on Low Gap Road by a sheriff who told us that a manhunt was going on nearby. A security guard at a pot-growing operation had shot at a deputy, then fled the scene. The sheriff, once he understood where the Circle C Ranch was, told my dad he had reason to believe the fugitive might be near or on their property. Was there a chance the man would find any weaponry there?

Nick soberly considered his answer. Sure, there were a few guns and rifles in the basement.

Anything else about the place that the sheriff's team should be aware of?

My dad looked at the uniformed man.

"Kittens," he said, after a pause. Even sitting next to him, I could not read his tone, whether he was giving the information ironically or just in shock at the idea of an armed man being chased by helicopters using thermal imaging technology. "There's a new litter of kittens; one of the cats gave birth a few days ago."

The sheriff eyed him, silently calculating—*There are some crazy people who live back here*—and then told my dad to turn us around. We could probably return the next day, but for now we were to head back into Ukiah. My friend kept exclaiming over what had happened. The earlier wine-tasting outing had been fun, but an armed hunt for a pot farm guard made for a better story, one she could "dine out on for days" back in London.

It was too hard to set up the context for this story, so I didn't try, and conversation between my passenger and me slowed over the last stretch of 128 as we approached the coast. Those ten miles or so take you through another ecosystem shift: the sky closes over as the road dives into a thick forest of towering redwoods. It is the marine fog they love. Your car shrinks as you go, and just as your human scale is revealed to be a paltry one, the Navarro River emerges on the road's south side and guides you to the Pacific. The route meets Highway 1, and the view immediately has the drama of Mendocino County: rocky cliffs, crashing waves, a cloud-pressed horizon.

The hitchhiker seems like a character I dreamed. She was called Summer or January; I can't see her edges or even her face. What I have left is an impression of her warm, scratchy voice and her heartfelt thanks, when I dropped her off at the bridge just before Mendocino— above the long, bankside beach where hounds of all kinds run in sandy ecstasy as Big River pours toward the sea—saying that she felt lucky that I had been her ride, and wishing me a good visit with my dad. She had something in her of Clarence, the angel in *It's a Wonderful Life*, who proves to George Bailey that his existence has been worthwhile, that the world would have been a colder, harder place without him. Maybe I was worthwhile, too, for making these visits to see my fading father. Her patchouli lingered in the car's atmosphere after I drove down and parked by the beach to let my dog run. He played with the slow-moving current, getting wet and gross and happy, while I held on to a sense of accomplishment from my small good deed, helping a traveler get where she was going.

4.

FALTERING MINDS

✦

IF I WANT TO HEAR HIS VOICE AGAIN, I GO BACK TO HIS written words. I have so many of them. *Mrs. Sylvia Thomson, Sylvia Brownrigg Thomson . . .*

Some are dated after significant events, like our gathering in Mendocino when he turned sixty, in 1992. At that celebratory weekend, Mike made the announcement that his wife was pregnant. Seven months later a baby boy was born. They called him Nicholas.

> 12/22/92
> Harbor House
> Elk, CA

Dear Sylvia,

Words become illusionary—thank you, for coming out, for coming up, for being here with Mike and Valerie and me.

I never thought I'd see 60 years—I mean, old Daddy Kings (??), life, etc. But, ooops! Just peeked over the wall to 61—can be done.

All this energy . . . to and fro, back and forth and really good things, loving things, fuel to the very same and best in us, in me—from you—awkwardly put but you know.

> Thanks, old girl, I love you very much,
> Dad

6/6/11

Dear Syl,

Whew! Just got off the cross-trainer . . .

. . .

Got a CT scan tomorrow—the hospital has had ROOMS (all equipped and ready to go) for years and they're finally hooked up to the Mother Ship. Though, I did kind of enjoy being pushed outside on a gurney, the mist a-cooling . . . oh, oh, I was gonna write "shroud" but that certainly won't do! Let's call it Lachrimae Christi (Phoenician spelling!). . . .

Fog hangs over the dunes, the ocean, doing nothing, nothing more than slowly rolling over the far hills and, forgetfully, allowing an errant ray of sun to shine through.

. . .

Much love to you all—and a clap on the back to Sam and to Romilly—

Dad

5/19/13

. . . Well, 80 years are chugging along—I think of things that probably a great deal of people do when they reach 80. I mean, you can sort of sigh and think, Thank God I got this far—now what? CF opposing paragraph! [arrow to lines about aches and pains and a bone scan coming up] A little fear, regret isn't far away. I doubt I've left any footprint in the world and suddenly it doesn't seem to matter so much—I think of family and friends and know how fortunate I've been. Big, spoiled brat!

If Sedge is there, give him my warm regards. He's a unique, wonderful fellow. Hey, and you're pretty wonderful too, Syl, my lovely daughter.

All my love
Dad

A neurologist would know more about this, but when I think of my dad's decline, and of other vulnerable brains—those of friends or of writers we admire, who get played by Judi Dench in the movie—I won-der if there are not as many ways for our minds to falter as there are fal-tering minds. Do we each put our own spin on it? "Happy families are all alike; every unhappy family is unhappy in its own way." Tolstoy's line gets quoted so often because particularity appeals to us: we don't want to be like everyone else. I know that clinically significant similarities are drawn between sufferers of Alzheimer's or of alcohol-related dementia, yet it still seems true to me that every elder whose personality disinte-grates, disintegrates in their own way.

It is like weevils have eaten away at the neurons. You take the shirt out of the closet and it's full of holes. I could see my dad, when he was still trying to have conversations and comment on the world, hunt around for words and not find them. He learned to laugh or shrug it off, like a forehand that goes into the net, a mangled chord at the keyboard. When Valerie asked me to help get him dressed some mornings when I visited, I would put on shirt after shirt for him—he wanted them to keep coming. T-shirt followed by sweatshirt followed by fleece. None was quite enough.

Different capacities drop out: speech, self-awareness, humor. Mem-ory, of course. Reading goes; watching TV and listening to music stick around. I think the children of parents who cease to recognize them—the Adam whose mother calls him Hugo, after the gardener; the Mark whose father plaintively asks where Mark is—have it especially rough, because even in middle age, parental denial of your self wrecks equilib-rium. On the other hand, a parent who calls you by the name of the dog or your brother, but basically knows who you are and greets you with fondness and trust—still wanting to make you laugh, open to your making him laugh—is easier to bear. Does a person still sound like themselves, even if they cannot speak like themselves? That was true of Nick, and if I visited him often in his last years, it was not just because I loved him, and knew any encounter might be the last, but also because the flood of his affection was so welcome: a late end to a much earlier drought. Maybe it is like sleep deprivation: the body stores up the need.

The slippages about names or gender did not bother me. In any case, Nick had been careless with my daughter's name since before his memory loss was evident, not infrequently mixing hers up with that of Mitt Romney (to be corrected sharply by my stepmother). When I went up with our family dog, Bruin, for as long as he and their mildly frantic border collie were able to get along without mayhem breaking out, my dad talked to our big brown labradoodle in a friendly way, as he generally did with dogs. "Good girl," he said, patting Bruin's head, then questioningly, to me, "Girl . . . ?" Over and over again.

"Actually, boy—Bruin's a big bear of a guy," I found a few different ways of saying.

"Right, right—sorry, old man," he chuckled, petting and soothing. "I didn't mean to cut your balls off."

It's a bit like being drunk, too. Things slide around: words, reactions, intentions. Sometimes when you are around people who are stoned, you feel stoned, too. That happened with my hitchhiker—not a contact high, but a dreaminess brought on by her company. Sometimes when you are around people drinking, it is as if you were drunk: you let your guard down, freeing yourself to be funny or seductive or blunt. And when you are around someone in cognitive decline, your own thoughts begin to wander and drift. By the time I was heading home from Fort Bragg, I would often feel disoriented, unable to finish a mental sentence. Driving back down Highway 1, close to grassy ledges above the roiling ocean, I could imagine how easily a car might stray over and crash on the rocks. Had I just seen my dad—was it the last visit—when might I come again—what had happened? Behind all that slip-sliding away, I was wondering who my dad was now, though scratch that question to find the one beneath it: Who had Nick ever been?

Though some of these difficulties felt distinctive, many were, I recognized, almost generic for people my age. I was like a thousand of my peers with older parents, advance-grieving their loss. Was it heartbreaking for me to see this strong, once tree-felling man brought low, forced to shed his old-world chivalries like holding a door open for his daughter, and be talked to in the patient tones people use for a child? Of course. He fell sometimes, and had to remain on the floor till the paramedics could come out and get him up. He fried up coffee beans in a pan, burning them and smoking up the kitchen. He got angry, frustrated with the kind people who came to help, without whom he was more and more trapped. He took to calling one of his steadfast caregivers, a good-humored, diminutive woman named Kitty, "Fidie Fiduco." She never knew why. She liked it, though it was unclear if it was a hidden insult. Some riff on cats and dogs, is my guess.

Yet Nick was mostly comfortable and in a beautiful place, and how many people get that lucky when they are "in their dwindles," as Julia Child called the last stages of her husband's life? My dad had been married for almost fifty years to a smart, loving, and uncompromising partner; he lived by the ocean and had two fond kids who came to see him, sometimes accompanied by various grandchildren, in whom he might not have much specific interest but whose jokes or tennis playing or cooking he enjoyed.

"Days of gracious," to use his phrase again about past periods of ease and glory—adventurous travel, cider parties at the Circle C, healthier finances—but he might just as well have used it to describe his concluding years. "I pray that every blessing in life might be yours," Nick's grandmother Beatrice wrote to him in 1939, when he was turning seven, as she signed off her wartime letter to him. In a certain light, it looks like her prayers were answered.

5.

WHAT'S YOURS?

✦

OUR LAST LESSONS ABOUT PEOPLE ARE IN HOW THEY leave. The life story hinges on the death story.

With courage, I would say. That's how Nick faced his dying. Emotionally, my dad was an avoider; we never talked of anything that had gone on between us, but physically and philosophically he was tough. He took things head-on, shoulders squared. No bullshit. He had always been interested in the big picture, the arc of the life: he thought like a novelist even if he did not fully become one. When Valerie's father died, after a grim period of weakening, Nick became reflective and considered how he might face similar straits. He wrote to me in 1993:

> Oh Syl, what a sad, ugly business it is, an ailing, infirm parent . . . Valerie's bearing up realizing (almost) that the figure on the bed is only a pale ghost of the man she knew as father. A man in restraints with boxing gloves on his hands so he cannot remove the feeding tube which he has managed to do, anyway. What a moral, ethical, metaphysical quagmire—sometimes, very privately, I question how and what we are taught about the meaning and value of life. I don't mean to imply psychopathic shallows but it is fascinating, this reverence for the state of being called life that we share . . . She'll be returning after Christmas to tidy up his affairs and I'll probably go, too. I write all this being all too aware of my age, not alarming, to be sure, and yet,

yes, yes, I could succumb to any of this stuff, could go ga-ga, be propped up or tied down, drool and gaze vacantly, soil my sheets and hope, in moments of lucidity, I would not recognize the horror and/or pity in your face and others.

On receiving the diagnosis of a return of his liver cancer in 2016, after the discovery of a new, inoperable tumor, Nick made a few stark decisions. He threw out his meds, all of them. He was done taking pills. There were chemo options for his condition, and he ought still to take something for his diabetes, but he wasn't doing any of that. This was a conscious decision, one that made his doctor unhappy, as well as my stepmother, but there was nothing anyone could say to change his mind.

At the start he made an equally deliberate decision to welcome back an old friend: wine. It was easy; they still had countless bottles in the basement that he could reach at any time of day or night—including a few of their own Circle C vintage. Many of Nick's male friends were inaccessible: his compadre Gus in New Mexico, who had sobered up years before, was dead, and he and his oldest friend, Bob, had dropped out of touch. So Nick reconnected with one who had been faithful just as long. Really, when you go that far back and strike up a relationship again, it's as if no time has passed at all.

A year or so into his AA period in the later 1980s, Nick wrote to Lucia about a drive he made from the ranch to Mendocino—along the same dirt road we took on a few early-morning fishing trips, when I was a kid. He described how in previous years he would have had a shot of something to fortify him before the drive out, a glass of wine or two at lunch by the coast, and something extra to make him loose for the drive back to the ranch. I cannot imagine his mother, a lifelong lover of drinks of all kind, having much interest in her son's twelve steps, whether he made a fearless moral inventory or amends to those harmed; or in his newfound ability to enjoy a sober jaunt to the coast. The one time I traveled with my grandmother, a ten-day cruise around the Gulf of Bothnia, stopping at pretty villages in Finland and Sweden, our voyage began with each of us unpacking in our small shared cabin. Lucia held up an opaque plastic liter-sized container. It had no label. "Mine's brandy," she announced. "What's yours?"

After enough alcohol, the boundaries dissolve and your caring dissolves with them. This state isn't what Americans, in particular, would call healthy, but it has its uses. Not caring, when you are in a steady relationship with alcohol, is the easiest, best thing. That might be why Nick went back to alcohol, after his second cancer diagnosis: so as not to care. One of the caregivers—the word's multiple meanings busy this part of the story—used to give him anti-anxiety medication when he became agitated, calling it his "happy pill," though it did not make him all that happy. I think drinking did.

On our visits, I generally took him out for a daytime meal in town, to give Valerie a few morning hours alone. We ate food he could name or not, always with salsa or salt or sugar heaped on. I knew *those pink things* were shrimp, a dish he loved, and that if we went to the nearby roadside diner he would prefer *huevos rancheros* to the house special called the Hippie Scramble, which was full of veggies. I might tell him a story, to which he would listen with interest, about the red flannel hash he used to cook at the Circle C in a big cast-iron pan, potatoes and onions and beets and bacon, in his version. The advantage of going to the diner was that he could not order wine there. They didn't have any—though he usually asked, just in case.

One morning, after a full late breakfast, back in the car he gave me careful directions to another place he wanted to show me in town. As I followed his suggested turns I realized he was steering us toward the Italian bistro. "But we've just eaten, Dad," I said. "Let's go here another time, okay? Or for dinner, later?" He was insistent. I parked the car and helped him out onto the sidewalk, all while trying unsuccessfully to persuade him we could return another day. The place opened at eleven; as soon as they unlocked the doors, we went inside, sat at a table guided by a person on the waitstaff who recognized Nick, and before long he was enjoying a glass of Sauvignon Blanc.

By now there had been a collective decision—by my stepmother, the caregivers, and my brother and me, though we had slightly different parameters—to let the question of alcohol slide. We had discussed ways of locking bottles away from his reach, but it seemed impractical and we could not agree on how it might work. Wine was better avoided, as it deepened his confusion and sometimes threw him off-balance, yet if it wasn't actually killing him, as it seemed not to be, he might as well have a glass or two for the pleasure of it. More than that caused trouble. There was the morning I got up early, wakened around five by a blaring radio, along with another voice coming from the kitchen. "You can't always get what you want!" he belted along with Mick Jagger while attempting to do the dishes. A near-empty bottle of Cabernet stood on the kitchen table. I think from then on, I stayed at the motel down the road when I came up. Like Nick, I had always needed a quiet stretch of solitude in the mornings to make the rest of the day work.

Some sense memory stayed with my dad that wine permitted flirtation, so at the bistro that day he laughed with the waitress, who indulged him. Afterward we visited the photographers' cooperative, where he and I gazed at coastal vistas, night skies, an old walled city's inviting alley. Wired on coffee as well as my worry of whether I was keeping him safe, I felt my mind jagged and a little broken, as though his dementia were contagious, and he and I might wander around this room of photographs indefinitely, dreaming our separate ways onto a wildflowered seaside trail or a misty path under giant redwoods, having forgotten when we were due home, or for that matter where home was.

6.

WHAT'S AHEAD

+

PLACES WITH ART WERE HAVENS ON OUR OUTINGS. NICK
had always loved going to galleries; he took lifelong pleasure in painting
and sculpture. Having never visited me in New Haven, he made a point
of coming out, solo, to Baltimore when I was in graduate school at Johns
Hopkins. I was twenty-five, studying fiction with a somewhat dad-like
figure, and a writer Nick admired, the incomparable John Barth. (Was
this visit an amends-making trip on Nick's part? He said nothing of the
kind, but it had that effect.) The two of us went to the Baltimore Museum of Art to see the Cone sisters' collection of post-impressionist art,
and there, in front of a pair of weathered boots, painted by Van Gogh,
we had what I think of as one of our first moments of adult connection.
He helped me appreciate the texture and beauty of that muted work, in
its browns and grays and blues. One boot is open, the leather lace loosened and snaking across the lower quarter of the canvas, the other boot
tipped over, showing its studded sole. You fill in for yourself the details
of the man who walked in them. If my dad had not stopped in front of
that painting, I doubt I'd have noticed it.

My mother and Nick developed, at a late date and separated by vast
time and distance, quite similar aesthetic tastes. After decades in which
it was impossible to imagine them ever as a couple, I found something
oddly soothing in these strange harmonies. (There is a comical story
of my mother reiterating to me, within the last ten years, that she and
Nick should never have married—no longer blaming him as she once

fiercely had, but acknowledging the marriage was simply a mistake. Nothing good had come from it. I said to her, teasing the obvious omission, "Well, a couple of good things came from it, at least?" to which Linda's authentic, instinctive answer was "No, really. Nothing.") My mother and father both loved radio and radio personalities, enjoyed botanical gardens and plant catalogs, and collected, in a small way, varieties of landscape paintings. It was like the way twins separated at birth and reunited later find they have developed identical hobbies or have the same favorite authors. When I asked my mom recently if going to galleries together had been one of the (few) shared pleasures in their marriage, she could not recall such a link. Perhaps Nick's fictional alter ego, Winston, having an intense affair with a sexy Florentine artist in his novel *Moebius Curve* explains why my mother might not remember their enjoying a love of art together. She has said more than once that the year they lived in Italy, when Mike was a toddler—the last year of their marriage—she often felt she was going mad with distress. I was conceived there, during that spring. Born back in California.

Around his Fort Bragg kitchen table one afternoon, in this last phase, I showed my dad a small photobook with my kids in it. Pictures were still fun to look at together. Linda was in a few of them, too; I hadn't had time to edit her out. My dad paused over her image; the photograph stirred something in him, and he found a way to speak his appreciation for all that she had done for Michael and me, for raising us, for being such a good mother. He did not use her name, but he knew who she was. This was a first, after fifty years, so I learned that, too: people forgive, even after the point when they might seem to have forgotten. And they can be forgiven, too. Post-divorce, Gawen had told his own mother, Beatrice, not to express regret about his having married Lucia, though it ended so swiftly in divorce. No, Gawen said: it was just life, it had taught him something, he had moved on. If my grandfather had lived, maybe he could have imparted that lesson to his own son. But Nick got to it his own way, via survival, intermittent sobriety, and luck.

My dad's love of image and texture and color predated his dementia and lasted right through it. Perhaps art is like music that way. De Kooning kept painting even after the onset of Alzheimer's, and a musician I know cares for an elderly friend who has great holes in her memory but can still sit down and play Bach. At the south end of Fort Bragg, in an area back behind a gallery, was the open studio where artists formed blown glass into luminous, sea-shaded pieces, and my dad liked for us to wander over and see the colors melting, taking shape in the fire. The people there knew Nick and were happy to let him watch them, as long as I kept him safe from the flames. We developed a workaround for his ongoing hunger to acquire—at the gallery, a piece could be "held" at the front desk for a later purchase that never came.

While he could, though, Nick continued to buy watercolors, photographs, prints. He did not read anymore, but his eyesight was fine, and he took pleasure in gazing. The pictures were nearly all landscapes, offering places to travel without the company of a human figure. He curated a shifting arrangement on the weathered wood wall of the bedroom upstairs where he now slept alone, my stepmother having moved down to the ground floor due to wounded knees and perhaps the beginning of her retreat from Nick, as he retreated from her. He liked showing the different artworks to me and my kids, if I brought them, and when the information was retrievable he would tell you where the piece had come from, why he chose it. A sepia-toned church in the Southwest; a bright, thickly painted sky with stars; an intimate garden. (He had once introduced me to the precise and vibrant flowers of Redon, a painter he loved.) There was one small night horizon, oil on wood about ten inches square. "It makes you think of what's ahead," he said to me, and I understood him to mean the light at the end. Whatever lay beyond. My dad was not religious, but you never knew; there might be something there.

I have that picture now in my own room, hanging on a wall across from where I sleep. I like the colors and the space in it—the opening, the scratchy mystery—and occasionally the painting reminds me of what I learned from my dad about endings. It is not as though he meant to teach me anything. He was never that kind of parent. I picked up a few tips anyway. Not to deny what is coming, since it doesn't help you or buy you more time; if anything, denial lets you waste the diminishing days you have left. How to occupy and appreciate the present—a good meal, ocean air out on the deck, petting the dog, the steadfast love of your spouse. My dad's illness was very hard on my stepmother, as it always is on the partner, for whom the sufferer saves his secret and worst aggressions, the built-up fears. In arguments, she gave it back to him as she always had. Yet the two did still have occasional deep conversations in which the old Nick was briefly back. They could speak of death, and of what he wanted. I think those few stretches of light kept her going, and allowed her to resolve that we should do all we could to help him stay at home until the end. Even if there were occasional mornings when he packed himself up, prepared to go back to some other home, elsewhere.

7.

THE DEATH STORY

✦

OUR DAD OUTLIVED THE GLOOMY PROGNOSIS HE WAS given by a good year, or year and a half. His stubborn, pill-tossing-out instinct proved sound, and the renewed wine habit did not seem to harm him, either. "I stopped predicting a likely timeline for your dad a while ago," one of Nick's doctors said when asked the sotto voce question of how we should plan for what lay ahead. Discussions on whether to move him came and went. He would not be moved.

On his eighty-fifth birthday, I went out to lunch with Nick and one of his caregivers, Rick, at a wharf-side restaurant in Fort Bragg's Noyo harbor, from where we had taken those predawn fishing trips. My dad and brother and I left the Circle C at a thick, black four in the morning, and dawn was still a faint suggestion when the intrepid Brownrigg party drove the curving road down into the harbor. Valerie stayed home with the dogs. Our dad insisted we get a good breakfast in us before going out onto the ocean, so we piled in eggs and hash browns before leaving the narrow channel on a vessel that puttered us out into the open waters. Once the waves got stronger and the boat ride rockier, I felt vaguely seasick and promptly fell asleep on deck, so my brother commandeered my fishing rod as well as his. Fish were caught and we got to keep them, snapper probably, packed in ice for the drive back. It was a fun outing, and one on which I got a decent nap. My dad and brother always did love to fish together.

For his birthday, along with his cod and chips, my dad wanted a glass of wine. Rick ordered the kind he liked, and then he and I mostly talked, Rick describing his old rock band in the nineties, and how hard it was to make a living as a musician in that area anymore. A couple of male caregivers were in the rotation, kind, low-key men who were fond of Nick; they made each other laugh, and he trusted them. My dad listened to Rick's stories curiously, as if they were being told in a language he was not fluent in, while I enjoyed looking out through the broad pane windows to the water, where small boats were still going out and coming back. On a lucky day you might see a few seals swimming lazily by; those were the sightings that used to make my daughter happiest when she was small.

We returned to the house, where my stepmother had gathered a colorful bouquet of cards into a basket on the kitchen table. She had alerted friends far and wide about Nick's eighty-fifth, and got a great response. She showed him the collection and read a few out loud, from friends in San Francisco or Southern California or farther afield, his brothers, her Michigan family, old pals from Ukiah. My dad said little and looked somber. He may have been overwhelmed by all the love or baffled by it. Sometimes he had a habit of turning inward, focusing quietly on what his body was doing, burping, digesting: he paid attention to his inner workings, as if feeling them gradually slow down. Maintaining his dignity took a lot of effort.

He did not live to see his eighty-sixth. Through the spring and summer I often thought each visit must be the last, but he carried on into September, at which point the caregivers with hospice experience could see signs he had entered into the final stretch. As our dad's arc completed, my brother and I were able to make a final visit together. For a while before then, the only name Nick had had left to call anyone was "Mike." The two of us stood by the hospital bed set up in the living room, saying the loving things you say at the end, whether the words are fully heard or understood or not. Our dad was not speaking anymore, but I do remember his fire-blue eyes staring at us, and the something like fear in them. Their dog could tell what was happening, too. The energetic, affectionate border collie first stopped going near his bed; then she stopped going into the room that contained our dad's bed, though because of the house's open plan, this meant also staying out of the kitchen, where her food was. Finally, she would not come inside the house at all, even to eat. To ensure she would not run away or come to any harm, my stepmother found a kennel to look after the dog while my dad finished dying.

It was the other male caregiver, a gentle fellow named Shawn, on overnight duty. Nick took a solitary moment to go, with no one watching, as Shawn dozed on the couch nearby. When he woke up to check at about three in the morning, my dad was gone.

In the morning, my stepmother called Mike, then me. She arranged for our dad's body to be collected and cremated. She has his ashes in an urn, next to those of one of their beloved dogs. (Like mother, like son: Lucia stipulated that her ashes be mixed with those of her last dog, Mandy, and they be scattered together in Switzerland. Tall order.) We have not yet discussed a scattering. Maybe one day we will.

My son has idiosyncratic objects, talismans, from his three grandfathers. Bow ties and fishing flies from his dad's dad in Seattle; a Latin dictionary from Philip; and, from Nick, one of his landscape paintings and an old wooden tennis racket. One weekend morning the year before he died, we all gathered in a town just north of Healdsburg for brunch and conversation, near some tennis courts where my son and I played a few "exhibition" games for Nick's entertainment. My dad had been a great fan of the sport since he was young, playing and watching it. The main coaching tip I recall from one of the few times I rallied with him as a teenager, in Ukiah, was to "stop being such a lead-ass," good advice though I didn't much like the phrasing. Sitting on a weathered wooden bench after that weekend brunch, leaning on his cane and wearing a silvered mustache those days, Nick looked very much like an old colonel, coming down from the highlands to catch a set or two at the club. He delighted to see his left-handed grandson hit the ball so well. A few times he had told Sam about one of his own best match-ending strokes, in a mixed doubles tournament, the backhand passing shot down the line. In his eighties, his stiff right arm could still make the sweeping backhand gesture, in the telling.

I have some of my dad's pictures, and a few of his books—his copy of *On the Road*, a literary touchstone for him, signed drunkenly by both Kerouac and Neal Cassady. He did not exactly mean it for me, but Valerie generously gave it along with some of his writings. In the end, he was not a leaver of things. There are hundreds of pages of his letters to me, and if I get tired of rereading those, I can always go back to his father's love letters to his mother, in which Gawen calls her "Darling little Lucia who I love so much, my sweet little baby, my adorable Lucia." I even have letters Nick wrote to Linda, in that brief fictional-seeming period in which my biological parents loved each other. (My mother kept them.) I have not done more than glance at those—it's too much of a paradigm shift away from the established legend of their mutual loathing.

But, in spite of that 2012 lunch he and my brother and I had in Healdsburg, sketching out distant financials, there were no messages from our dad in the aftermath. There were no secrets revealed in his will, as there had been with Gawen. For further understandings we would have to turn back to Beatrice, and her scrapbook. Or use our imaginations.

To his friend Gus, soon after the move to the Circle C:

6/1974

I also dug what you said about journals and envy you, remembering, uneasily, how I still could not sugar charlie that mass of manuscripts accumulated in Los Altos and Italy, all that pretentious shit and pathetic strivings. Next time we get into Bekins for any reason I'm gonna extract it and burn it, leaving a few of the stories and all of my journals, let Michael and Sylvia experience what traumas they will from Daddy's mad ravings. Like when I read my father's second novel and felt really let-down, so indulgent, petty and rife with phantasy it was and so totally lacking the discipline of an editor let alone author. Odd, I think as we grow older and our children learn us better, some psychic exchange takes place analogous to our own selves vis-à-vis Life and as we give we die and, giving to our children, their illusions die, too, as do ours of ourselves. Eternal cycles, perpetuating.

Nick did not leave us his journals. If at one time he considered papers for Mike and me to comb through after his death, he scrapped that idea. Perhaps their years at the Circle C cured Nick of the idea of literary inheritances. Maybe he just didn't feel like thinking about it. He made peace with the decisions he made, I believe around the time he edged so close to a second divorce: to quit drinking, to stop writing, to stay married.

The January after he died, I drove up with my son and daughter to gather at the house in Fort Bragg. Mike and his wife and kids met us there, and, as you might expect with Brownriggs, my children were introduced to two new relatives—our uncles, Victor and Peter, my dad's Brosies, who had traveled from Virginia and from Oregon. The Brosies were warm and joshing, telling stories of fishing trips they had taken together over the years and how Nick used to play a mean boogie-woogie on the piano. Everyone then lapsed, inevitably, into outlandish tales about Lucia. Their mother always made for the best dark comedy. She stole the show, long after she had left the stage. I played a recording of a song my dad taught me when I was a kid, "Walking My Cat Named Dog." It had reminded him of his elegant silver-and-white cat named Baby Ball, who moved with them from Telegraph Hill up to the Circle C. My brother spoke, with love and frankness, about how Nick had and had not been around as a father. And my son read aloud from Kerouac's *Dharma Bums*, a scatological section that had reminded him of his grandfather. It featured repetitions of the word *asshole*, an eyebrow-raising choice but one of which I think my dad would have approved. More than once the subject came up of Nick's foul mouth, his f-bombs, as Victor referred to them, reminding me of the phrase from Watergate tapes days, "expletive deleted," which I had borrowed for my children's book so that the story would be readable by grade schoolers. The dad character in *Kepler's Dream* had that among other things in common with mine.

At a later, fuller memorial with people from Ukiah and Mendocino and Fort Bragg, Valerie arranged for a bluegrass trio followed by a pianist who played Beethoven, and she asked me to bring up a photograph of Gawen to add to a table display of photographs. Some of their friends learned for the first time about Nick's English background, and my brother made brief, sheepish reference to our appearance in Debrett's. (Mike, as the sixth baronet, is there now along with his children; I am off the record.) A quick way to irritate my dad had been to express fascination with his English family, when occasionally people who had met Lucia and heard about her presentation at court probed him for further details. The 5TH BT plates were really intended as a joke for himself. But you cannot control the story any longer, after you've gone. That is one of the things I have learned in this writing.

Another has to do with gifts for your descendants. Some offerings may not reach their mark, at least not when you wanted them to; others may be received gratefully, in spite of being accidental. He may not have planned to, but our dad did, in the home stretch, bequeath us Gawen and Beatrice. Our ancestors, if you want to call them that. Like a craft kit, the materials to build our own story of the family.

What he never thought to impart was any awareness of beginnings. Not of his, and not of mine. It's hardly surprising. He himself had none, and mine were always associated with his departure. I was born, he left. Or he left, I was born. I was never quite sure of the order. Either way, the two events were bound together.

I saw a photograph recently that my mother found and gave to me. It was new to me. Nick is holding me as an infant, in the Los Altos Hills house. His head is tilted up at the camera, the camera being I guess my mother, and there is no happiness or love on his face, rather a look of wariness, a readiness to guilt, as this slightly hunched, clean-shaven, dark-eyed man cradles a small white bundle in his arms. The expression is haunting—you could write a book about it—but the incredible thing to me is the act. He did hold me. It's good to know.

ACKNOWLEDGMENTS

DAYS OF GRACIOUS...

Where to start?

That was the first problem, one I talked about with Dan Gunn in his classroom, Peggy Orenstein on the trail, and Ann Packer over the phone, when I began to imagine how I might interbraid these diverse stories.

Through readings and comments early and late, and all along the way, these astute writers and unfailingly kind friends have made this book possible. My gratitude to them is boundless.

Years ago, my brother, Michael, and I had a Burlingame lunch together, and when we finished I felt encouraged to pursue our grandfather's story. Mike and my stepmother, Valerie Brownrigg, are at the heart of this tale and my ability to complete it. I hope they feel my love and affection for them in its pages. Valerie's generosity about materials of Nick's helped me understand him more deeply as a writer, and her sharing of other Brownrigg facts and lore furthered my knowledge of Gawen. It is a great treat still to hear her stories about the Circle C. I owe deep thanks to Mike and Valerie, whose memories will be different from mine but who will, I hope, recognize these landscapes and the people in them. As well as the dogs.

I can't express all that comes from my mother, Linda, except to say that without her not a word of this would be possible. It was a specific joy to read aloud a few early chapters at her Oxfordshire table, where she added and clarified various details. My mother encouraged me, as she has from the start, in my storytelling, as did my late stepfather, Philip Lewis. That is the foundation on which I write.

Anna Webber, my deft and indefatigable agent, believed in my ability to write about my grandfather in Kenya and bring that history to light. I'd never have continued without her thoughtful suggestions and her patient support of my work. Her sense of humor has saved me more than once. Also, she introduced me to the great poetry of Adam Foulds.

Jack Shoemaker has been the ideal editor for this curious, personal book: he knows Beats as well as writings about Kenya, and over many brilliant years published writers important to Nick and to me, both.

Jack's narrative instincts are unmatched, and his editorial directions helped at crucial points make this a better book. It was my greatest luck that he became its champion.

The Counterpoint and Catapult teams have been fantastically thorough, friendly, and helpful: Laura, tracy, Dan, Yukiko, Wah-Ming, Megan, Rachel, Andrea, Vanessa. To all, my huge thanks. And as well to Alyson Sinclair and all at Nectar Literary.

This is largely a story about letters, but it was conversation that made the work possible. Talks with and careful readings from Lisa Kennedy, Pam Thompson, Blakey Vermeule, Ann Cummins, Pam Dick, Claire Messud, Katy Emck, Nick Jenkins, Susanne Pari, Stephen Pelton, Paula Rae Gibson, Anne Raeff, Lori Ostlund, and Sasha Natapoff kept me going, as did inspiring exchanges with my Lightfast colleagues Christel Dillbohner, Monica Scott, and Danae Mattes.

In England, Hermione Lee has in her invariably engaging work and conversation pointed this fiction writer toward ways of writing (real) lives; Dr. Christine Nicholls kindly welcomed me to her Oxford home and shared details about her upbringing in Kenya; and Merlin Holland told me a few stories about meeting my grandmother Lucia in London in earlier years as we pieced together the relation between his father and my grandmother. Julian Barnes has illuminated the ways of grief, and the formal potential of standing fiction and nonfiction side by side. And I appreciate Neal Pearson's offering of his research into Gawen Brownrigg and Obelisk Press more than twenty years ago.

In Berkeley, my work was made easier by the organizational efforts of Emily Denny, Madeline McCormick, and Aynaz Alia Faruqui, all of whom helped place some order on the mass of family materials in the scrapbook and the letters.

At Banff and after, novelists Jennifer Haigh and Peter Behrens offered essential guidance and response to my work in progress. To Kelly Sicat and Judy Dennis at lovely Villa Montalvo, thanks for a welcoming place of artistic community last spring. And I am grateful for the stewardship of the Batten House by Elaine Richardson and others at the Albuquerque Museum Foundation.

Lastly: this is a book about family, and a few have a special role in these stories.

The Yus come at the start, as Connie Young Yu's kindness toward me when I was young was a gift, the Yus' warm home a haven. That Jessica and I still joke about the tales she and Jennifer and I made up together, and that Jessica and her daughter are both storytellers, too, gives me another reason to feel good about chickens; we might never have met without them.

The Engels: Peter and Victor, my dad's Brosies, gave us as adults a sense of where, and who, our father had come from, and share that house style of comedy that runs through all of us. Also, they're great fishermen.

The Bartons: Bob, with stories of his and Nick's decades of friendship and pictures from Carmel; Jessica, Sabrina, and of course, Adam, who knew Nick and the Circle C from a different angle and who could also tell me how winches work. Adam's boyhood affinity for Little Rhino helped bring that creature into the story.

Jo and Helen Lewis offered their kindnesses with Philip's illness, in both countries, as well as their enthusiasm about this writing, and Marty Burchell gave help to Nick and Valerie, and Mike and me, through Nick's last years. Kitty, Shawn, and the late, lovely Rick took care, in every sense, of my dad as he faded. I loved that each one of them could laugh with him, too, a part of caregiving that goes undermentioned but makes the end so much more bearable as it comes.

The Lovelaces: Lillian, for finding the scrapbook in the first place, and ensuring it reached Linda and then us; Cynthia, for her longtime, gracious support; and my Lovelace cousins, especially poet and translator Olivia and visionary Carey, for giving me a feeling of creative connection to family.

And, of course, the Thomsons. Thank you to Henry, who coined the nickname Santa Claus for Nick and had his affection from their first meeting, and to Sedge, for sharing his own memories. I could always hear the warmth in my dad's voice when he was talking or writing about Sedge. The great panda!

Finally, to my own two Thomsons, who don't have Brownrigg in them by name, but do under the surface: this is your history too, Sam and Romilly. I'm leaving it for you, with all my love, whenever you want it.

Here you go.

Gawen

Nick

FAMILY TREE

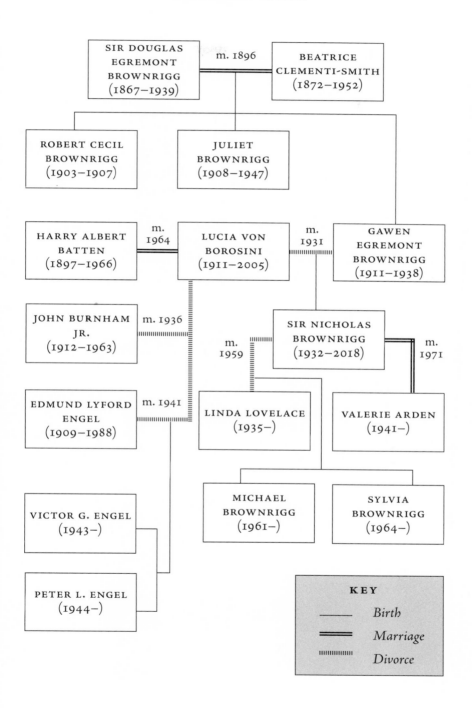

READINGS

Chimamanda Ngozi Adichie, *Notes on Grief*

Hilton Als, *The Women*

David Anderson, *Histories of the Hanged: the Dirty War in Kenya and the End of Empire*

Julian Barnes, *Nothing to be Frightened Of*

Julian Barnes, *Levels of Life*

Juliet Barnes, *The Ghosts of Happy Valley: Searching for the Lost World of Africa's Infamous Aristocrats*

Nicholas Best, *Happy Valley: The Story of the English in Kenya*

Karen Blixen (Isak Dinesen), *Out of Africa*

Karen Blixen (Isak Dinesen),*Shadows on the Grass*

Beatrice Brownrigg, *The Life and Letters of Sir John Moore*

Beatrice Brownrigg, *The Well of Life: Prayers for Children*

Rear-Admiral Sir Douglas Egremont Brownrigg, *Indiscretions of the Naval Censor*

Gawen Brownrigg, *Star Against Star*

Gawen Brownrigg, *Later Than You Think*

Keggie Carew, *Dadland*

Terry Castle, *Boss Ladies, Watch Out! Essays on Women, Sex and Writing*

Lisa Cohen, *All We Know: Three Lives*

K. M. de Silva, *A History of Sri Lanka*

Max Frisch, *I'm Not Stiller*

Le Comte de Janzé, *Vertical Land*

Joan Didion, *Slouching Towards Bethlehem*

Caroline Elkins, *Imperial Reckoning: The Untold Story of Britain's Gulag in Kenya*

Adam Foulds, *The Broken Word*

James Fox, *White Mischief*

Atul Gawande, *Being Mortal*

Victoria Glendinning, *Vita: The Life of Vita Sackville-West*

Merlin Holland, *The Wilde Album: Public and Private Images*

Vyvyan Holland, *Son of Oscar Wilde*

Alan Hollinghurst, *The Sparsholt Affair*

Gerald Horne, *Mau Mau in Harlem? The US and the Liberation of Kenya*

Elspeth Huxley, *The Flame Trees of Thika*

Jomo Kenyatta, *Facing Mount Kenya: the Tribal Life of the Gikuyu*

Jack Kerouac, *On the Road*

Jack Kerouac, *The Dharma Bums*

Hermione Lee, *Virginia Woolf*

Yiyun Li, *Where Reasons End*

Helen Macdonald, *H is for Hawk*

Beryl Markham, *West With the Night*

Blake Morrison, *And when did you last see your father?*

Alice Munro, *The View from Castle Rock*

C. S. Nicholls, *Red Strangers: the White Tribe of Kenya*

C. S. Nicholls, *A Kenya Childhood*

C. S. Nicholls, *Elspeth Huxley: A Biography*

Ngũgĩ Wa Thiong'o, *Decolonising the Mind: the Politics of Language in African Literature*

Ngũgĩ Wa Thiong'o, *Dreams in a Time of War*

Ngũgĩ Wa Thiong'o, *In the House of the Interpreter*

Barack Obama, *Dreams from my Father*

Michael Ondaatje, *Running in the Family*

Neal Pearson, *Obelisk: A History of Jack Kahane and the Obelisk Press*

William Peterson and Nicole Blaisdell Ivey, eds., *Gus Blaisdell Collected*

Anthony Powell, *A Dance to the Music of Time*

Vita Sackville-West, *The Edwardians*

Sathnam Sanghera, *Empireland: How Imperialism Has Shaped Modern Britain*

Dorothy Sayers, *Gaudy Night*

Paul Spicer, *The Temptress: The Scandalous Life of Alice de Janze and the Mysterious Death of Lord Erroll*

Thomas Tweed, *Blind Mouths: A Novel*

Alexander Waugh, *Fathers and Sons*

Evelyn Waugh, *Decline and Fall*

Evelyn Waugh, *Vile Bodies*

Evelyn Waugh, *Black Mischief*

Evelyn Waugh, *Scoop*

Evelyn Waugh, *Waugh in Abyssinia*

Sara Wheeler, *Denys Finch Hatton*

Virginia Woolf, *Jacob's Room*

Virginia Woolf, *Orlando*

SYLVIA BROWNRIGG is the author of several acclaimed works of fiction, including the novels *Morality Tale*; *The Delivery Room*, winner of a Northern California Book Award; *Pages for You*, winner of a Lambda Literary Award; and *The Metaphysical Touch*; and a collection of stories, *Ten Women Who Shook the World*. Brownrigg's works have been included in the *New York Times* and *Los Angeles Times* lists of notable fictions and have been translated into several languages. Her novel for children, *Kepler's Dream*, written under the name Juliet Bell, was published in 2012 and adapted into a feature film. Brownrigg lives with her family in London and in Berkeley, California. Find out more at sylviabrownrigg.com.